Pears Encyclopaedia
of
Myths and Legends

Pears Encyclopaedia
of
Myths and Legends

Northern Europe

Southern and Central Africa

BY SHEILA SAVILL

ADVISORY EDITOR: PROFESSOR GEOFFREY PARRINDER

GENERAL EDITORS: MARY BARKER AND CHRISTOPHER COOK

PELHAM BOOKS

First published in Great Britain by
Pelham Books Ltd,
52 Bedford Square,
London WC1B 3EF
1977

ISBN 0 7207 0931 8

Picture research by Philippa Lewis.

Filmset and printed in Great Britain by
BAS Printers Limited, Wallop, Hampshire and
bound by Redwood Burn Ltd, Esher

Contents

Illustrations

Black and White Plates

Frontispiece: Wayland's Smithy, a prehistoric stone circle near Uffington, Berks. (*Photo: A. F. Kersting.*)

The Turoe Stone, Co. Galway. This third-century Celtic cult stone, decorated with leafy curvilinear patterns, bears a striking resemblance to the ancient *linga* stones of India. (*Photo: Commissioners of Public Works in Ireland.*) p. 19

Janiform Celtic statue, *c.* fifth century, from Boa Island in Lower Lough Erne, Co. Fermanagh. (*Photo: C. M. Dixon.*) p. 21

An Elizabethan concept of Queen Boudicca addressing her troops. Illustration to Holinshed's *Chronicles*, 1577. The British Library. (*Photo: Ray Gardner.*) p. 22

The Three Mothers. This second-century Romano-British relief shows the goddesses carrying trays of loaves and fruit. The Corineum Museum, Cirencester. (*Photo: Photoresources.*) p. 23

Pillar decorated with bas-relief of severed heads, from the Celto-Ligurian temple, Entremont, Bouches du Rhône. Musée Granet. (*Photo: Jean Roubier, Paris.*) p. 24

The portico of the Celto-Ligurian temple at Roquepertuse, Bouches du Rhône, with niches for severed heads or skulls, brooded over by a huge bird reminiscent of the Irish Badhbh. Musée d'Archaeologie Borély, Marseilles. (*Photo: Jean Roubier.*) p. 25

The twelfth-century stave church of Lom, Norway, its roof decorated not only with the Christian cross, but with the gaping dragon heads of pagan myth. (*Photo: Norsk Telgrambyrā, Oslo.*) p. 27

Enamelled handle of a Celtic Irish bowl found in a Viking tomb at Miklebostad, Norway. The design on the 'tabard' may represent the five *cóigedh*, Ulster, Leinster, Munster, Connacht and, in the centre, Meath. Bergen Museum, Norway. (*Photo: Yan Zodiaque, Jean Dieuzaide, Toulouse.*) p. 33

The Hill of Tara, Co. Meath, site of the religious and political capital of Celtic Ireland. Until the mid-sixth century a new king's marriage with the Spirit of Ireland was celebrated here at a ritual wedding feast. (*Photo: the Irish Tourist Board.*) p. 35

Effigies of King Lud (Lludd) and his two sons from the old Ludgate, London, now in the vestry porch of St Dunstan's, Fleet Street. This nineteenth-century etching of the figures is by Sir Richard Hoare. The Guildhall Library, London. (*Photo: the Guildhall Library.*) p. 38

The coast of the Isle of Man, traditional home of the Irish sea-god Manannán mac Lir. (*Photo: J. Allan Cash.*) p. 39

Statue of the dying Cú Chulainn in Dublin Post Office. (*Photo: the Green Studios, Dublin.*) p. 43

Derdriu and her nurse, the wise woman Lebhorcham. Woodcut illustration by John D. Datten to *Celtic Fairy Tales*, London 1892. The London Library. p. 46

A page from the story of Pwyll in *The Mabinogion and Other Welsh Tales from the Red Book of Hergest*, a facsimile edition by Rhys and Evans, Oxford, 1887. The London Library. p. 48

Pwyll drives off Arawn's hounds from the stag. Illustration to Lady Charlotte Guest's *Mabinogion*, London 1838–49. The London Library. p. 49

A giant bearing a magic cauldron rises from the Lake of the Cauldron watched by the Irish King Matholwch. Lady Charlotte Guest's version of the *Mabinogion* tells how the giant, displeased by Matholwch's treatment of him, went off to Britain, taking the cauldron to Bendigeidfran, King of Britain. Illustration to Lady Charlotte Guest's *Mabinogion*, London 1838–49. The London Library. p. 52

Culhwch takes the magic razor and comb from the head of Twrch Trwyth. Illustration from Lady Charlotte Guest's version of the *Mabinogion*, London, 1838–49. The London Library. p. 55

The last page of a copy of Geoffrey of Monmouth's *History of the Kings of Britain*, from the late fourteenth-, early fifteenth-century manuscript of the *Red Book of Hergest*. Jesus College Library, Oxford. (*Photo: the Bodleian Library, Oxford.*) p. 56

Sir Gawain takes leave of King Arthur and Queen Guinevere. Illustration from the fourteenth-century French manuscript *Roman de Lancelot du Lac*. Bodleian Library Ms. Douce 199 f. 151 v. (*Photo: Bodleian Library.*) p. 57

The ruins of Glastonbury Abbey, traditionally founded by Joseph of Arimathea when he brought the Holy Grail to Britain. Some said King Arthur was buried in the abbey. (*Photo: J. Allen Cash.*) p. 58

A vision of the Holy Grail appears to the Knights of the Round Table. Illustration from the fourteenth-century

flower. Museum of Antiquities, Newcastle-upon-Tyne. (*Photo: Photoresources.*) p. 104

Bas-relief from a pillar dedicated to Jupiter by the 'sailors of Paris', A.D. 14–37, shows the god Esus cutting branches from a tree and is partnered by the relief of Tarvos Trigaranus, p. 126, with whom Esus was associated in a myth now lost. Musée de Cluny, Paris. (*Photo: Photoresources.*) p. 106

The White Horse of Uffington, a prehistoric hill figure possibly sacred to the Celtic goddess Epona. (*Photo: Ashmolean Museum Oxford.*) p. 107

Late romanesque pier in the crypt of Freising Cathedral, Germany, depicting the wolf-man Fenrir. (*Photo: Bildarchiv Preussischer Kulturbesitz.*) p. 108

Panel from the Franks Casket showing, left to right: Weland in his smithy; Weland and the Swan Maidens; the Adoration of the Magi. British Museum. (*Photo: British Museum.*) p. 109

Prehistoric temple at Stonehenge, Wiltshire, built, according to legend, by Merlin. (*Photo: The British Tourist Authority.*) p. 110

Chalk figure on the Gogmagog hills, Cambridge, allegedly depicting a Celtic deity, but, according to some authorities, a nineteenth-century work. (*Photo: Director in Aerial Photography, University of Cambridge.*) p. 111

Guinevere ill in bed sends a ring to Sir Lancelot. Illustration from the fourteenth-century French *Roman de Lancelot du Lac*. Bodleian Library Ms. Douce 199 f. 44v. (*Photo: Bodleian Library.*) p. 112

Detail from the Gundestrup Cauldron showing a god brandishing two deer. (*Photo: Photoresources.*) p. 113

Gunnar, Brynhildr's husband, in a snake pit, playing his harp with his toes. Twelfth-century carving from Hylestad Church, Setesdal, Norway. University Museum, Oslo. (*Photo: Werner Forman Archive.*) p. 113

Sir Lancelot (*left*) and his son Sir Galahad in a boat. The anonymous knight in white armour is a divine messenger, summoning Galahad to go forward alone on the last stage of the Grail Quest. Illustration from the fourteenth-century manuscript *Quête du Saint Graal*. The British Library Ms. Royal 14E iii f. 134 v. (*Photo: the British Library.*) p. 116

King Leir from Holinshed's *Chronicles*, 1577. The British Library. (*Photo: Ray Gardner*) p. 117

Merlin teaching his magic arts to the Lady of the Lake. Illustration to the early fourteenth-century *Lestoire de Merlin*, from Bologna. The Bodleian Library Ms. Douce 178 f. 249. (*Photo: the Bodleian Library.*) p. 119

Merlin astride a black horse brings together King Arthur's army. Illustration to the early fourteenth-century *Lestoire de Merlin*, from Bologna. The Bodleian Library Ms. Douce 178 f. 195. (*Photo: the Bodleian Library.*) p. 119

Reginn mends Sigurdr's sword; twelfth-century carving

from Hylestad church, Setesdal, Norway. University Museum, Oslo. (*Photo: Werner Forman Archive.*) p. 122

Sigurdr kills the dragon Fáfnir; twelfth-century carving from Hylestad church, Setesdal, Norway. University Museum, Oslo. (*Photo: Werner Forman Archive.*) p. 124

Whetstone-sceptre from the Sutton Hoo ship burial, decorated at either end with typical Celtic heads. Illustration from British Museum's *The Sutton Hoo Ship Burial*, 1970. (*Photo: British Museum.*) p. 125

Bas-relief from a pillar dedicated to Jupiter by the 'sailors of Paris', A.D. 14–37, shows the bull Tarvos Trigaranus and three cranes. Musée de Cluny, Paris. (*Photo: Photoresources.*) p. 126

Scene from a recent production of Wagner's *Tristan and Isolde* at the Royal Opera House, Covent Garden, London. (*Photo: Houston Rogers.*) p. 128

Wayland's Smithy, a prehistoric stone circle near Uffington, Berks. (*Photo: A. F. Kersting.*) p. 130

Twelfth-century figure of Wotan supporting a vault in the crypt of Königslutter church, Brunswick, W. Germany. (*Photo: Bildarchiv Preussischer Kulturbesitz.*) p. 131

'The three weird sisters' beneath a tree. Illustration to Holinshed's *Chronicles* 1577. The sisters probably represent a folk memory of Wyrd and her sister Fates. The British Library. (*Photo: Ray Gardner.*) p. 132

Royal pyramids dating from the third century B.C. to the fourth century A.D. in the North Cemetery of Meroë, second city of that name and capital of Kush. (*Photo: Werner Forman Archive.*) p. 137

Illustration from an eighteenth-century Ethiopian manuscript shows God in a cloud watching the building of the Tower of Babel. British Library, Oriental Ms. 590 f. 10 r. (*Photo: the British Library.*) p. 138

Ruins of the great mosque at Kilwa, Tanzania. (*Photo: Werner Forman Archive.*) p. 139

Prehistoric rock carvings of antelopes, Tassili, Algeria. Similar carvings and paintings of ritual significance are found in many parts of Africa and have been made until modern times by the Bushmen. Musée de Préhistoire et d'Ethnographie de Bardo, El Dejeziar (Algiers). (*Photo: Werner Forman Archive.*) p. 140

Female ancestor figure of the *Bambara* people, Mali. Museum of Mankind, British Museum. (*Photo: British Museum.*) p. 142

Divining bowl used for detecting witches, *Bavenda* people, N. Transvaal, S. Africa. Museum of Mankind, British Museum. (*Photo: British Museum.*) p. 143

Olokun, the *Yoruba* sea-god, Nigeria. Rijksmuseum voor Volkenkunde, Leiden. (*Photo: Rijksmuseum voor Volkenkunde.*) p. 146

Wood carving of a figure used in rain-making ceremonies by the *Dogon* people of Mali. At other times such figures are

Colour Plates

Foreword

In modern times comparative studies of religion and mythology, strongly supported by psychology, have revealed again the importance of myths. And one 'fact' that confronts us immediately is that myths have universally been thought to express truth, not mere detail of present existence but primordial and eternal reality. The myth is real and sacred, and it serves as an example in providing a pattern for human behaviour and an explanation of its mysteries. These elements can be seen in great modern myths. In Communism, quite apart from economic theory, there is a revival of Jewish and Christian mythical themes in the redemptive role of the innocent, the proletariat, the inevitable struggle of good and evil, and faith in a coming Golden Age. At a lower level the Nazi myths, held recently by millions of intelligent and educated people, propounded the myth of the chosen people, the master-race, and tried to revive Nordic paganism with its doom of the world and destruction in chaos. Other myths, about the Empire on which the Sun never Set, or the American Way of Life, had their potency but were also subject to the weakness of modern mythology in not being sufficiently anchored in age-old symbolism and therefore inadequate to represent lasting reality. But psychology has shown also that the dreams and fantasies of modern men, formerly dismissed by rationalists as nonsensical, often repeat great themes of mythology and produce their effect upon the unconscious and half-conscious behaviour of individuals.

An authoritative and comprehensive collection of myths such as this book provides, therefore, is of absorbing interest and topical significance.

This volume begins with the setting of the myths, relates them in detail, and provides comprehensive index and bibliography. It is a splendid work, for reading and reference, and enlightened by illustrations. When the four volumes are completed they will be an unrivalled and up-to-date source for knowledge of these age-old mythologies.

GEOFFREY PARRINDER
Professor of the Comparative Study of Religions,
King's College, University of London

General Introduction

The standard reference book of world myths, *The Mythology of All Races* (ed.: Louis Herbert Grey and John Arnott MacCulloch), appeared between 1916 and 1932. It comprises thirteen weighty volumes and its price, approaching one hundred pounds, puts it beyond the means of most readers. Moreover, although this great work, which has recently been reissued, contains material of lasting importance and interest, much new knowledge has become available since it was compiled. The researches of the linguist and archaeologist have extended our knowledge and understanding of the myths and legends of the ancient civilisations, such as Sumer, Greece and China. Anthropologists and ethnographers have done the same for those of Africa, and parts of the Americas, Oceania and Australia. A number of books offer information on particular aspects of this new knowledge, but much of it remains tucked away in specialised libraries, the pages of learned journals and academic theses. Here therefore we have aimed to provide up-to-date yet reasonably compact volumes for the growing number of readers who share our interest in this perennially fascinating subject.

This volume is the second of a proposed four which the publishers plan to issue. Each volume contains two chapters, each dealing with the myths and legends of a particular region:

Vol. 1
    Chapter 1 The Ancient Near and Middle East
    Chapter 2 Classical Greece and Rome
Vol. 2
    Chapter 3 Northern Europe
    Chapter 4 Southern and Central Africa
Vol. 3
    Chapter 5 Ancient Iran, India and S.E. Asia
    Chapter 6 Northern and Eastern Asia
               (Tibet, China, Korea, Japan)
Vol. 4
    Chapter 7 Oceania and Australia
    Chapter 8 The Americas

Each chapter is divided into four parts. The first gives a brief introduction to the historical, religious and cultural background of the region's myths and legends, the second outlines the chief stories of each area, in so far as these are known, or, as in the case of Africa and India, offers a representative selection from them. The third part of each chapter consists of an index and glossary, referring particularly to the numbered paragraphs of the second part and also including brief details of many other myths and legends of the region. Finally comes a bibliography and guide to further reading. This pattern is based on that devised for the original section of Greek myths and legends, first published in *Pears Cyclopaedia*. Many readers said how helpful they found the scheme, which enables any character or story easily to be pinpointed.

Examples of reference:
   23 refers to paragraph **23** of part 2 of the current chapter;
   4.1 refers to chapter 4, part 1:
   4.3 refers to chapter 4, part 3;
   vol. 2: 4.2.**23** refers to volume 2, chapter 4, part 2, paragraph **23**;
   vol. 3:7.3 refers to volume 3, chapter 7, part 3.

These four volumes as a whole contain many references to Jewish and Christian myths and legends, but for two reasons no specific chapter is devoted to them. The first is that the chief Jewish and Christian myths and legends, which are all we would have had space to include, are already very easily available in that best-selling work *The Bible*. The second is that the thousands of myths and legends concerning patriarchs, rabbis, saints, relics and miracles belong to various regions of the world. Readers seeking a more detailed survey are referred to L. J. Ginsberg: *The Legends of the Jews*, Philadelphia, 7 vols. 1909–46, and G. Everly, *Christian Mythology*, London, 1970.

The terms *myth* and *legend* are often used rather ambiguously. Here *myth* is a fictional narrative, often involving supernatural persons; legend is a traditional story with perhaps some historical foundations.

In speaking of fictions we do not imply that myths and legends offer false images of the world. They have a serious function and express a people's feelings and intuitions about the significance of their lives, the nature of human relationships and human potentialities for good or ill.

It used to be thought that myths were stories devised to explain or to accompany rituals, but, although the evidence suggests that many did originate in this way, it is now accepted that the theory does not account for the origin of all myths, whose genesis remains a matter of speculation.

In the last century it was popular to think of myths as no more than naïve attempts to explain the existence of natural phenomena. The validity of this approach was wittily undermined by Andrew Lang in a satire offering 'proof incontrovertable' that Mr. Gladstone was no more than an expression of a solar myth. Some myths certainly embody poetic 'explanations' of natural phenomena, but this in itself could not account for the fascination they continue to hold for highly educated minds, fully aware that, for example, the sun does not either sail across the sky in a boat nor ride across it in a chariot drawn by fiery steeds.

Certain mythological paradigms (mythologems) and symbols such as those of the flood, the theft of fire, the monster/dragon in its cave, the ladder from earth to heaven, appear to have a very widespread and potent significance for mankind. This fact was noted by Jung and forms the basis of his influential theory of the Collective Unconscious, which has done much to illuminate our understanding of the world's myths and legends.

More recently, studies of animal behaviour have led to the suggestion that perhaps some of the power of these archetypal images is analogous to that of the stimuli which provoke automatic responses in less highly developed species. A newly hatched chick will immediately cower if it sees a hawk or even an image of hawk shape, though it shows no fear of gulls or similar birds.

Each society gives its own particular form to such 'archetypal images' or stimuli, for myths and legends are expressions of communal feelings and intuitions.

During the past century scholars have made us increasingly aware of the important part myths and legends have played in shaping our own culture. The influence of Greek and Roman mythology had long been acknowledged but critical consideration of Jewish and Christian myths and legends was taboo, while very little was known of those earlier stories of the Near and Middle East from which many of our most compelling myths seem to have originated. Not did we know much of the myths and legends of primitive peoples, or of the geographically remote Chinese and Indians.

The disciplines of archaeology, linguistics, psychology, anthropology, ethnography, sociology, comparative mythology, comparative religion and religious history have all played a part in helping to extend our knowledge and understanding of the world's myths and legends. Some of their discoveries and theses are discussed in the introductions to the various chapters.

It is impossible in a work of this size to incorporate detailed discussion of various theories regarding the provenance and significance of individual myths and legends, but wherever possible we have included brief details, and referred the reader to the appropriate scholarly works.

The following general studies are particularly recommended:

CAMPBELL, Joseph *The Masks of God*, 3 vols. New York: The Viking Press. 1959–65.

DUMÉZIL, Georges *Mythe et epopée*. 3 vols. Paris: Gallimard, 1974.

ELIADE, Mircea *The Sacred and the Profane*. New York: Harcourt Brace & World Inc. 1959.

——*Myths, Dreams and Mysteries*. Harvill Press. 1960.

——*From Primitives to Zen*. Collins. 1967.

HUXLEY, Francis *The Way of the Sacred*. Aldus/Jupiter Books. 1974.

JUNG, Carl *Psychology of the Unconscious*. Kegan Paul, Trench Trubner & Co. 1919.

——*Symbols of Transformation*. Vol. 5 of *Collected Works*. Routledge & Kegan Paul. 1956

——*Archetypes and the Collective Unconscious*. Vol. 9, Part 1 of *Collected Works*. Routledge & Kegan Paul. 1959.

JUNG, Carl and FRANZ, M. L. von (eds.) *Man and His Symbols*. George Allen & Unwin. 1964.

LÉVI-STRAUSS, Claude *Mythologies*. 3 vols. Translated as *An Introduction to the Science of Mythology*. Vol. 1 *The Raw and the Cooked,* Vol. 2 *From Honey to Ashes*. Jonathan Cape. 1970–73.

LOMMEL, Andreas *Masks Their Meaning and Function*. Paul Elek Books. 1972.

SCOTT-LITTLETON, C. *The New Comparative Mythology*. Revised ed. New York & London: University of California Press. 1974. (This book outlines the main ideas of Dumézil and critical reactions to them.)

CHAPTER 3

Northern Europe

PART 1

Introduction

Linguistic evidence suggests that almost all the early inhabitants of historic Europe derive from Āryan forebears who in prehistoric times spread northward and westward from the steppes of southern Russia. In Chapters 1 and 2 (vol. 1) we considered the myths and legends of the Āryan Hittites, Greeks and Romans. In Chapter 5 (vol. 3) we shall be concerned with those of the other great branch of the Āryan family, the Iranians and Indians. As Dumézil and his followers have shown, it is possible to suggest many interesting parallels between the myths and legends of these various Indo-European (Āryan) peoples. Some of them will be indicated in the course of the following chapter.

The Turoe Stone, Co. Galway. This third-century Celtic cult stone, decorated with leafy curvilinear patterns, bears a striking resemblance to the ancient *linga* stones of India. (*Photo: Commissioners of Public Works in Ireland.*)

THE CELTS

The first group of people to rise to prominence in Europe north of the Alps were the Celts, whose ancestors may have reached Bohemia and Bavaria by the late third millennium B.C. and gradually spread into Spain, Gaul and the British Isles, east along the Danube, south into Italy, Greece and Asia Minor.

It is generally agreed that there was no large-scale immigration into Britain between 2000 and 600 B.C., but scholars are divided as to whether the Celts reached these islands before 2000 or in about 600 B.C. The great antiquity of Irish traditions, which have many parallels with those of early Vedic India (vol. 3: 5.1.) leads some authorities such as Myles Dillon, to prefer the earlier date, but there is at present no conclusive evidence either for or against it.

Most of the Celtic peoples became absorbed into the culture of the Graeco-Roman world. Only in the British Isles—particularly in Ireland, which remained virtually untouched by Classical culture—were the ancient traditions of the Iron-Age Celts preserved and transmitted by word of mouth until, in the seventh century A.D., they began to be written down.

The men who committed them to writing were Christian scribes, ignorant of, or indifferent to, the religious significance of the tales they were recording and sometimes concerned to arrange them in a framework of their own devising (1). Nonetheless, Irish texts from the eighth to twelfth centuries preserve a mass of very ancient material, albeit in a somewhat confused and fragmentary form.

These early works can be divided into five main groups. The first is the mythical history of Ireland (1–19), contained mainly in two texts, the *Leabhar Gabhála Éireann* and an epic poem the *Battle of Magh Tuiredh* (Moytura), which records the names and attributes of many Celtic Irish deities. The second group of stories concerns the gods of the mythical Otherworld (34–47). Closely associated with it are a number of later *immrama* or 'voyage' tales. The earliest of them, the *Immram Curaig Maíle Dúin*, was to inspire the famous story of St. Brendan, *Navigatio Brendani* (see glossary: Bran, Brendan, Maíle Dúin). The late Christian *fís* or 'vision' stories such as the *Vision of Fursa* and *St. Patrick's Purgatory* represent a further development of this genre.

Cú Chulainn (48–63) is the hero of the third group of stories, known as the Ulster Cycle. This also includes the tale of Derdriu (70–74). Fourth comes another cycle whose hero is the great Fionn mac Cumhail (Finn mac Cool) (64–69), who, scholars generally agree, represents a late development of the earlier god Lugh (28–33). Finally comes a group of stories about the Irish kings including the tales of Cobthach Coel, Labhraidh Loingsech, Maíl Fothartaig and Cano (qq.v.).

In Britain, where Roman influence was more powerful, and as it waned the British were driven westward by the Saxons, fewer Celtic myths and legends have survived and those only in Wales. The extant Welsh stories begin some two hundred years after the earliest Irish material and are well on their way to degenerating into folklore. Nonetheless they contain much interesting material. There are many similarities between the Welsh and Irish tales,

Janiform Celtic statue, *c.* fifth century, from Boa Island in Lower Lough Erne, Co. Fermanagh. (*Photo: C. M. Dixon.*)

but it is difficult to determine which influenced the other or whether both versions of a particular story derive from some common original. We may however note that during the fourth century the southern Welsh kingdom of Dyfed was a bilingual Irish state. A second group of Irish emigrants settled on the west coast of Scotland establishing the kingdom of Dál Riata, which retained close links with its parent Irish kingdom, Dál nAraidi (38).

Between the fifth and seventh centuries, as pressure from the Saxons increased, settlers from Cornwall and Wales emigrated to Brittany and so re-established Celtic traditions in the Armorican peninsula, playing a part in the later development of medieval Arthurian romance (130–140) which sprang from the cross-fertilisation of ancient Celtic and medieval Christian culture.

Although no Celtic myths have survived from Continental Europe we have quite a lot of information about the customs and beliefs of the Gaulish people. This is an invaluable aid to our understanding of the myths and legends of their insular cousins, of whose culture, and particularly of whose religion, we know far less.

Some of the evidence comes from place-names, monumental inscriptions and archaeological discoveries. This is supplemented by the observations of Classical writers.

One of the earliest references to the Celts is Aristotle's caustic comment on the recklessness of their warriors, ready 'to take up arms to fight the waves.' It is thought that the very name *Celt* may derive from a verb meaning 'to fight' and Celtic belligerence certainly impressed both Greek and Roman, who remarked that it was by no means confined to the men. Celtic women were if anything the more terrifying. It is clear that the British Queen Boudicca, who 'struck fear into all who saw her' was by no means exceptional and some Irish stories suggest that women may even have played some part in the training of young warriors (30, 53).

Women certainly played a very important rôle in Celtic society. History speaks not only of Boudicca but of the great Brigantine Queen Cartimandua and in Irish myth it is Medhbha (q.v.), not her consort Aillil, who rules Connacht.

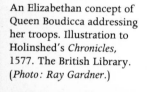

An Elizabethan concept of Queen Boudicca addressing her troops. Illustration to Holinshed's *Chronicles*, 1577. The British Library. (*Photo: Ray Gardner.*)

The Earth Mother

It seems that the authority of an Irish king was only ratified after he had engaged in a ritual marriage with the goddess Spirit of Ireland (q.v.), which Medhbha herself personified. In other Irish and Welsh tales the goddess is represented by the most beautiful woman in the land (**42, 44, 70, 121**). It is clear that these goddess-heroines represent a personification of the ancient Earth Mother and Branwen is specifically referred to as embodying one of her three aspects (**96**). Among the Celts as among other peoples (cf. vol. 1 : 2.2. **111–118**; 4.3 : Ala; vol. 3 : 5.2. **163–171**) the mother goddess is an ambivalent figure, at once the fount of life and its destroyer, or Queen of the Dead (**42–47, 100**). Her ambivalent nature finds its grimmest expression in Celtic stories in the character of the Mórríghan (q.v.), a fearsome battle goddess. It also seems to have been the inspiration for the many tragic stories of doomed love, for which the Celts are famed (**61–62, 66–69, 70–74, 105–108**, and glossary : Cano, Tristram).

The Earth Mother is commonly represented in both Celtic and Germanic myth by the Three Mothers. This triad of deities is characteristic of Celtic religion (see glossary : Badhbh, Brighid, Goibhniu) and possibly relates to the three divisions or 'functions' into which Dumézil suggests Indo-European societies were commonly divided : those of the priestly intelligentsia, the warriors and the agriculturalists. Caesar's observation that the Celts of Gaul were divided into *druids, equites* and *plebs* lends support to Dumézil's theory.

The Three Mothers. This second-century Romano-British relief shows the goddesses carrying trays of loaves and fruit. The Corineum Museum, Cirencester. (*Photo: Photoresources.*)

The Cult of the Head

Roman observers noted with horror the Celtic custom of decapitating their vanquished foes and nailing the severed heads above the doorways of their homes (cf. **51, 63**). It is clear from literary references (**99–100**) and archaeological evidence that the head had a particular cultic significance for the Celts. A sanctuary discovered at Roquepertuse (Bouches du Rhône) in France, dating from the third or fourth century, contains stone pillars with niches for heads or skulls. Above perches a huge stone bird. A number of skulls have been found in the vicinity, also stone carvings of heads, including one of a pair of severed heads divided by the beak of a carrion bird. Possibly this, and the bird on the monument, may represent a Gaulish battle goddess comparable with the Irish Badhbh (q.v.) who was usually thought of as assuming the form of a carrion crow.

The significance of the cult of the head seems to have survived well into the Christian era. The west doorway of St. Brendan's cathedral at Clonfert, Co. Galway, is carved with some twenty such heads, ten of them set in niches very similar to those at Roquepertuse.

Pillar decorated with bas-relief of severed heads, from the Celto-Ligurian temple, Entremont, Bouches du Rhône. Musée Granet. (*Photo: Jean Roubier, Paris.*)

The portico of the Celto-Ligurian temple at Roquepertuse, Bouches du Rhône, with niches for severed heads or skulls, brooded over by a huge bird reminiscent of the Irish Badhbh p. 99. Musée d'Archaeologie Borély, Marseilles. (*Photo: Jean Roubier.*)

Druids and Filidh

The intense importance the Celts attached to their religion greatly impressed Caesar, who gives some details of their gods and also describes the training of the *druids* who, he says, spent up to twenty years committing 'immense amounts of poetry' to memory and teaching younger members of their tribe.

It seems that the *druids* may have been at once priests, bards and law-givers, forming a class analogous to that of the Indian *brāhmans* (vol. 3 : 5.3.). Their eloquence was matchless and greatly prized. In Ireland even after the advent of Christianity the *filidh* (poets) continued in their rôles of poet and story-teller long after any religious function they may have fulfilled had been taken over by the Christian priests. It is for this reason that so many ancient stories continued to be preserved in Ireland when they were lost elsewhere.

THE NORSE–GERMANIC PEOPLES

To the north of the Celts other groups of Indo-European settlers had established themselves in Germany and Scandinavia. Between the fourth and sixth centuries A.D. they began to move south, Angles and Saxons into Britain, Franks into Gaul, the Vandals and Goths into central Europe, overwhelming the Graeco-Roman and Romano-Celtic cultures of those lands. By the middle of the eighth century the English and most of the continental Germans had been converted to Christianity and most of their myths and legends were lost. We must rely chiefly on the evidence of place-names and archaeology for information on the beliefs of the pagan Anglo-Saxons and Germans, but this material is supplemented by the writings of travellers, especially the Roman Tacitus, who greatly admired the German peoples, and also from the great Anglo-Saxon epic *Beowulf*. Although it dates from the Christian era this splendid poem preserves the tradition of the earlier pagan heroic age.

Most of the Norse-Germanic myths and legends which survive come from Scandinavia, which did not begin to be converted to Christianity until the tenth century. Sweden, which resisted longest, remained pagan for nearly two hundred years after that.

Like the Celtic myths and legends, those of Scandinavia were recorded by Christian scribes and are not wholly free of Christian influence. Some modern scholars regard the Norse *sagas* rather as historical novels than as true legends, but like the early Irish tales they preserve much valuable ancient material.

The twelfth-century stave church of Lom, Norway, its roof decorated not only with the Christian cross, but with the gaping dragon heads of pagan myth. (*Photo: Norsk Telgrambyrā, Oslo.*)

Apart from the *sagas* is a small collection of Icelandic poems about the heathen gods, but this *Codex Regius*, as it is called, has only forty-five pages. For the most part we are therefore obliged to rely on the work of an early thirteenth-century Icelandic scholar, Snorri Sturluson, who compiled an anthology of heathen stories known as the *Prose Edda*. Its authenticity can to

some extent be checked for we have other copies of some of the poems Snorri quotes. All suggest that he was a faithful, dedicated scholar, as well as a writer of lively wit.

Less entertaining and eloquent, but almost equally valuable for the student are the tales collected by the twelfth-century Dane, Saxo, in his *Gesta Danorum*.

How far the surviving material is literary and how far it records the beliefs of heathen Norse-Germanic peoples is difficult to determine. Moreover the beliefs and practices of the Norse-Germanic peoples were by no means uniform and it is unlikely that they were more static than those of any other group of people. How far and in what ways they changed we cannot for the most part tell.

There are a number of similarities between the extant texts and the stories recorded from the Graeco-Roman and Celtic civilisations. Some of these may be accounted for by the common Indo-European ancestry of these different peoples. Others may derive from cross-cultural influences. For example, the story of Mímir's head (156) may owe something to Celtic beliefs and practices, for we have no other evidence that the severed head had any cultic or magical significance for the Norse-Germanic peoples. They certainly offered human sacrifices to their gods, but literary and archaeological evidence suggests that although their victims were hanged or stabbed, or even buried alive in peat bogs, they were not mutilated.

One striking aspect of the Norse-Germanic myths is their references to *shamanistic* practices (see below). Whether these were adopted under the influence of Finno-Ugric peoples or during the course of the migration of the Norse-Germans from their southern homeland we cannot determine, but the myths of Óðinn in particular make it clear that such practices were of considerable importance in the Norsemen's lives (168–171) and in medieval times the Christian kings of Norway specifically forbad their subjects to travel to Finland to consult *shamans*, which suggests the old ways still exercised considerable power over men's minds.

Shamanism

The *shaman* is the name given by the Tungu people of the Siberian Arctic to their priestly magicians and seers, who practise a form of what is now popularly known as 'charismatic' religion. The word *shaman* (feminine: *shamanka*) itself means 'one who is excited or raised up' and the priest or priestess is held to have the power of entering the spirit world at will and commanding its denizens. In some cases the *shaman's* journey is symbolised by his climbing a ladder or tree. In others he is spoken of as flying, sometimes in bird form, or on a magical flying horse (171 and vol. 3: 6.2. 14–19; 55) He has the power to send his own spirit forth into any form (cf. vol. 3: 6.2. 124–125) to summon other spirits and to exorcise those who cause illness or other harm.

While in some cases the *shaman's* rôle is inherited he (or she) is usually summoned by particular spirits, usually much against his will and driven out into the wilds in great anguish of mind until at length he receives an ecstatic experience of enlightenment in which the secrets of the universe are revealed. The *shaman* now accepts his vocation and acknowledges his particular spirit aids.

Such ecstatic experiences are of course by no means confined to *shamans* and *shamankas,* nor are such priestly magicians found only among the Tungus.

African 'doctors' (see 4.1. medicine-men) and Haitian Voodoo priests (vol. 4) have a similar rôle, so do the 'spiritual healers' and exorcists of western Christian and spiritualist cults. We may however note that while such specialists are found among many other peoples, among the Mongols they were pre-eminent and in some regions yet remain so.

Two fascinating studies of *shamanism* from the viewpoints of the anthropologist and psychologist are Lewis's *Ecstatic Religion* and Sargant's *The Mind Possessed*. Eliade's classic *Shamanism and Other Archaic Techniques of Ecstasy* contains material of great interest to the student of mythology although the distinction Eliade makes between the *shaman's* ecstatic trance and spirit-possession is not now accepted by all scholars, since both phenomena are common to *shamanistic* cults.

THE FINNO-UGRIC PEOPLES

Unlike the other peoples whose myths and legends are considered in this chapter, the Finno-Ugric group are not of Indo-European stock. They may be divided into four main groups according to their geographical distribution. The first includes the Finns, Estonians, Karelians, Livonians and Lapps; the second the Cheremiss-Mordvin peoples of the middle and upper Volga; the third the Zyrians, Votyaks and Permyaks living in the Russian provinces of Vyatka and Perm; and the fourth the Voguls and Ostyaks of western Siberia. The Hungarian Magyars are usually included in this fourth group, since they also originated in western Siberia.

Although influenced by the beliefs of their Indo-European neighbours, the Balts, Slavs and Norse-Germans, all the Finno-Ugric peoples practised an animistic religion in which the *shaman's* power was supreme. Our chief source for their myths and legends is the *Kalevala*, a very late compilation made by the Finnish scholar Lönnrot at the beginning of the last century. It is based on folk-songs and cannot be taken as a reliable guide to the beliefs of the pre-Christian era although it undoubtedly reflects them to some extent.

THE BALTS AND SLAVS

Known to the Classical writers of the first and second centuries as the Venedi, a people living beyond the Vistula, the Balts and Slavs form the north-eastern branch of the Indo-European family of peoples. During the sixth century they expanded considerably, forming several groups.

The Slavs are usually divided into the Western Slavs, including the Poles, Czechs, Slovaks and Moravians, the Eastern Slavs or Russians, and the Southern Slavs comprising the Bulgars, Serbs, Croats and Slovenes.

The closely-related Balts were also divided into three groups, the Lithuanians, Latvians and Prussians.

Few myths or early legends of these people have survived, but notes on their deities and heroes are included in Part 4.

A NOTE ON SPELLING AND PRONUNCIATION

Names in the various Celtic dialects are usually modernised by writers in order to give a clearer idea of their pronunciation. The Old Irish Etain is thus rendered Édain since the 't' is pronounced as a 'd' and the accented vowels are long.

The Welsh 'll' should be pronounced as the *tl* in ket*tl*e.

The Norse-Germanic alphabet contains two unfamiliar letters 'þ' and 'ð'. The first is usually transcribed as 'th' and should be voiceless as in *th*in. The second is usually transcribed by English writers as 'd' but it should be pronounced as the voiced 'th' in *th*en. Here it is distinguished from the ordinary 'd' by being given in brackets as 'th' thus Ódinn (Óthinn).

The final 'r' of Norse names should not be pronounced as a separate syllable, as it often is in English, where Baldr commonly, but incorrectly, becomes Balder.

Vowels should be pronounced roughly as follows:

á as or in sw*o*rd
ǫ as o in st*o*p
ø as the French eu in p*eu*r
ae as ai in f*ai*r
au as ou in cl*ou*d

PART 2
Narrative Outlines

CELTIC MYTHS

The Invasions
1–19

1 No Celtic creation myths survive. Their place is taken by the Irish stories of the Invasions, which describe six groups of immigrants who formed the Irish landscape and comprise its various peoples. The stories were compiled by scribes who wished, among other things, to emphasise the supremacy of the royal house of Ulster, so the tale of the Invasions culminates in the arrival of the Sons of Míl Éspáine, the Ulstermen's traditional ancestors. The stories are contained in a twelfth-century manuscript entitled *Leabhar Gabhála Éireann (The Book of the Conquest of Ireland)*.

(i) THE FIRST INVASION: THE PEOPLE OF CESAIR
2 Before the Flood there came to Ireland a company led either by Cesair, daughter of Bith, son of Noah, or by Banbha (the Spirit of Ireland (q.v.)). Of these people all but one, Fintan, were drowned in the Flood. Fintan lived on; now as a falcon, now an eagle, now a hawk, and so saw all that happened in days of yore.

(ii) THE SECOND INVASION: PARTHOLÁN AND HIS PEOPLE
3 Now Ireland was inhabited by the Fomhoire (literally: 'sea giants'), a race of half-human monsters, each with a single leg and hand and three rows of teeth. (They are possibly intended to represent the original inhabitants of Ireland, whom the Celts overcame). These Fomhoire were defeated by Partholán and his people and exiled to the Hebrides and the Isle of Man; then Partholán's men cleared four plains and seven lakes were formed. Partholán built the first guest house, brewed the first ale and beer and established crafts and laws.

(iii) THE THIRD INVASION: THE PEOPLE OF NEMHEDH
4 After Partholán's people had been destroyed by the plague Nemhedh came to Ireland. His company cleared twelve plains and four more lakes were formed, but after their leader's death these people were conquered by the Fomhoire. Each Samhain (1 November) they were compelled to pay

their giant overlords a tribute of two-thirds of their wine, corn and children. Driven to despair the people of Nemhedh at last rebelled. Only one boat-load of them survived their attack on the Fomhoire's stronghold. Some of these survivors went to Greece, others to northern lands.

(iv) THE FOURTH INVASION: THE FIR BHOLG

5 In Greece the refugees multiplied and after many years again set sail for Ireland in three companies named the Fir Bholg, the Gailioin and the Fir Dhomhnann (the Gailioin being the Laighin of Leinster, the Fir Dhomhnann, who settled in Connacht, possibly relatives of the British Dumnonii).

6 The Fir Bholg, who were the leaders of the invasion, divided Ireland into five *cóigedh* (provinces, literally: *one fifth*) Ulster, Leinster, Munster and Connacht, with Meath in the centre (cf. Indian and Chinese concepts of the five cardinal points).

(v) THE FIFTH INVASION: THE TUATHA DÉ DANANN

7 Next, those refugees who had fled to northern lands (**4**) also returned to Ireland. During their exile they had learned much magical lore and now called themselves the Tuatha Dé Danann (People of the Goddess Danu). They were led by the Daghdha (**20–27**) and with them they brought four great treasures: the stone of Fál, which cried out when a true king sat upon it, the invincible spear of Lugh, the inescapable sword of Nuadha and the Daghdha's inexhaustible cauldron, that satiated all who supped from it.

The First Battle of Magh Tuiredh

8 The Tuatha Dé Danann demanded that their predecessors, the Fir Bolgh, resign the kingship of Ireland, or fight for it. The Fir Bolgh chose to fight, but were defeated at the First Battle of Magh Tuiredh and went into exile among the Fomhoire.

9 However during the battle the Tuatha Dé's king, Nuadha, lost an arm, and since the king must be physically unblemished (a common requirement of sacral rulers, cf. 4.3: Mujaji) Nuadha had to abdicate. The kingship passed to Bres, who had been brought up among the Tuatha Dé, his mother's people, although his father Elatha was a Fomhoire leader.

10 Bres proved at once tyrannical and mean, offering no entertainment to his followers and making even the greatest of them toil like slaves. The Daghdha, the great *druid*, he compelled to build him a fort. Oghma (q.v.) the great warrior, he made collect firewood. Eventually the tribe's *fili* (poet) Coirbre cursed him in a magical satire and Bres was compelled to abdicate. He deserted to his father's people, the terrible Fomhoire, and mustered an army against the Tuatha Dé.

11 Meanwhile, helped by Creidhne (the divine smith), the great leech Dian Cécht had made Nuadha an artificial arm of silver. Now restored to perfection he again became king, known thenceforth as Nuadha Airgedlámh (Nuadha of the Silver Hand, q.v.).

Enamelled handle of a Celtic Irish bowl found in a Viking tomb at Miklebostad, Norway. The design on the 'tabard' may represent the five *cóigedh*, Ulster, Leinster, Munster, Connacht and, in the centre, Meath. Bergen Museum, Norway. (*Photo: Yan Zodiaque, Jean Dieuzaide, Toulouse.*)

The Second Battle of Magh Tuiredh

12 While Nuadha was preparing to meet the challenge of Bres's diabolical army there came to his court the marvellous Lugh (**28–33**). Convinced of Lugh's superiority, Nuadha resigned the throne to him.

13 Under their new leader the Tuatha Dé made vigorous preparations for battle and went into combat armed not only with splendid magical weapons forged by the Trí Dé Dána (Three Divine Metalworkers), Goibhniu, Luchta and Creidhne (qq.v.), but reinforced by a battery of powerful charms and spells forged by Lugh. He appeared everywhere among his host in characteristic sorcerer's shape with one leg and one eye, chanting strengthening words of magic and heartening every warrior. Meanwhile any who were wounded or killed were speedily revived by Dian Cécht and his three children, who cast them into a magic well (cf. **21, 96, 98**).

14 In a final great stand, Lugh confronted the monstrous Balar, whose single eye could unman a host (cf. Kumbhakarna, vol. 3: 5.2. **134–135**). It took four men to lift his one eyelid but when they raised it against Lugh that mighty hero slung a stone straight into it and out through the back of Balar's skull, scattering the entire Fomhoire army, whose few survivors fled the country. They were hotly pursued by Lugh, Oghma and the Daghdha, determined to recover the Daghdha's magic harp, which the Fomhoire had stolen and carried off as booty.

15 Bres was taken prisoner and pleaded for his life, promising to ensure four harvests a year and continual milk from the cows. These offers were rejected, but his life was spared in return for his advice on what were the best times for ploughing, sowing and reaping.

16 Dumézil suggests that the story of this great battle is analogous to those in which the Indian Ashvins, Norse Vanir and Italian Sabines (vol. 3: 5.2. **100**); 3.2. **155–157**; vol. 1: 2.2. **440–443**) seek for recognition among the gods and rulers. Dumézil feels the myth should be interpreted as symbolising the interdependence of the three 'functions' of Indo-European society, which may here be represented by Lugh and the Daghdha in the first function, as priest-magicians, Oghma and Nuadha in the second, as warriors, and Bres in the third as the farmer. Dumézil suggests that those elements in the story which do not lend themselves to such an interpretation derive from subsidiary local considerations affecting the scribes who later edited the material and confused the Tuatha Dé's challengers with the traditional Fomhoire demons, and, although far from universally accepted, this theory does offer a helpful insight into a story with many puzzling features. One may however feel that the reconciliation of the Tuatha Dé and the Sons of Míl (**18–19**) is a more telling example of reconciliation between the various 'functions' to which Dumézil refers.

(vi) THE SIXTH INVASION: THE SONS OF MÍL ÉSPÁINE

17 The Sons of Míl Éspáine came to Ireland from Spain, landing on the feast of Beltene (1 May). They were led by the *fili* (poet) Amhairghin. Defeating a Tuatha Dé army they set out for the capital, Tara. En route they

met the three goddesses Banbha, Fódla and Ériu, wives of the Tuatha Dé's three kings, Mac Cuill, Mac Cécht and Mac Gréine. The Sons of Míl promised each lady in turn that the land should bear her name if she favoured them. Ériu told Amhairghin that the Sons of Míl would conquer Ireland and rule there forever but she warned Donn (q.v.), the Sons of Míl's discourteous king, that neither he nor his heirs would enjoy the land. Soon after this Donn was drowned and buried on the island of Tech Duinn, to which he now welcomes dead warriors.

18 At Tara the three Tuatha Dé kings disputed the Sons of Míl's right to Ireland and asked the *fili* Amhairghin to judge between their claims. Amhairghin ruled that the Sons of Míl should be put out to sea again to beyond the ninth wave (a magical boundary). When, having done so, they tried once more to land the Tuatha Dé sent an enchanted wind against them. Calling upon the Spirit of Ireland Amhairghin caused the wind to drop. The sea grew calm. The Sons of Míl came to land and defeated the Tuatha Dé at the Battle of Tailtiu.

The Hill of Tara, Co. Meath, site of the religious and political capital of Celtic Ireland. Until the mid-sixth century a new king's marriage with the Spirit of Ireland was celebrated here at a ritual wedding feast. (*Photo: the Irish Tourist Board.*)

19 Determined not to be exiled, the defeated Tuatha Dé used their magic arts to deprive the conquerors of both corn and milk, until at length the Sons of Míl agreed to divide the land with them. The Tuatha Dé received the underground half and their leader the Daghdha then gave each of their chiefs a *sídh* (earth barrow) for his dwelling. There the Tuatha Dé remain. (See also **12–16**).

Irish Deities, Heroes and Heroines
20–74

(i) THE DAGHDHA

20 The Daghdha ('Good God'), leader of the Tuatha Dé, combines elements of a sky-father, war-god and chthonic fertility deity with those of a powerful magician. Possibly he may represent a development of the early Indo-European sky-father, who among most Indo-European peoples seems to have been superseded by a triad of deities.

21 The Daghdha is called Eochaidh Ollathair ('Eochaidh the Great Father') and Ruadh Rofhessa ('Mighty and Most Learned One'). His equipment includes a magic Otherwordly cauldron, a huge club and a magic harp. The first satiates all who sup from it, and references to similar cauldrons in both Irish and British stories suggest that it probably also has the power to heal those wounded and revive those dead who are placed within it (see also **13, 96, 98**).

22 With his club, like Thórr with his hammer (**176–180, 188**), the Daghdha kills his enemies and resurrects his dead friends. It is said that he also determines the weather and controls the harvest (cf. glossary: Perkūnas).

23 On the feast of Samhain before the Second Battle of Magh Tuiredh he had appointed to meet the Mórríghan, goddess of battle (see p. 23 and glossary: Badhbh). He came upon her as she stood astride the River Unius washing the bloody corpses of those foredoomed to die. After the Daghdha had had intercourse with her she promised to help the Tuatha Dé in the coming battle.

24 Subsequently Lugh sent the Daghdha to scout out the Fomhoire positions and to try and arrange a postponement of the engagement. The Fomhoire received him derisively, mocking his great appetite for 'porridge' by preparing an enormous stew of sheep, pigs and goats seethed in eight measures of milk and an equal quantity of mead. Pouring it all into a hole in the ground they declared that if he failed to eat every single drop he should be slain forthwith.

25 The Daghdha took a ladle, so huge that a couple could have slept within it side by side, and spooned up the 'porridge'. Having emptied the hole he ran his finger over the gravel that lined it, licked the finger and promptly fell asleep.

26 Rested, he took one of the Fomhoire women, and so satisfied her that she promised to use her magic arts to help the Tuatha Dé's cause.

27 Like Thórr in **178–181**, the Daghdha is here treated as a grotesquely comic figure, yet leaves no doubt as to his ultimate authority and success.

(ii) LUGH

28 Lugh (Gaulish: Lug; British-Welsh: Lludd) seems to have been one of the most important of all the Celtic gods. He is almost certainly to be identified with the deity Caesar referred to as the Gaulish 'Mercury'. His name means 'shining one' and he seems ultimately to have derived from a Mitra-Varuna prototype (vol. 3: 5.3.). His name is found in dedications at Avranches in Switzerland, at Asma in Spain and forms a common element in French place-names as well as appearing in the Dutch Leiden and Silesian Liegnitz.

29 In Ireland Lugh is the patron of the Harvest Festival, Lughnasadh, held on 1 August. Its sites at Carmun and Tailtiu are associated with fertility goddesses and the story of Conn Cétchathlach (q.v.) also associates him with the lovely goddess, Sovereignty of Ireland (see glossary and cf. **121**), who is probably a version of the ancient Earth Mother.

30 It is said that Lugh came to Ireland from across the sea. He spoke with a stammer—that is, not native Erse. According to one story his foster-mother was the wife of one of the Tuatha Dé and trained him to bear arms, but he is also said to have been reared in the Otherworld by the sea king Manannán mac Lir (**34–41**). His grandfather was Balar, that Fomhoire leader whom he slew in the Second Battle of Magh Tuiredh (**14**).

31 As the Tuatha Dé were preparing for that battle Lugh arrived at their stronghold, where Nuadha their king was feasting his warriors. Lugh asked for admittance. The gate-keeper enquired what he could offer, but it seemed he had no new gift to bring the Tuatha Dé. He was a healer, but Dian Cécht was a splendid healer (**13**), a wright, but the Trí Dé Dána were splendid metalworkers (**13**). In the end Lugh claimed that unlike the Tuatha Dé's specialists he was a polymath (*samildánach*). Immediately the gate was open to him and, recognising his obvious superiority, Nuadha at once resigned the kingship to him. Armed with the gifts of his foster-father Manannán—a wonderful spear, a great sling, a helmet of invisibility and the marvellous shield later owned by Fionn mac Cumhaill (**64–69**)—Lugh now led the Tuatha Dé into battle and drove the Fomhoire from the country. (See **13–16**).

32 A Welsh story of Lludd may represent the gradual decay of this great Celtic god's importance. Here Lludd is presented as King of Britain, a great and generous soldier who rebuilt the city of London. Since he lived there for most of the time it came to be known as Caer Lludd (Lludd's Fort) and so Caer Lundein and, after foreigners arrived, as Lundein or Lwndrys.

33 The Welsh hero-magician Lleu (**101–108**) is probably another degenerate version of this god. Fionn (**64–69**) is another.

Sir Richard Hoare

Effigies of King Lud & his Sons.

Effigies of King Lud (Lludd) and his two sons from the old Ludgate, London, now in the vestry porch of St Dunstan's, Fleet Street. This nineteenth-century etching of the figures is by Sir Richard Hoare. The Guildhall Library, London. (*Photo: the Guildhall Library.*)

The coast of the Isle of Man, traditional home of the Irish sea-god Manannán mac Lir. (*Photo: J. Allan Cash.*)

(iii) MANANNÁN MAC LIR

34 The Celts probably had several sea deities but apart from the rather vague Tethra, who is mentioned as fighting beside the Fomhoire (**13–16**), the only sea-god of whom we have any information is Manannán mac Lir ('Manannán Son of the Sea'). His home is said to be the Isle of Man, described in terms of an earthly paradise, but he is also associated with the paradisal island Emhain Abhlach ('Emhain of the Apple Trees') usually identified with the Isle of Arran.

35 Medieval Irish writers tried to establish Manannán as an historical figure. Cormac mac Cuilennáin (fl. A.D. 900) declares he was a wonderful navigator and merchant from the Isle of Man, whom both British and Irish came to regard as a god. While of course doing nothing to establish the historical character of the merchant-sailor, this account does lend weight to the possibility that Manannán and the Welsh Manawydan fab Llŷr (**86–92, 100**) represent the Irish and British aspects of one god.

36 Manannán is Lord of Tír Tairngiri ('the Land of Promise'), an Otherworld realm, and is characteristically dressed in a green cloak fastened with a silver brooch, a satin shirt, a gold fillet and golden sandals, though when he wanted to lure King Cormac mac Airt to visit Tír Tairngiri he assumed the guise of a warrior and so appeared to Cormac on Mayday morning as the king stood on Tara's ramparts at dawn. He told him that he came from a realm where falsehood, decay, old age and death were unknown and in exchange for the promise of three wishes gave Cormac a bough of three golden apples which produced exquisite healing music when it was shaken. A year later Manannán claimed his three wishes and stole away the king's wife and children. In his pursuit of them Cormac was overtaken by a mist and then as it cleared came to a wonderful palace set in a lovely plain. Here he was entertained by a handsome warrior and a charming girl and told them of his loss. Lulled asleep by the warrior's singing he woke to find his wife and children restored to him. The warrior revealed himself as Manannán and presented the king with a wonderful golden cup. Next morning Cormac and his family found themselves lying on the grass outside their home at Tara with the golden apples and cup beside them. (See also glossary: Conn Cétchathlach).

37 When Bran (q.v.) set out to journey to Tír inna mBan (the 'Land of Women', another supernatural realm), he met the great sea-king Manannán driving his chariot across the waters and singing a beautiful air, describing how (though Bran believed himself to be rowing over the sea) to Manannán the waters formed a flowery plain, its salmon appeared as sprightly calves and lambs, while the waves were to him flowering shrubs, the seaweed (?) fruit trees.

38 Manannán was believed to use his power of shape-changing to control re-incarnation. From time to time he fathered mortal children, who are in a sense his *avatars* (vol. 3: 5.2. **108** ff). It is said that when Fiachna Lurgan, King of Dál nAraidi, went to Alba (Scotland) to fight against the Saxons with his ally Aedán mac Gabráin, King of Dál Riata, a nobleman appeared to Fiachna's queen, who had remained behind in Ireland, and told her that unless she would bear him a son Fiachna should die next day. The queen perforce consented to lie with this stranger. In the morning he had disappeared and was seen that day on the battlefield in Alba, where he overcame all the Saxons, enabling Fiachna and Aedán to win a great victory.

39 When Fiachna returned home, his wife told him all that had befallen, for she knew by the poem that the stranger had left for her that he was none other than Manannán.

40 Three days after her child Mongán was born Manannán came and took him to the Land of Promise, where he remained until he was twelve, or, some say, sixteen.

41 Mongán, whose historicity is unquestioned, ruled at Molyinny on Lough Neagh early in the seventh century, so this strange tale of his birth is probably post-Christian.

(iv) ÉDÁIN AND MIDHIR

42 Édáin Echraidhe, daughter of King Ailill, the most beautiful woman in all Ireland (i.e. the personified Spirit of Ireland, see glossary and cf. **70, 121**) was wooed by Oenghus Mac ind Og (see glossary: Oenghus) for his foster-father Midhir, a god of Tír Tairngiri (the Land of Promise). Although he lived in the *sídh* of Brí Léith (Co. Longford) Midhir was, like Manannán, associated with rebirth (cf. **38**).

43 His first wife Fuamhnach was jealous of his new bride Édáin and turned her into a pool of water. That changed into a worm, the worm into a huge and astoundingly beautiful fly whose music and perfume suffused the air. Midhir was wholly content to have Édáin's presence with him in this lovely and unusual form. The jealous Fuamhnach therefore resorted once again to magic and, raising a wind, had Édáin whirled off to a rocky coast, where, for seven years, she lay helpless, buffeted by the waves, until at last Oenghus found her and placed her in a crystal bower. There she was happy again, which Fuamhnach could not endure. Again she drove Édáin away and at length the beautiful fly fell into a woman's wine cup and was swallowed. So, 1012 years after her previous birth she again became incarnate, now as Édáin daughter of Édar, an Ulster hero.

44 Now Eochaidh Airemh became King of Ireland, but his warriors could not do him honour while he remained unmarried. He therefore sent out to seek the most beautiful woman in the land and Édáin eventually was chosen as his wife.

45 Learning of this, Midhir went to Tara to reclaim her, but she refused to leave Eochaidh without his consent. Midhir therefore challenged the king to a chess contest. He allowed Eochaidh to win the early round and accepted the forfeits imposed, building the king a great causeway across the bogs of Meath.

46 When that was finished Midhir returned to Tara for the final match of the contest. This he won and chose as his prize a kiss from Édáin. A month later, when he came to claim it all doors were barred against him. The king sat feasting with his warriors. Suddenly, in all the splendour of Tír Tairngiri, Midhir stood in the midst. Seizing Édáin he flew through the smoke hole in the roof and, in the form of swans, they disappeared.

47 Eochaidh and his host pursued them to the *sídh* of Brí Léith and began to dig it up. Midhir came out to them and promised to return Édáin to the king. There then appeared before Eochaidh fifty women, all dressed alike, and each seemingly his wife. Although he chose carefully the Édáin he chose was in fact his daughter. Only long after did he discover his mistake and by that time Édáin had born him a son, the hero Conaire Mór.

(v) CÚ CHULAINN

48 Chulainn's mother was Deichtine, sister or daughter to Conchobhar mac Nessa, King of Ulster (see also **70–74**). Some say his father was Lugh (**28–33**). According to others it was Conchobhar himself. Twin foals born at the same moment as the hero later became his famous steeds, Black of Saingliu and Grey of Macha.

49 As a boy Chulainn was named Sédanta. His first great deed took place at Conchobhar's court at Emhain Mhacha, where he defeated all fifty of the youths in the king's service.

50 Later, attacked by Culann the Smith's fierce hound, Sédanta threw his ball down its gaping throat and, seizing the animal before it had recovered from the shock, he dashed its brains out. Culann complained at the loss and Sédanta therefore promised to act as his guard dog for as long as he needed one. So he gained his popular title Cú Chulainn, 'Culann's hound'.

51 Offered the chance either of fame or a long life, Chulainn chose fame. Taking up arms on the day which, according to prophecy, would assure him the fame he sought, he went out to do battle with the three terrible sons of Nechta Scéne (cf. vol. 1 : 2.3 : Horatii; vol. 3 : 5.2.33; 5.3 : Thraetauna; Trita; Āptya. He killed them all and on his way home captured a stag and tethered a whole flight of swans. The heads of his defeated enemies dangled from his chariot, the stag ran behind, the tethered swans flew overhead. Approaching Emhain Mhacha he was still possessed with the indiscriminate fury of battle (cf. *berserkir* and vol. 1 : 2.3. : Horatii).

52 To calm his frenzy, Mughain, Queen of Ulster, led her women naked to meet him. Overcome with embarrassment, Cú Chulainn averted his eyes and was immediately seized by the king's warriors and ducked in three tubs of icy cold water to cool him down. The first tub straightaway burst, the water in the second boiled, but that in the third merely grew warm. Now calm and clothed by Mughain herself, the hero entered the royal household.

53 As his wife Cú Chulainn wished for Emer, Forgall's daughter, and in order to prove himself worthy of her went to the east, beyond Alba (Scotland) to become a pupil of the Amazonian prophetess Scáthach. While he was there he fought and conquered Scáthach's rival Aífe and took her as his mistress. She bore him a son, Conlaí or Conall.

54 After Cú Chulainn had returned to Ireland the boy, who had also become Scáthach's pupil, was sent after his father, with strict orders not to reveal his identity to any single warrior who challenged him. As he approached the shore in his bronze boat the Irish heroes, amazed by his magical deeds, sent a champion, Conall Cernach, to challenge him. Conall was quickly overcome, so Cú Chulainn himself went out against the lad, despite the pleas of Emer, his wife, who warned him that the boy could only be his own son.

55 When Conlaí refused to reveal his name, Cú Chulainn attacked him and, although only with great difficulty, at last succeeded in giving him a mortal wound. Dying, the lad revealed his name.

56 Cú Chulainn took the body in his arms and showed the men of Ulster his son. (cf. Hildebrand (i) and vol. 3 : 5.3 : Sohrāb).

57 In vivid contrast to this tragic tale is the story of *Bricriu's Feast (Fled Bricrenn)*. Based on an earlier ribald tale, *Scéla Mucce Maic Da Thó* (the *Story of Mac Da Thó's Pig*), it tells how Cú Chulainn came to be judged champion of all Ireland.

58 The malicious Bricriu ('Poisoned Tongue') gave a feast for all the men of Ulster and Connacht (traditional rivals). Since it was the privilege of the most notable warrior present to carve the roast, there was much competition for this honour, and Bricriu secretly persuaded Loeghaire Buadhach ('Loeghaire the Triumphant'), Conall Cernach and Cú Chulainn all to claim the champion's privilege. A brawl ensued. Eventually it was agreed that the three heroes would seek judgment in Connacht and there Queen Maeve (Medhbha) gave the palm to Chulainn. However on their return to Emhain Mhacha, Loeghaire and Conall refused to acknowledge the verdict, saying Chulainn had bribed the queen. All three were therefore sent to the great Cú Roí mac Dáiri, King of Munster. He also chose Cú Chulainn, but again the two defeated warriors refused to accept the verdict.

59 One evening when all the men of Ulster were in the king's hall at Emhain Mhacha, there entered a rough giant and challenged in turn Loeghaire, Conall and Cú Chulainn first to cut off his head and then on the following evening to allow him to retaliate in kind. All three agreed and taking the first turn, Loeghaire beheaded the great oaf. Picking up his head the giant tucked it under his arm and went out. The next evening he returned to claim his reward. Loeghaire welched on their bargain. When Conall's turn came he did the same, but when Cú Chulainn, having in turn beheaded the giant, was called to pay the price, he knelt down and awaited the blow. Touching him lightly on the neck with his axe, the giant bade him rise, for he was indeed the champion of Ireland. (See also glossary: Gawain).

60 Now the giant revealed himself as none other than Cú Roí mac Dáiri, come to reaffirm the judgement which the two proven cowards had previously found unacceptable.

61 On another occasion, when Cú Chulainn and his men were raiding the Otherworld (here depicted as Scotland) Cú Roí mac Dáiri again appeared in disguise and offered to help them. With his aid they managed to capture a marvellous cauldron (cf. **13, 21, 96, 98, 137, 139**) and also three magic cows and the beautiful Bláthnad. The heroes failed to keep their promise to share the spoils with Cú Roí, so he seized the lot and when Cú Chulainn tried to prevent him from leaving with the booty the great sorcerer buried Chulainn up to his armpits and shaved off all his hair, so that Chulainn had to go into hiding for a year!

62 On the feast of Samhain he planned revenge and conspired with Bláthnad, whom Cú Roí had married, to trap her husband (cf. **106–107**). Cú Roí was murdered and Bláthnad became Cú Chulainn's but the dead king's poet Fercherdne avenged him. Noticing Bláthnad standing on the verge of a cliff, he caught her round the waist and jumped over the edge, killing them both.

63 Cú Chulainn himself was foredoomed to an early death, having chosen fame in preference to longevity. Overcome by his enemies' magic he bound

Statue of the dying Cú
Chulainn in Dublin Post
Office. (*Photo: the Green
Studios, Dublin.*)

himself to a pillar so that he might die honourably still upright, and when they saw hooded crows alight on his shoulders his foes, recognising the Mórríghan and her sisters (see glossary : Badhbh), closed in upon him and cut off his head.

(vi) FIONN MAC CUMHAILL (FINN MAC COOL)

64 The poet and seer Fionn became the leader of a famous warrior troop, the *fian*, at the age of eight by defeating the terrible Aillén mac Midhna, who annually at Samhain came to Tara and, first bewitching all the warriors with enchanting music, burned down the court. In the year that Fionn came to Tara however, when Aillén began to play, Fionn pressed his magic spear's point into his forehead and so remained immune to the charm, then, as Aillén drew near, breathing out fire, Fionn stepped forward and beheaded him.

65 Fionn's supernatural wisdom may have been derived from drinking Otherworldly wine, but according to most accounts it had a different origin. One day, while cooking his master's food, Fionn happened to touch the Salmon of Wisdom with his thumb. Ever afterwards he had only to bite that thumb to learn what the future held.

66 As an elderly widower Fionn became betrothed to the beautiful Gráinne, but she loved Diarmaid ua Duibhne and on the night of her wedding drugged Fionn and his company ; then, casting a *gessa* spell on Diarmaid, she induced him to elope with her to a wood in Connacht.

67 There, besieged by Fionn, they were helped by Diarmaid's foster-father, the god Oenghus, who rescued Gráinne, while Diarmaid, in a single tremendous leap, jumped straight over the heads of all his attackers, and so escaped. Even now however he did not break his oath to Fionn and take Gráinne as his mistress. Only her contemptuous mockery at length persuaded him to this disloyal act.

68 Gráinne bore him four sons and through the good offices of Oenghus the couple were at length reconciled with Fionn. However, there came a day when Fionn and the rest of the *fian* including Diarmaid, went to hunt the magic boar of Beann Ghulban. Not even the fact that it had been prophesied that the boar, his foster-brother, would bring about his end, prevented Diarmaid from joining the hunt, and although he managed to slay the beast, he was himself mortally gored.

69 His life could only be saved if Fionn, who had the healing gift, would give him water from his own hands. Reluctantly Fionn fetched some, but, remembering Diarmaid's treachery, he let the water trickle through his fingers. Returning for more, he again let it fall and by the time he returned with the third handful Diarmaid was dead (cf. **61–62, 101–108** and see glossary : Cano ; Tristram).

(vii) DERDRIU (DEIDRE) AND THE SONS OF UISNECH

70 The *druid* Cathbhadh prophesied that Derdriu, daughter of Fedlimid, King Conchobhar's *fili*, would be extraordinarily beautiful, but the cause of much suffering in Ulster. At her birth some therefore wished to kill her, but the

Derdriu and her nurse, the
wise woman Lebhorcham.
Woodcut illustration by
John D. Datten to *Celtic
Fairy Tales*, London 1892.
The London Library.

king, Conchobhar, decreed that she should live and when she was old enough he himself would marry her (the king always marrying the most beautiful woman in Ireland, cf. **42, 121**).

71 Derdriu was brought up in strict seclusion by the wise woman Lebhorcham. One day, watching her foster-father flay a newly slain calf, she saw a raven stoop in the snow to drink the spilled blood and remarked that a man whose hair was as black, whose blood was as red and whose skin was as white would be most lovable. Learning from Lebhorcham that Naoise, son of Uisnech, had just those attributes, she immediately determined to meet him. This she contrived to do one day as he was passing by and left him in no doubt that she found him most attractive.

72 Naoise, who knew of Cathbhadh's prophecy and Derdriu's betrothal to the king, was reluctant to be drawn, but she threatened to make him a laughing stock and so, to preserve his honour, he fled with her to Scotland, accompanied by his two brothers, Ardán and Ainnle.

73 After some time the Ulstermen persuaded Conchobhar to call a truce and ask the fugitives to return home, sending the heroes Ferghus mac Roich, Dubthach and Dubthach's son Cormac to guarantee their safety. However, when Derdriu and the Sons of Uisnech returned to Emhain Mhacha, Conchobhar broke his sword and had the young men slain by Eoghan mac Durthacht and his men. Enraged at the treachery, Ferghus, Dubthach and Cormac attacked and burned Emhain, killing three hundred of the Ulstermen before deserting to Conchobhar's great enemies Ailill and Queen Medhbha of Connacht (q.v.).

74 For a year Derdriu pined, never once lifting her head. Then Conchobhar asked her what she most disliked in the world. She replied Conchobhar himself, and after him Eoghan mac Durthacht. The king vowed that since she had spent a year with him, she should now spend the next with Eoghan. Next day, forced to travel between them to the assembly of Mhacha, she threw herself from the chariot, dashing her brains out against a rock.

Heroes and Heroines of Britain and Wales
75–140

(i) PWYLL AND PRYDERI
75 This story is found dispersed among the first, third and fourth 'branches' of the *Mabinogion*. Many scholars follow Professor Gruffydd in believing that originally Pryderi was the hero of a cycle of tales, but that by the time the *Mabinogion* was assembled its compiler had only fragments of the material and, being ignorant of the original, diffused the story of Pryderi among three of the four branches of his book.

76 While out hunting one day Pwyll, Lord of Dyfed, encountered Arawn King of Annwn (the Otherworld) and to atone for having insulted him by driving off his hounds from a stag, agreed to spend a year in Annwn and despatch Arawn's enemy Hafgan. Arawn then changed their appearances so that each resembled the other and they parted.

A page from the story of Pwyll in *The Mabinogion and other Welsh Tales from the Red Book of Hergest*, a facsimile edition by Rhys and Evans, Oxford, 1887. The London Library.

77 Pwyll behaved most honourably for never did he lie with Arawn's wife though they shared a bed and she supposed him, from his appearance, to be her husband. At the year's end, having killed Hafgan, Pwyll returned home and found that Arawn had ruled Dyfed with unprecedented wisdom. When Pwyll explained to his lords all that had happened they gave him the title Pwyll Head of Annwn.

78 While out riding one day, Pwyll saw the beautiful Rhiannon, daughter of Hefeydd the Old, whose beauty enchanted him. They made a tryst. So, at the year's end Pwyll went to Hefeydd's house and there they feasted.

79 There came in a handsome, richly dressed youth and asked of Pwyll a boon, which he, unthinking, granted, only to discover the youth wished for Rhiannon, for he was Gwawl fab Clud, her rejected suitor.

80 Though angry, Rhiannon had to comply, but suggested they postpone her meeting with Gwawl for a year. She then advised Pwyll to have ready on the night of this meeting one hundred men hiding in the orchard. He himself should come in to her wedding feast shabbily dressed, carrying a bag she would give him, and ask for enough food to fill it. They would trick Gwawl into treading the food down into the sack and so capture him in it. Then, blowing his horn Pwyll should summon his men.

Pwyll (*right*) drives off Arawn's hounds from the stag. Illustration to Lady Charlotte Guest's *Mabinogion*, London 1838–49. The London Library.

81 All happened as planned and as Pwyll's men came one after another into the hall they began to kick the bag, playing the game of 'badger in the bag' until Gwawl begged for mercy and when he promised to withdraw his claim to Rhiannon and never to seek vengeance, he was freed.

82 Pwyll married Rhiannon and they lived happily, but after three years still had no child. Pwyll's lords asked him to take another wife, but he refused, and before the end of the year Rhiannon bore him a son.

83 On the night of his arrival Rhiannon's waiting-women fell asleep and the baby disappeared. To save themselves from blame the women smeared the sleeping Rhiannon with blood and claimed she had murdered the child. Believing her innocent Pwyll refused to divorce her but she, rather than wrangle against the women to establish her innocence, did penance for a year by carrying all who approached the castle.

84 The baby was found on the doorstep of his home by Teyrnon Twryf Liant, Lord of Gwent Is-Coed. He named the child Gwri. After a year, learning of Pwyll and Rhiannon's loss and struck by the child's likeness to Pwyll, Teyrnon concluded the boy must be his and took him to the king.

85 Now the child was named Pryderi and became the foster-son of Pendaran Dyfed. He grew up handsome and brave, a great warrior, much loved by his people, and married Cigfa, daughter of the great Gwyn Gohoyw (Gwyn Gloyw).

86 Pryderi went with Bendigeidfran to Ireland against Matholwch (**96–100**) and was one of the seven who returned, to find that the Island of the Mighty (Britain) had been conquered by Caswallawn, son of Beli, disinheriting Pryderi's cousin Manawydan fab Llŷr (see also **35**), Bendigeidfran's brother and heir. So Pryderi gave Manawydan his own mother Rhiannon for a wife and with her the seven *cantrefs* of Dyfed, so that Manawydan was no longer a landless man.

87 One night as Pryderi and Manawydan and their wives were feasting at Arberth there came a peal of thunder, then a cloud and finally a brilliant light, enveloping them all. When it vanished they found all their houses, men and beasts had disappeared too. They four only were left. However the woods were stocked with game, the streams with fish and for two years they lived happily; then, growing tired of this lonely life, Pryderi and his cousin decided to go from town to town earning their bread.

88 One day, as they were out hunting in the forest their dogs disappeared into a *caer* (earthen barrow). Pryderi entered to seek them, against Manawydan's advice, and there was fast bound by a spell.

89 After waiting till dusk, Manawydan went home and told Rhiannon what had happened. Immediately she went to the *caer* and seeing a door in it, invisible to Manawydan, entered it. She too was caught. That night the *caer* vanished and she and Pryderi with it.

90 When Cigfa, Pryderi's wife, realised she and Manawydan were now left alone, she was much distressed but he, reassuring her, swore to be her friend. Having neither dogs to hunt with nor any means of support, he became a shoemaker and prospered, so that after a year they were able to return to Arberth and there establish three crofts. These Manawydan sowed with wheat.

91 When the harvest in the first was ripe, he came to reap it and found all had been eaten. The same happened with the second, so on the third he kept a watch and at night saw a host of mice come to devour the corn. One of them he caught and took home vowing that next day he would solemnly hang it for theft. Cigfa tried to dissuade him from so ridiculous an act but he persisted.

92 While he was preparing the gallows next day there came first a poor clerk, then a richly dressed priest and finally a bishop with his retinue, the first people other than Cigfa that Manawydan had seen for a year. Each offered him money to save the mouse but all he refused. The clerk and priest went their ways, but the bishop persisted, offering anything Manawydan could name. Manawydan demanded that Rhiannon and Pryderi be returned and that the spell on their land be lifted. The bishop agreed, confessing that the mouse was his wife and he himself Llwyd fab Cil Coed, who had cast a spell on them all to avenge Pwyll's treatment of his friend Gwawl son of Clud. So Llwyd removed the enchantment, Rhiannon and Pryderi were returned and the lands of Dyfed restored to their former state.

93 Now Pryderi had some magic swine, given to his father by Arawn of Annwn. Gwydion, servant to Math fab Mathonwy, Lord of Gwynedd, told his master of these swine and promised to obtain them for him. He went to Dyfed with eleven companions, all disguised as bards. Pryderi received them hospitably.

94 Gwydion told of his errand and promised next morning to show Pryderi a fair exchange for the swine. Secretly he created by magic twelve splendidly caparisoned stallions, twelve greyhounds with golden collars and twelve golden shields. After consulting with his lords, Pryderi agreed to the exchange and Gwydion drove off the swine, very hurriedly, for he knew that after two days the enchantment would fail.

95 When it did, Pryderi and his host set out in pursuit. Math raised an army to meet his invasion and after two bloody battles it was agreed that Gwydion should meet Pryderi in single combat to decide the issue. With his magic arts Gwydion overcame the good king and slew him at Maen Tyriawg (Maentwrog). So Pryderi died.

(ii) BRANWEN
96 Branwen, daughter of Llŷr, sister to Bendigeidfran (Bran the Blessed) King of Britain, was one of three Mothers (q.v.) of the island. Matholwch King of Ireland wooed her and Bendigeidfran gave his sister to him together with a magic cauldron (cf. **7, 13, 21**). But while the King of Ireland was in the Island of the Mighty (Britain) an insult was offered him by Efnisien, Bendigeidfran's half-brother, and on his return home Matholwch took his revenge, treating Branwen cruelly.

97 Learning of her suffering, Bendigeidfran and the Men of the Island of the

A giant bearing a magic cauldron rises from the Lake of the Cauldron watched by the Irish King Matholwch. Lady Charlotte Guest's version of the *Mabinogion* tells how the giant, displeased by Matholwch's treatment of him, went off to Britain, taking the cauldron to Bendigeidfran, King of Britain. Illustration to Lady Charlotte Guest's *Mabinogion*, London 1838–49. The London Library.

Mighty set out for Ireland to rescue her. Bendigeidfran was so huge that no ship could carry him, so he waded through the sea, appearing from the distance like a great mountain, while his fleet seemed like a forest moving beside him.

98 When they landed in Ireland a great battle ensued. At first Matholwch's forces were in the ascendant, for each night they put their dead and wounded into the magic cauldron which restored them to full health and vigour (cf. **13**). However Efnisien succeeded in destroying the cauldron and so the Men of the Island of the Mighty proved the victors, and there was no one left alive in Ireland but five pregnant women hiding in a cave.

99 Of the Britons, only seven survived and their king Bendigeidfran was mortally wounded in his foot. At length he commanded the seven to cut off his head and take it to the White Mount of London and there bury it, for so the Island of the Mighty would be guarded against all its foes.

100 So Pryderi (**85–95**), Manawydan (**35, 86–92**), Glifieu, Taliesin, Ynawag, Gruddieu and Heilyn came with Branwen to Britain bearing Bendigeidfran's head. And when they landed Branwen sat down to rest. She looked towards Ireland and then around at the Island of the Mighty thinking that these two lands had been lain waste for her sake, and her heart broke and she died.

(iii) LLEU AND BLODEUEDD

101 The fourth branch of the *Mabinogion* in which this story appears is extremely confused and the tale of Lleu and Blodeuedd interwoven with that of Pryderi (**85–95**). It seems however that it was originally a combination of two popular mythical types, the story of the doomed hero and that of the unfaithful wife, and it is in some respects closely related to the tales of Fionn mac Cumhaill and Gráinne and of Cú Roí and Bláthnad (**66–69, 61–62**).

102 Knowing that his brother Gilfaethwy desired King Math's footholder (a court post held by a maiden), the beautiful Goewin, Gwydion fab Dôn, the king's bard, used his magic arts to contrive a quarrel between Math and Pryderi Lord of Dyfed (**93–95**). While Math was away fighting Pryderi, Gilfaethwy was able to abduct Goewin, whom he and his brother ravished. On his return Math punished them by condemning them to three years in animal forms, the first as deer, the second as swine, the third as wolves.

103 Having expiated his crime, Gwydion sought to provide the king with a new footholder and put forward his sister Aranrhod. However, as she stepped over the wand (a rite to attest her virginity) two bundles dropped from her. One was a golden haired baby, who was christened Dylan. He immediately set off for the sea, whose nature he assumed, being ever after known as Dylan Eil Ton (Dylan Son of the Wave).

104 The second bundle, which Gwydion hastily concealed in a chest, was a second baby. Gywdion adopted him, but after four years could not resist bringing him to show Aranrhod, who embarrassed by the reminder of her shame, cursed the boy, saying he should have no name until she herself gave him one, implying she never would. However, by disguising himself and the lad, Gwydion tricked her into naming him Lleu Llaw Gyffes (Bright-one-with-the-nimble-hand). Later, when Aranrhod swore Lleu should never bear arms until she gave him some, she was again tricked into providing them. Finally she cursed Lleu a third time, saying he should never have a woman to wife until she bestowed one on him.

105 Gwydion and Math therefore evaded the curse by making Lleu a wife from the flowers of oak, broom and meadowsweet. They named her Blodeuedd ('Flowerface').

106 Though beautiful, she was unfaithful to Lleu and took the hunter Gronw Bebyr for her lover. At Gronw's suggestion she set out to discover how her husband might be slain and at length persuaded him to tell her that he was vulnerable to a spear that had been worked for a year at Mass time on Sundays if he were standing with one foot on the back of a billy goat, the other on a bathtub.

107 After trying for a year Blodeuedd managed to contrive that Lleu should be in this position and Gronw, furnished with the necessary spear, stood in hiding and cast it at him. Wounded, Lleu changed into an eagle and flew away.

108 Gwydion sought him, tracking him down by following the sow who was feeding on the maggots that dropped from the eagle's putrifying wound. He found the dying hero perched in a tree and healed him. Blodeuedd he changed into an owl. Gronw, Lleu killed.

(iv) CULHWCH (KULHWCH) AND OLWEN

109 Culhwch's mother Goleuddydd lost her reason during her pregnancy and wandered the countryside. As the time for her delivery approached sanity returned. She came to herself in the middle of a herd of swine and was so frightened that she immediately fell into labour. The child being born in a pig run was named Culhwch (*hwch*: pig).

110 Culhwch's stepmother swore he should love only Olwen, daughter of the Chief Giant, Ysbaddaden, and Culhwch went to the court of his cousin King Arthur (**116–130**) to ask his help in winning this maiden. Glwelwyd, who kept the gate of Arthur's court, declared that never in all his long and varied career had he seen so handsome a man as this youth.

111 Arthur granted his cousin a boon and, learning of Culhwch's desire, confessed he had never heard of Olwen or her father but would send messengers to seek them. At the year's end however all returned unsuccessful.

112 Now Cei (Kay), Bedwyr (Bedivere), Cynddylig the Guide, Gwrhyr the Interpreter, Gwalchmei fab Gwyar, and Menw fab Teirgwaedd formed a party to help Culhwch in his quest. The company was chosen for its extraordinary gifts. Cei could remain nine days and nights without breathing or sleeping. He could change his height at will and his body temperature was so high that during a storm he never got wet and in cold weather his companions could kindle a fire from him. Bedwyr, though he had only one hand, was faster with his sword than three others fighting together. Gwalchmei never gave up any quest upon which he had started and Menw was a master of spells, which would preserve the party in heathen lands.

113 At length the company came upon a shepherd whose wife proved to be Culhwch's aunt. Though she had lost twenty-three of her twenty-four sons to the giant Ysbaddaden she agreed to help Culhwch meet Olwen, who came every Saturday to wash her hair at the woman's cottage.

114 When they met, Olwen told Culhwch to ask her father for her and not flinch from any conditions he might set. Three days Culhwch and his friends went to Ysbaddaden's castle. Each day he told them to return on the morrow and then, as their backs were turned, threw a poisoned stone at them, but they being quick always caught it and threw it straight back, gravely incommoding the giant. On the fourth day he therefore agreed to Culhwch's suit and imposed on him three tasks. These involved first, felling and burning a thicket, ploughing its ashes into a field and sowing that with flax; second, obtaining a variety of provisions for the wedding feast; and third, obtaining various preparations and pieces of equipment to barber the giant. Among these was a razor and comb from between the ears of the great boar Twrch Trwyth.

115 Innumerable conditions were imposed and as Ysbaddaden mentioned each, he told Culhwch it was impossible to fulfil. Each time the hero replied he could do it easily. Finally he swore fully to complete all the tasks with the help of his cousin King Arthur. So he did and returned to Ysbaddaden's castle with all the giant's enemies. There Ysbaddaden was killed and Culhwch slept with Olwen and she was his only wife for the rest of his life.

Culhwch takes the magic razor and comb from the head of Twrch Trwyth. Illustration from Lady Charlotte Guest's version of the *Mabinogion*, London, 1838–49. The London Library.

(v) KING ARTHUR

116 Although early Celtic writings contain a few passing references to Arthur, the eleventh-century *History of the Kings of Britain*, by Geoffrey of Monmouth, gives the first coherent narrative.

117 King Uther Pendragon became infatuated with Ygerna, wife of Duke Gorlois of Cornwall. Merlin (q.v.) so altered the king's appearance that even Ygerna believed him her husband when secretly he came to her in the castle at Tintagel. That same night Gorlois was killed in battle against Uther's troops, so the king married Ygerna. Arthur was their son.

The last page of a copy of Geoffrey of Monmouth's *History of the Kings of Britain*, from the late fourteenth-, early fifteenth-century manuscript of the *Red Book of Hergest.* Jesus College Library, Oxford. (*Photo: the Bodleian Library, Oxford.*)

Sir Gawain takes leave of King Arthur and Queen Guinevere. Illustration from the fourteenth-century manuscript *Roman de Lancelot du Lac*. Bodleian Library Ms. Douce 199 f. 151 v. (*Photo: Bodleian Library*.)

118 On his father's death the fifteen-year old prince was chosen as king and at once led the army against the Saxons, defeating their leader Colgrin and a mixed force of Saxons, Scots and Picts at the Battle of the River Douglas. Colgrin took refuge in York but Arthur was obliged to abandon his siege of that city and return to London.

119 Now he sought the aid of Hoel, King of Brittany, his cousin (or possibly his nephew), who landed at Southampton with a great army. Together, Arthur and Hoel beat the Saxons at Lincoln, at Caledon Wood (q.v.), and at Bath. They put down the Scots, Picts and Irish in Moray and toured Loch Lomond.

120 Next the two kings raised the siege of York. Arthur restored that city to its former glory and returned their lands to the three dispossessed Yorkist princes Loth, Urian and Auguselus.

121 Having now restored the whole kingdom, Arthur married, taking as his bride Guinevere, a lady of noble Roman descent, ward of the Duke Cador. She was the most beautiful woman in Britain (cf. **42, 70** and see glossary: Ireland, Spirit of).

122 Arthur then sailed to Ireland and, defeating its king Gilmaurius, conquered that island. Hearing of his great prowess and fearing his might, Doldavius and Gunhpar, the kings of Gotland and the Orkneys, came and did him homage.

123 Now Arthur began to invite the most distinguished men of other lands to join his court. The fame of his knights spread to the ends of the earth.

124 He decided to conquer Europe and began with Norway, which he gave to Loth of Lodonesia. Sailing thence to Gaul, he defeated and killed the Tribune Frollo and took Paris. With Hoel's aid Arthur had within nine years conquered the whole of Gaul. He held a court in Paris and established the government of that kingdom on a legal footing.

125 Now at Whitsun Arthur decided to hold a plenary court at the City of the Legions (Caerleon-on-Usk) and to it came representatives of all Europe.

126 Summoned to Rome by Lucius Hiberius to meet the charge of attacking the empire, Arthur, with 183,300 men, crossed to France and marched southwards. En route he had a vision of a dragon fighting and conquering a bear, and decided it represented his conflict with the emperor, though some of his entourage interpreted it as meaning he would fight and overcome a giant.

127 A giant he did defeat and kill at Mt. Saint Michel. He also routed the imperial troops at Saussy and was about to march on Rome when he heard that his nephew Mordred, son of Loth, whom he had left as his regent in Britain, had usurped the throne and taken Queen Guinevere as his mistress.

128 Returning home, Arthur landed at Richborough, where he fought and defeated Mordred. At the Battle of Winchester he defeated him again and pursued him to the River Camlan in Cornwall, where they fought a third time. Mordred was slain and Arthur taken to the Isle of Avalon so that his mortal wounds might be healed. Before leaving the king gave the crown to his cousin Constantine, son of Cador, Duke of Cornwall. That was in the year 542.

129 The belief that Arthur would return to inaugurate a golden age (cf. vol. 3: 5.1. Zoroastrianism; 5.2. **114, 194–195**; 5.3. Saushayani; 6.2. **56**; *St. Luke* 21. ix–xxviii, and *Revelation* 21–22) was well-established in both England and France by the early twelfth century and persisted at least until the later part of the nineteenth, though accounts of how and where the king would reappear varied considerably. In the *Vita Merlini* Geoffrey of Monmouth had called Avalon the Isle of Apples (cf. **34**), which suggests an Otherworldly realm, but some fifty years later in 1190 or 91 Avalon had become identified with Glastonbury, where Arthur's body was said to have been exhumed. In other stories he is said to lie sleeping at Cadbury in Somerset, in a cave on Craig-y-Dinas, near Snowdon, or even in another cave on Mount Etna (a story probably deriving from the Norman occupation of Sicily).

The ruins of Glastonbury Abbey, traditionally founded by Joseph of Arimathea when he brought the Holy Grail to Britain. Some said King Arthur was buried in the abbey. (*Photo: J. Allan Cash.*)

(vi) THE DEVELOPMENT OF THE ARTHURIAN LEGENDS

130 Stories of King Arthur and his knights have become some of the most potent of all European myths and legends, forming the bases of innumerable stories, poems, plays and operas, not only in Britain and France, but also particularly in Germany, as well as occurring in most other western European countries. One of the earliest tales is Chrétien de Troyes' *Le Conte de Grail* (1190). It was followed in the thirteenth century by the German Wolfram von Aeschenbach's *Parzival*, in the fifteenth century by Sir Thomas Malory's *Le Morte Darthur*, in the nineteenth by Tennyson's *Idylls of the King* and Wagner's *Parsifal, Lohengrin* and *Tristan*, in our own century by T. S. Eliot's *The Waste Land* and John Arden and Margaretta D'Arcy's *Island of the Mighty*. Besides such work lies a host of more or less popular 'historical' romances, every year bringing forth more examples.

131 The early development of these tales resulted from the cross fertilisation of Celtic and Christian material in which the king's band of knights becomes the Christian company of the Round Table dedicated to chivalry and the quest of the Holy Grail.

The Round Table

132 The Round Table is first referred to by the early twelfth-century writer Wace in his *Roman de Brut*, written in French but quickly translated and expanded in Layamon's *Brut*, written 1189–99.

133 According to Wace, Arthur's barons quarrelled over precedence and the king therefore 'made the Round Table'. Layamon says the quarrel arose during a Christmas feast and resulted in the death of several men. Shortly afterwards while visiting Cornwall, Arthur met a foreign carpenter who had heard of the brawl and offered to make a portable table at which 1600 could sit without anyone having precedence over another. Arthur commissioned the piece, which was finished in six weeks.

134 Other versions of the story however credit Merlin with the work, while in some Anglo-French romances the table, which now seats but 150, is the gift of Arthur's father-in-law, King Leodegrance. One seat at this table, the Siege Perilous, or Seat of Danger, was reserved for the knight who was to seek the Holy Grail.

The Grail Quest and the Fisher King

135 The Holy Grail was said to have been the dish from which Jesus had eaten the lamb at the Last Supper. It had also been used to catch drops of Christ's blood as he hung dying on the cross. Eventually it was brought to England by Joseph of Arimathea, who established a church at Glastonbury. His descendants, the Fisher Kings, guarded the grail in their Castle Corbenic, where it was hid from prying eyes.

136 Associated with the grail was a bleeding lance, sometimes identified with the lance of Longinus, said to be that with which Jesus' side was pierced by the centurion (*St. John* 19. xxxiv).

137 In later versions the association of the grail and the bleeding lance remains, but the grail itself is said to be the cup from which Jesus and his disciples drank at the Last Supper (*St. Matthew* 26. xxvii–xxviii). It brought about many miracles when Joseph of Arimathea brought it to Britain and fed the saint and his followers when they were in prison. Subsequently how-

A vision of the Holy Grail appears to the Knights of the Round Table. Illustration from the fourteenth-century French manuscript *Roman de Lancelot du Lac*. Bodleian Library Ms. Douce 199. (*Photo: Mansell Collection.*)

ever it disappeared to be seen thenceforward only by a few who were 'pure in heart' (a condition medieval Christian writers defined as 'celibate'). So, the magical dish or cauldron of the Celtic tradition (**13, 21, 96, 98**) became transformed into a symbolic cup of the Eucharist.

138 In Chrétien de Troyes' early version of this myth the mysterious vessel is housed in Grail Castle, guarded by a Grail Keeper. The wounded Fisher King of the castle has been maimed 'through his thighs' and feeds only from a magical dish. As a result of the king's injury the land has become infertile and will revive only if the king be healed. This can happen only if there be a knight brave enough to face all the dangers of the perilous journey through the 'land of wailing women' to Grail Castle and then wise enough to ask a certain question, which will break the enchantment to which the Fisher King and his land are captive.

139 Scholars are generally agreed that this strange tale derives from an ancient fertility myth and we may note that although one early writer derives the Fisher King's name from the fish symbol of Christ, it also has associations with the sea-god, who in Celtic myth is a king of the mysterious Otherworld to which selected heroes journey, and the Welsh *Preiddeu Annwn* describes a journey made by King Arthur to this Otherworld in search of a magic cauldron. (See glossary: Annwn, Bran and Conn Cétchathlach).

140 In medieval Arthurian legends the Grail Quest is undertaken by Sir Lancelot of the Lake, Sir Galahad, Sir Perceval and Sir Bors. (See glossary: Galahad, Lancelot, Perceval).

NORSE–GERMANIC MYTHS

Cosmological Myths
141–161

(i) THE CREATION

141 The story of the world's creation given by Snorri Sturluson in the *Prose Edda* and the anonymous poem *Vǫluspá* combines elements from at least three distinct accounts. In the first, life forms at the meeting point of heat and cold in the salty sea and from its sacrifice comes the world we know. In the second the World Cow licks Búri and his sons from the ice. In the third the giant Bergelmir survives a cataclysmic flood to found a new race. Possibly the Bergelmir story is a late invention by Snorri and based on the Biblical Flood myth, but we may notice that it also has much in common with the Vedic story of Manu (vol. 3: 5.2. **74–75**) and other evidence from the northern

Sir Galahad enters a tournament, riding so fast that he not only unseats Sir Gawain but, unable to draw rein, beheads Gawain's horse. Illustration from the fourteenth-century manuscript *Quête du Saint Graal*. The British Library Ms. Royal 14 E iii, f. 125 a. (*Photo: the British Library.*)

sagas suggest that the Norse-Germanic peoples, like the Indo-Āryans, believed in a cyclical pattern of events in which a recurrent catastrophe destroyed the world and all but one or a few of its inhabitants, who miraculously survived to found a new race.

142 At first there existed only the southern Múspellheimr, a region of fire and light, and Niflheimr the northern land of ice and snow. Between them lay the empty waste Ginnungagap. Here where sparks from Múspellheimr met the icy floes of Niflheimr and slowly thawed them, there appeared beneath the melting ice a giant named Ymir. The first man and his wife grew from the giant's left armpit. From his feet came the Frost Giants.

143 Ymir was fed by the primordial cow Audhumla (Authhumla). Like all cattle, she enjoyed licking salt and from the salty sea ice her lapping freed the man Búri, whose son Borr married Ymir's daughter Bestla and became the father of the Aesir, Ódinn (Óthinn), Vili and Vé.

144 These gods killed Ymir. The giant's blood poured out, flooding the world and killing all the Frost Giants except Bergelmir, who sailed away in his boat and became the father of a new giant race.

145 From Ymir's corpse the three Aesir formed Midgardr (Midgarthr, literally 'the middle earth'), the world of men. They made its seas and lakes from his blood, earth from his flesh, mountains from his bones, rocks and pebbles from his teeth, jaws and smaller broken bones. From Ymir's eyebrows the gods then made a wall to protect Midgardr from the Frost Giants. Taking his skull they made the dome of the sky, supported at the world's four corners by four dwarfs (cf. vol. 3: 5.2. **47–48, 56**, and 6.2. **58–60**).

Viking 'hogsback' stone from Heysham, Lancs., showing four dwarfs supporting the sky and possibly illustrating a Norse-Germanic creation myth. (*Photo: Werner Forman Archive*.)

Illustration from a late seventeenth-century manuscript of the *Prose Edda* showing *left*: Ódinn at the door of Valaskjálf, behind which rises Yggdrasill, chewed by the nanny-goat Heidrún and the hart Eicybyrmr; *right*: Midgardsormr about to swallow Thórr's baited line. Staatsbibliothek, Berlin. *(Photo: Bildarchiv Preussischer Kulturbesitz.)*

Phallic, bronze figurine, probably of the Norse-Germanic god Freyr. Statens Historiska Museum, Stockholm. *(Photo: Werner Forman Archive.)*

Above: 'The Wooing of
Grunhilde, the mother of
Hagen' : Arthur Rackham's
illustration for Wagner's
*Siegfried & the Twilight of
the Gods (trans.)* London,
1911. *(Photo: Cooper-
Bridgeman Library.)*

Right: the mortally
wounded King Arthur sits
in a meadow while Sir
Bedivere returns Excalibur
to the Lady of the Lake.
Illustration from the early
fourteenth-century *Roman
de Lancelot du Lac et de la
mort du Roi Arthur.* British
Museum Mss. Add. 10294,
vol. 94. *(Photo: Cooper-
Bridgeman Library.)*

(ii) THE CREATION OF MAN

146 The gods Ódinn, Hoenir and Lódurr were walking on the seashore when they came upon two trees. From them they made the man Askr ('Ash') and the woman Embla (possibly 'Elm'). Ódinn gave them spirit, Hoenir gave them intelligence and Lódurr bestowed their senses and bodies. (There is some dispute among scholars as to the exact meanings of the words here rendered as 'spirit', intelligence', 'body', 'senses').

147 The gods also created dwarfs, like maggots in Ymir's flesh, the earth. They ordered Night and Day to drive across the sky in their chariots and two blond children, the girl Sun and the boy Moon, they also ordered to drive across the skies. These children are pursued by wolves and one day the biggest of them will succeed in catching and swallowing Sun. Then the world will end. (See also **158–161**).

Bronze Horse drawing a chariot with a gold-plated disc, thought to represent the chariot of the sun, found at Trundholm on the isle of Zealand. The National Museum, Copenhagen. (*Photo: National Museum, Copenhagen.*)

(iii) YGGDRASILL THE COSMIC TREE

148 Another ancient creation myth is suggested by the story of Yggdrasill.

149 In the beginning existed the great ash tree Yggdrasill. One of its three roots reached to the domain of the Aesir and at its foot lay the Well of Urdr, the spring of Fate, guarded by the three Norns, Urdr (Urthr), Verdandi (Verthandi) and Skuldr ('Fate, Being and Necessity'). Daily they watered the tree and plastered it with clay from the spring, so preserving its life.

150 Yggdrasill's second root reached into Jọtunheimr, the land of the Frost Giants, and beneath it was the Spring of Mímir, whose water gave wisdom to all who drank it. The third root passed into Niflheimr, kingdom of the goddess Hel, the land of the dead. Beneath this root gushed the spring Hvergelmir, source of all rivers.

151 At the tree's foot curled a huge snake, Nidhọggr (Nithọggr), and many smaller serpents all constantly gnawing its roots. On its topmost bough perched an eagle with a hawk on its head. This eagle was the serpent's inveterate foe. Between them scurried the squirrel Ratatoskr, carrying insulting messages.

152 Yggdrasill was also menaced by goats which nibbled its branches and young shoots. From its boughs, which encompassed earth and heaven, fell the dew.

(iv) ASGARDR (Asgarthr)

153 Having formed Midgardr the Aesir built themselves a home, Asgardr, and commissioned one of the giants to encircle it with a wall. This the giant promised to build within a year asking in return to be given Sun and Moon and the goddess Freyja for his wife. When with the help of his wonderful stallion Svadilfari (Svathilfari) he seemed likely to finish the job in time, which all the Aesir had thought impossible, the Aesir commissioned Loki to find some way of preventing it, lest having Freyja the giant would grow too powerful. The wall was therefore never finished.

154 The wall was guarded by the silent Hemdallr, who carried a great trumpet *Gjallarhorn* to warn the Aesir of approaching danger. Between the earth and Asgardr the gods built the rainbow bridge Bifrọst.

(v) THE WAR IN HEAVEN

155 The Aesir fought a great battle with the Vanir (gods of fertility). At length a truce was declared and the two sides met to make peace. They all spat into a cauldron and from it made Kvasir, a being of such wisdom he could answer any question. However two dwarfs slew him and from his blood mixed with honey they brewed the Mead-of-Inspiration (q.v.). This Ódinn by his magic arts managed to steal and take to Asgardr. Whoever drank of this mead was inspired and spoke words of great wisdom and composed poetry, which was thenceforth known as 'Kvasir's blood' or 'Ship of the dwarfs'.

156 Another story says that when the truce was declared the Vanir and Aesir exchanged hostages, so the two greatest Vanir, Njọrdr (Njọrthr) and Freyr, went to live in Asgardr. The Aesir sent the handsome Hoenir—

Woodcarving from the stave church at Urnes, Norway, suggesting the Yggdrasill gnawed by the hart Eicybyrmr or the goat Heidrún. (*Photo: Werner Forman Archive.*)

prototype of the 'strong silent man'— and wise Mímir as their hostages. Since Hoenir never spoke a word the Vanir felt they had been badly treated and took their revenge by killing Mímir, whose head they returned to Asgardr. Óðinn sang charms over it and gave it the power of speech. From thenceforth he consulted it in any crisis, for Mímir was the fount of all wisdom.

Detail from the south side of the tenth-century Viking cross at Gosforth, Northumberland, showing Óðinn on Sleipnir and, below, the wolf-man Fenrir. (*Photo: C. M. Dixon.*)

157 Neither of these stories is very clear as it stands and though Dumézil suggests the myths express a common Indo-European theme of conflict arising from the gods of the third 'function's' desire to be recognised on equal terms by the other divinities (cf. the Ashvins, battle with Indra vol. 3: 5.2. **100**) one cannot but reflect that in these Norse accounts the Aesir seem to get the best of the battle, except for the fact that the two greatest Vanir become numbered among the inhabitants of Asgardr.

RAGNARØKR

158 The 'doom of the gods', a story popularised in Wagner's *Götterdäm-merung,* will be foreshadowed by a time of anarchy on earth, in which men will perform all manner of foul and unnatural crimes. The great wolf Fenrir (see **147** and glossary) will catch and swallow the sun and moon and the bitter *fimbulvetr* shroud the world for three long years. The stars will fall; mountains crumble in earthquakes and all the monsters imprisoned in the underworld break loose.

159 Spouting venom, Midgardsormr (Mithgarthsormr), the world serpent (**194–195, 198–202**) will rise from the ocean and flood the earth. Across the turbulent waters will come *Naglfar,* a ship made of dead men's nails, with Loki at its helm, bearing the Frost Giants to fight the gods. Surtr, the fire fiend, will lead his hosts from Múspellheimr shattering the rainbow bridge Bifrǫst and join the giants and monsters congregated on the plain of Vígrídr (Vígríthr) before Valhǫll (Valhalla).

160 Summoned by Heimdallr's horn the gods will ride out behind Ódinn and his host. Each finds himself pitched against his mortal foe: Ódinn against the terrible wolf-son Fenrir; Thórr against Midgardsormr, Freyr against Surtr, Tyr (q.v.) against the hell-hound Garmr; Heimdallr against Loki. All but Surtr will die. Then he will throw fire over the whole world, burning the corpses and destroying all mankind, and as the flames reach up to the heavens all sinks beneath the sea.

161 But Earth will rise again fresh and green from beneath the waters, and the daughter of the sun-goddess drive across the heavens in her mother's place. Baldr (**223–235**) returns from the dead to rule the sons of the gods and from Yggdrasill's (**148–152**) sheltering branches emerge Líf and Lífdrasir to repeople the world.

The Norse-Germanic Deities
162–235

(i) TÎWAZ, WODAN AND ÓDINN (ÓTHINN)
162 The great Norse god Ódinn seems to have combined characteristics of two deities known to the Germans as Tîwaz and Wodan or Wotan (Anglo-Saxon: Woden). Tîwaz, the Sky Father, was a fearsome god of justice (cf. Vedic Varuna: vol. 3: 5.3.; Iranian Ahura Mazda: 5.2. **1–6**) as well as Lord of Battle. By the first century after Christ Tîwaz's position was it seems being challenged in Germany by the war-god Wodan.

163 Wodan or Wotan was thought of rather in terms of the Vedic Indra, as leading a troop of warriors across the sky. His host was comprised of the souls of dead warriors and his name means 'Master of Fury' (*wode*). In Britain he was known as Wotan or Grim and his function as leader of the Wild Hunt survives in the story of Hern the Hunter (see also glossary: Cernunnos). It is clear that as master of the powers of darkness and death

Ódinn's ravens Huginn and Muninn, carved on an early twelfth-century pier in the church at Königslutter, W. Germany. (*Photo: Bildarchiv Preussischer Kulturbesitz.*)

Wodan had a *shamanistic* character. This is even more evident in stories of his Norse counterpart Ódinn.

164 The sacrificial rites associated with Tîwaz and Wodan are similar to those we know were performed in Ódinn's honour and in Norse myths Ódinn has become the Sky Father as well as the terrible battle-god. This gradual eclipse of the father deity by a younger god, often a god of war, is a common feature of Indo-European mythology (vol. 1: 2.2. **1–10**; vol. 3: 5.1: Indo-Iranian deities; 5.2. **94**; 5.3.: Varuna; and cf. vol. 1: 1.2. **20–28**).

165 Óðinn was known as 'the All Father', as well as leader of the Aesir. He was also called 'the One-eyed' for he had sacrificed one of his eyes in exchange for the right to drink from the Spring of Mímir (**150, 156**). His other names were Father of Battle, God of the Hanged, and God of Cargoes. He lived in the silver-roofed hall Valaskjálf where stood the Hliðskjálf (Hlithskjálf), the seat from which he could survey all the worlds, but he also journeyed constantly over the earth on his wonderful eight-legged horse Sleipnir and was brought information by his two ravens Huginn and Muninn (Thought and Memory).

166 As Father of Battle Óðinn stirred up strife with his great spear *Gungnir*. He determined the outcome of all conflicts and in tenth-century Norwegian poems is envisaged as deciding that his favourite warriors shall die in battle so that they may become part of his personal band in Valhǫll (Valhalla), feasting all night on pork and mead, milked from the goat Heiðrún, and sallying forth to do battle all day.

167 However, like the German Wodan, Óðinn was regarded with mixed feelings, for whereas Tîwaz had been a sternly just god, neither of his successors could, it seems, be relied on. Many references are made to Óðinn's treachery. He promised Haraldr Hilditǫnn (Harald Wartooth), King of the Danes, that he would protect him in return for the souls of all those the king slew, but then stirred up strife between Haraldr and his friend King Ringr, taught Ringr how to draw up his troops into the all but invincible wedge formation and during the ensuing battle took the place of Haraldr's charioteer and, flinging the Danish king from the chariot, stabbed him to death.

168 On the other hand, Óðinn was generous to his favourites and bestowed a magnificent sword upon the Volsung Sigmundr and a splendid horse on Sigmundr's son Sigurðr (the German Siegfried, hero of Wagner's *Götterdämmerung* (**236–246**).

169 Óðinn's title 'God of the Hanged' seems to be of twofold significance. We know that people, especially defeated enemies, and animals were hanged in his honóur, often being stabbed or speared as they dangled from the tree. Sometimes their bodies were later burned. Old Norse writing refers to sacrifices being dedicated with spear, hanging and burning and there are many later accounts of such rites.

170 The story of Óðinn himself stabbed and hanged from Yggdrasill, which appears in the poem *Hávamál*, was once thought to have been derived from Christian sources, but is now believed to refer to the symbolic death of the *shaman*, by means of which he penetrates hidden wisdom. Nine days did stabbed Óðinn hang from the tree, without food or drink, sacrificed to himself; then, peering down he took the runes of knowledge and was set free.

171 Yggdrasill was also referred to as Óðinn's 'steed', which may be a reference to the *shaman's* symbolic ascent of a tree or ladder to commune with the heavens. Other references to his *shamanistic* character occur in the *Ynglinga Saga,* which speaks of his ability to send out his spirit in the form of an animal or bird, speeding to far-off lands. His eight-legged flying horse Sleipnir is also typical of the *shaman's* mystical steed. Ellis Davidson how-

Memorial stone from
Alskog, Tjangvide,
Gotland, shows Ódinn
riding Sleipnir, attendant
women and a flying figure
with a spear, who may be
Valkyries and, to the left, a
building probably denoting
Valhalla, a symbol of the
grave. Below is a death
ship. (*Photo: Antikvarisk-
Topografiska Arkivet,
Stockholm.*)

ever suggests that this may be not only an image of the *shaman's* power of
'flight', but also incorporates a reference to the bier, which the Gond people
of central India refer to as an eight-legged horse. She notes that on Sleipnir
Ódinn journeys to the Niflheimr to consult a dead seeress and on another
occasion Hermódr (Hermóthr) was sent down to this kingdom of Hel on
Sleipnir in search of his brother Baldr (**226**). In the late *Egils Saga ok Ásumndar* Ódinn leads a giantess down to the underworld and we know from other
sources, Tibetan for example, that one function of the *shaman* was to conduct
the souls of the dead to the next life.

172 Ódinn was also very active on the earthly plane and, like his Greek counterpart Zeus (vol. 1: 2.2. **26**), fathered many heroes on human women.

The Valkyries

173 Associated with Ódinn were the Valkyrja (Valkyries) whose name means 'Choosers of the Slain'. They included Hildr, Hlǫkk and Gudr (Gurthr), whose names all mean 'Battle', Herfjǫturr ('War-fetter'), and the beautiful Brynhildr (**240–243**).

174 In many Old Norse stories they are armed horsewomen and, from comparatively early times, among both Scandinavian and Germanic peoples they were also conceived of as terrifying figures riding wolves. One Viking Irish poem refers to them as weaving the fate of men in bloody entrails. They bathed battlefields in blood and are once spoken of as rowing through a sea of blood as more blood rains from the skies.

175 It is possible that the Valkyrja were associated with the priestesses who chose human victims for Ódinn's sacrifices and performed the ritual slaughter, as described by the tenth-century Arab traveller, Ibn Fadlan.

Sixth-century silver and bronze-gilt pendant from Tura, Lapland, possibly intended to represent a Valkyrie. Statens Historiska Museum, Stockholm. (*Photo: Werner Forman Archive.*)

Silver amulet of the ninth to tenth century, in the form of Thórr's hammer. National Museum, Copenhagen. (*Photo: Photoresources.*)

(ii) THÓRR

176 The huge Thórr, son of Fjǫrgynn, was the gods' champion. Wearing iron gloves, he wielded his terrible hammer *Mjǫllnir*, protecting Asgardr against all enemies. His other weapon was his *Belt-of-Strength*. Thórr's irascibility was famous and those who offended him risked having a thunder-bolt hurled at their heads or a gale drive their ships onto the rocks as Thórr angrily puffed out the bristles of his great red beard. Like Zeus and Indra (vol. 1: 2.2. **28**; vol. 3: 5.2. **94–100**) he is associated not only with the fear-

Four figures arranged in a swastika pattern on a Pictish graveslab, seventh-ninth century. Meigle Museum, Perthshire. (*Photo: C. M. Dixon.*)

some power of the storm but also with its fertilising rain and his hammer is both thunderbolt and phallic symbol (cf. glossary: Perkūnas). It was, it seems, held to afford its wearers protection, for many hammer charms have been found and the hammer sign and allied *swastika* also appear on inscriptions invoking Thórr's blessing on the dead. The *swastika* also appears on Anglo-Saxon funerary jars. It seems to have been a fire emblem and possibly signified Thórr's lightning. It was especially popular among the Germanic tribes.

177 The dual nature of the hammer symbol is particularly evident in the stories of Thórr's journey to Utgardr (Utgarthr, **187–196**) and of his fight with Thrymr (**180**).

178 Thrymr stole *Mjǫllnir* and refused to return it unless Freyja (**218–221**) became his wife. Heimdallr suggested that Thórr disguise himself in a bridal veil and, attended by the resourceful Loki, travel to the Giants' home, Jǫtunheimr, to recover the precious weapon. Thórr was reluctant to assume such a costume as a bridal veil but eventually consented.

179 The two disguised gods received a joyful reception from the Frost Giants but Thórr nearly gave himself away at the marriage feast by eating not only eight salmon but an entire ox, washed down by three cups of mead! Loki hastily explained that 'Freyja' had so longed for Thrymr that she had been unable to touch food for eight days. When Thrymr was somewhat startled by the glaring eyes he glimpsed behind the bridal veil as he stooped to kiss his betrothed, Loki quickly added that Freyja had been unable to sleep either!

180 At length, according to custom, *Mjǫllnir* was laid in the bride's lap to hallow the marriage. Seizing his weapon, Thórr slew Thrymr and all the guests.

181 Possibly this comic tale is the Norse version of that fertility myth otherwise expressed in terms of the dying god or goddess who is rescued from the underworld (cf. **88–92, 276–279**; vol. 1: 1.2. **40–52, 105–109, 152–157**; 2.2. **111–115**).

182 Other giants slain by Thórr included Geirrødr (Geirrøthr) and the builder of Asgardr's wall (**153**). Of particular interest is his duel with Hrungnir, whose head and heart were of stone. Drunken Hrungnir boasted he would sink Asgardr beneath the sea and abduct both Freyja and Thórr's golden-haired wife, Sif. He challenged the furious Thórr to a duel.

183 The Frost Giants created Mǫkkurkalfi ('Mist-calf'), a man of clay, to support their champion and Hrungnir advanced brandishing a great whetstone and guarding himself with a stone shield. Thórr came out wearing his iron gloves and *Belt-of-Strength*, brandishing *Mjǫllnir*, and attended by his servant, the farmer's son Thjálfi (**188**).

184 Hrungnir hurled his whetstone, Thórr his thunderbolt. *Mjǫllnir* shattered the whetstone and smashed Hrungnir's skull. Pieces from the stone flew everywhere, one lodging itself in Thórr's forehead.

185 Gróa, a *vǫlva* (seeress), tried to charm the fragment out but while she was doing so Thórr began to speak of the occasion on which he had brought her husband, Aurvandill, out of the Frost Giants' kingdom in a basket and, when the man suffered a frostbitten toe had amputated it and hurled it into the sky, where it became the star Aurvandill's Toe. Fascinated by the story the *vǫlva* forgot to finish her spell, so the piece of stone remained in Thórr's forehead.

186 Possibly this tale is associated with the ritual kindling of fire. References to 'god-nails' in the pillars of Thórr's temple occur in *Eyrbyggja Saga* and the seventeenth-century pagan Lapps had a temple to the thunder-god where the image had a nail and a flint in its forehead, which were used to kindle light. Several *sagas* refer to the association of fire with Thórr's rituals particularly in hallowing land to him, and the late *Kjalnesinga Saga* says the fire in his temple was never allowed to go out. We know that the sanctuaries of the Old Prussian thunder-god Perkonis (see Perkūnas) also contained such fire.

187 Thórr was not always depicted as invincible. In the *Prose Edda* Snorri describes the god's comic journey to Utgardr (Utgarthr), a giant kingdom.

188 Thórr set out accompanied by Loki. En route they stopped at a farm where Thórr slaughtered a number of goats (his sacred animal) for a meal. Afterwards, he spread out the goatskins and bones and, raising his hammer above them, blessed them, restoring all to life. One however was lame for the farmer's son had broken its leg bone for the marrow. This caused Thórr such annoyance that the farmer hastily offered his son and daughter, Thjálfi and Rǫskva, as servants to the god.

189 After travelling all day through a great forest, the party came at night-fall to a building with a gaping opening along one of its sides. This they entered and lay down to rest, but were soon disturbed by an earthquake. Creeping further into the hall they found a passage leading off to the right. In this they hid while Thórr guarded the entrance. All night their rest was disturbed by a terrible roaring.

190 At dawn they stole out to find a huge sleeping giant and realised that the roaring was the noise of his snores, while their shelter had been his glove. Thórr hastily began to buckle on his *Belt-of-Strength*, but just then the giant awoke. He seemed amiable and told them his name was Skrymir ('Big Fellow'). Picking up his glove he suggested he carry all the party's luggage, and packed it in his sack. So huge were his strides however that he soon was lost to view and when at dusk they at last caught him up it was to find him once more fast asleep.

191 Unable to unfasten the sack containing their provisions Thórr hammered Skrymir on the head. He opened an eye, remarked that a leaf had hit him and promptly went to sleep again. A second blow he took to be an acorn. Hungry, Thórr and his party spent another sleepless night.

192 In the morning Thórr took a third, furious, swipe at the giant's head, putting such power behind the blow that his hammer sank up to its shaft in Skrymir's skull. The giant sat up, said that a bird seemed to have dropped something on his head. Rising, he bade Thórr and his company farewell, warning them to mind their manners when they came to Utgardr, for there they would find giants even bigger than he.

193 When they at length reached the huge hall of Utgardr, the giant king Utgardar-loki (Utgarthar-loki), after commenting disparagingly on their puny appearance, invited them to display their skills.

194 First, Loki engaged in an eating competition with one Logi, but although Loki ate quickly Logi ate even faster and consumed not only the food but also all the bones and the eating trough to boot! Thjálfi raced against Hugi, who beat him hands down. Thórr then attempted to empty at a single draught the horn of wine he was offered. After three huge drinks he had only slightly lowered the level of its contents. Utgardar-loki then suggested that Thórr might try to lift his cat. Thórr grasped the huge grey monster and, exerting all his strength, managed to lift one of its paws. More was beyond him. Now Utgardar-loki suggested Thórr try to wrestle with his old foster-mother. Thórr approached this aged crone, but could not throw her. She easily forced him onto one knee and might have thrown him too but the king intervened and stopped the contest.

195 Next morning, after royal entertainment, the travellers were taken to the gate by Utgardar-loki himself. Before bidding them farewell he explained that they had been deceived, for Loki's opponent had been Fire (*logi*), Thjálfi's Thought (*hugi*), while Thórr had been trying to drink the sea (and had appreciably lowered its level). The cat he had attempted to lift was the serpent Midgardsormr (**198–202**) in disguise, while the aged crone against whom he had wrestled was Old Age (*elli*).

196 Outraged by this trick, Thórr swung his hammer, but king and hall instantly disappeared, leaving Thórr and his companions alone in the forest.

197 Thórr's battle with the world serpent Midgardsormr is the Norse version of the widespread myth of the storm or fertility god's contest with a monster (cf. **271**; vol. 1: 1.2. **1, 22–26, 83–88, 100–102**; and vol. 3: 5.2. **95–96**) and is told in the *Edda* poem *Hymiskvida*.

198 Thórr's struggle with Midgardsormr in cat form seems to have resulted in his defeat, yet Utgardar-loki's comments implied awe at the great god's achievement. Thórr's other encounter with Midgardsormr also seems inconclusive, but again there are suggestions that Thórr did in fact succeed, though appearing to have failed.

199 Taking the form of a youth, Thórr went to the giant Hymir and asked to accompany him on a fishing expedition. Hymir sent him to fetch some bait. Thórr cut off the head of the giant's largest ox.

200 Once in the boat Thórr rowed so swiftly that Hymir grew nervous lest they disturb Midgardsormr. He was even more apprehensive when, instead of stopping at the usual fishing ground, the youth continued out to sea and at length cast his line baited with the whole ox-head.

201 Before long Midgardsormr took the bait. Exerting all his strength, Thórr drew in the line and, eventually, having stamped holes in the boat's hull and braced himself against the seabed, he at length hauled the monster to the surface. Serpent and god glared balefully at each other. Thórr raised his hammer; but just as the blow descended the terrified Hymir cut the line and Midgardsormr fell back beneath the waves. Furious, Thórr swept the giant overboard and, leaving him to flounder, himself waded back to the beach.

202 The serpent's malevolent character is evidently the motive for Thórr's action, yet both Utgardar-loki and Hymir imply that his overwhelming success would bring disaster to the world, for Midgardsormr curls round it, holding it in its place. Only at Ragnarøkr will he break free and then the

Eighth-century bronze plaque from Solberga, Ostergotland, showing Thórr fishing for Midgardsormr. Statens Historiska Museum, Stockholm. (*Photo: Werner Forman Archives.*)

Bronze die for making helmet plaques shows two warriors in boar's head helmets. The die is one of several found at Torslunda on the Baltic island Öland, and dates from the sixth century. Statens Historiska Museum, Stockholm. (*Photo: Photoresources.*)

world will be destroyed. The purpose of Thórr's contest seems therefore less to kill the monster than to assert his power over it. In their final battle at Ragnarøkr they slay each other (**158–161**).

(iii) NJǪRDR AND SKADI
203 Njǫrdr, the chief Vanir, lived at Noatun ('the boat enclosure'). He governed both the sea and its winds, helping fishermen and sailors. His name is the Old Norse equivalent of Nerthus, whom Tacitus describes as a Danish fertility goddess carried round the countryside in a wagon and worshipped on island sanctuaries. Human sacrifices seem to have been made to her in bogs and possibly these account for the Iron Age corpses discovered in Danish peat cuttings and described in Glob's *The Bog People*.

204 Various theories have been advanced about the relationship between Njǫrdr and Nerthus. Possibly they were aspects of the same figure. Freyr's cult (**208–213**) certainly seems to have embodied rites common to both. Possibly however the two deities were regarded as brother and sister, like Freyr and Freyja (**207–221**).

205 According to Snorri, Njǫrdr's wife was Skadi, daughter of the giant Thyázi (q.v.), whose death she sought to avenge by attacking Asgardr. Preferring not to fight a woman the Aesir offered to allow her to chose a husband from among the gods. When she agreed, hoping to win Baldr (**223–235**), they hid themselves so that all she could see was their feet and she found she had selected Njǫrdr. Their marriage was unusual, for she disliked living by the sea and Njǫrdr found the inland mountains intolerable. In winter therefore they parted, he returning to the sea, she hunting over the snowy mountainside.

206 A similar but apparently happier union took place between a giantess and Njǫrdr's son Freyr.

(iv) FREYR

207 Freyr fell in love with Gerdr (Gerthr), daughter of the giant Gymir, whom he had glimpsed while sitting on Ódinn's Hlidskjálf seat (**165**). His friend and servant Skírnir went down to the giants' Underworld kingdom to woo Gerdr for him, offering her gifts of golden apples and the great ring *Draupnir* (q.v.). She rejected them, only consenting to become Freyr's wife when Skírnir threatened to cast a spell on her and exile her to a cave on the edge of the world, where she would 'wither like a thistle'.

208 Gerdr did not accompany Skírnir back to the upperworld but agreed to meet Freyr nine days later in his sacred grove.

209 Possibly their marriage represents the union of earth and sky. The references to apples and the sacred grove suggest a fertility rite and we know from other sources that ritual union played an important part in Freyr's cult.

210 The *Flateyjarbók* tells how the Norwegian Gunnarr Helmingr fled to Sweden after offending King Oláfr Tryggvason. At Freyr's temple he was attracted by the god's wife, the young priestess, and when the time came for Freyr's autumn progress to bless the land, Gunnarr was invited to accompany it, although the priestess felt Freyr might dislike it. The party found itself caught in a blizzard and all but Gunnarr abandoned the god and his wife. Gunnarr led the wagon on for a while, then stopped to rest. The priestess said Freyr would attack him if he did not continue, and indeed the god descended from the wagon and fought the hero. In desperation Gunnarr called upon King Oláfr's god (i.e. the Christian god), and with his help overcame the other, who departed. Gunnarr destroyed Freyr's image, dressed himself in the god's ornaments and took his place.

211 When the party at length arrived at the feast being held in Freyr's honour, the people were delighted that their god could now share their food and drink. They were even happier when he asked for rich clothing and gifts rather than human sacrifices, but their pleasure reached its peak when they found the god's wife was pregnant.

The Green Knight picks up his head, which Sir Gawain has just severed, at King Arthur's
Christmas Feast in Camelot. Illustration to *Sir Gawain and the Green Knight, c.* A.D. 1400
British Library Cotton Collection, Ms. Nero Ax. *(Photo: Cooper-Bridgeman Library.)*

Above: a tapestry,
c. A.D. 1100, from Skog
church, Hälsingland,
Sweden, thought possibly
to show the deities Óðinn,
Thórr, Freyja (small back-
ground figure) and Freyr.
Statens Historiska Museum,
Stockholm. (Photo:
Photoresources.)

Right: The horned god and
attendant animals from the
Gundestrup cauldron.
This god is usually
identified with the Celtic
Cernunnos. National
Museum, Copenhagen.
(Photo: Werner Forman
Archive.)

212 Just at this time King Oláfr sent to command Gunnarr's return, so the young man took his wife and all the booty and secretly stole away.

213 Freyr's fertility cult was also especially associated with horses and boars, well-known ancient fertility symbols. There are several references to horses named Freyfaxi dedicated to him, and the dwarfs made him a golden boar called Gullinbursti ('Golden-bristled'). It shone in the dark and could outrun the fastest horse.

214 To Norse and Germanic peoples the boar seems to have had a protective function as well as being a fertility symbol and war helmets were decorated with its image. King Athlis of Sweden won such a helmet, called *Hildisvín* (Battle-swine), the name of the golden pig owned by Freyr's sister Freyja.

215 As we have seen, the story of Njǫrdr's and Skadi's marriage suggests the union of fertile sea and icy mountains, wintry underworld and fructifying sky. Freyr's association with the sea also combines the ideas of death and fertility. He was said to have had a magic boat named *Skídbladnir* (Skíth-blathnir), which when not in use could be folded into his pocket, but was capable of expanding to carry all the Aesir. It could sail in any direction and always had a following wind.

216 We know that ships had a potent significance for the Norsemen and until modern times they have been kept in churches and carried in religious processions. In Denmark they are used in the ceremony of blessing the fields. At the same time they were also associated with death, for, as many *sagas* tell, dead heroes were sent out to sea in their burning ships. Archaeological discoveries such as that of Sutton Hoo show that ship burials were also well known. Possibly Freyr's own burial was of such a type.

217 When Freyr died his death was concealed for three years. He lay in a tumulus whose door had three holes through which the priests offered gold, silver and copper.

(v) FRIGG, FREYJA AND GEFJUN

218 Freyr's sister Freyja was the chief Vanir goddess and the one of whom we know most, but Ódinn's wife Frigg seems to have been closely associated with her. Some writers even confuse them. Both were fertility goddesses and they seem to have been complementary figures, Frigg the maternal, Freyja, promiscuous, emblem of fertility. Her importance to the world's vitality is suggested by the Frost Giants' constant attempts to win her and the Aesir's horror at this possibility (**153, 178**).

219 Like Mediterranean fertility goddesses (cf. vol. 1: 2.2. **111–115**), Freyja is also associated with the underworld, although we know little of her function there. The *Grímnismál* says that half of those warriors slain in battle go to her hall Fǫlkvang, while Ódinn receives the rest in Valhǫll (**166**).

220 Freyja's most precious possession, one of the 'Treasures of the Gods', was the wonderful *Brísingamen*, a splendid piece of jewelry, possibly a necklace, which the dwarfs gave her in return for her sleeping with them one by one.

221 Freyja's carriage is said to have been drawn by cats, possibly because

Twelfth-century wall-painting, Schleswig Cathedral, W. Germany, shows Freyja as a witch or *shamanka* riding a striped wild cat or tiger. (*Photo: Bavaria Verlag.*)

Twelfth-century wall-painting from Schleswig Cathedral, W. Germany, shows Frigg riding a broomstick and, like the illustration of Freyja (*opposite*), suggests the derivation of medieval witches from the earlier *shamankas*.
(*Photo: Bavaria Verlag.*)

cats were also associated with the *vǫlva* seeresses, who practised a kind of trance divination known as *seidr*, which Freyja was the first to teach. These *vǫlva*, who were, it seems, *shamankas*, wore animal costumes, including gloves of catskin. Additional evidence of Freyja's *shamanistic* associations are found in references to her ability to turn herself into a falcon.

222 Gefn was one of Freyja's names. The Vikings told of another goddess with the related name Gefjun. Rather like Freyja, she had a beautiful necklace, a present from a lover. Gefjun was particularly associated with agriculture. It is said that Ódinn sent her to find some land. Gylfi, King of Sweden, said she might have as much as she could plough. Gefjun therefore became a giant's mistress and conceived four huge sons. These she transformed into oxen and ploughed the whole of Sjaelland (Zealand) isolating it from the Swedish mainland. Then she went to live at Leire with Ódinn's son Skjǫldr (Scyld), first king of Denmark.

BALDR

223 No myths about Baldr are known among Germanic peoples although the second *Merseburg Charm* (a ninth-century pagan spell) mentions him in association with Wodan. His name means *lord*. Snorri calls him Ódinn's blond son, beloved of the gods, but Saxo, who describes him as 'sprung secretly from celestial seed', speaks of him as a hero, and he may well have been thought of as a warrior of celestial birth, like Skjǫldr (**222**). Early Skaldic lays refer to him in this sense. The popular conception of him as a shining sky-god derives from Snorri.

224 The beautiful Baldr was troubled by ominous nightmares and the Aesir sent Frigg to ask all things on earth to swear they would never harm Baldr. Subsequently the gods amused themselves by hurling spears and stones at him and seeing him invulnerable to them all. However Loki, disguised as an old woman, discovered that Frigg had omitted to ask any promise from the delicate mistletoe plant. Loki then took a dart of mistletoe wood and gave it to Hǫdr to throw at Baldr, guiding the blind god's aim. The dart pierced Baldr, who fell dead.

225 The gods built a great funeral pyre on Baldr's ship *Hringhorni*. Beside him they lay his wife Nanna, who had died of grief at his loss. On the pyre too they placed his horse and many treasures, including Ódinn's great ring *Draupnir*. Then the pyre was lit and a giantess pushed *Hringhorni* off its rollers and it floated out to sea on the tide.

226 At Frigg's request Ódinn's son Hermódr took his father's great stallion Sleipnir and rode down to the Niflheimr, land of the dead, to rescue his brother's spirit. After nine days he came to the River Gjall (Resounding River), which encircled the underworld. Modgudr (Mothguthr), guardian of its golden bridge Gjallarbrú, told him that Baldr had crossed the previous night accompanied by five troops of dead horsemen.

227 Sleipnir easily leaped Helgrind, the gate of the underworld, and Hermódr came into the Hall of Hel and saw Baldr his brother sitting in the place of honour.

228 Hermódr explained his mission to Hel, goddess of the underworld, who said that if all things in the world, living and dead, wept for Baldr he might return to Asgardr. Otherwise he must remain with her. The brothers parted, Baldr giving Hermódr many gifts, including the ring *Draupnir* to return to their father Ódinn.

229 The gods asked all things to weep for Baldr and it seemed that all did, even the stones and metals of earth exuded frosty tears, but the giantess Thǫkk refused, saying that as Baldr had been no use to her, alive or dead, he might stay where he was.

230 Believing Thǫkk to be none other than Loki in disguise, the Aesir determined on revenge and though Loki fled, turning himself into a salmon, they eventually netted him. He was bound across three stones held down with the entrails of one of his own sons, and placed beneath a serpent's open mouth which dripped venom into his face. Sigyn, his devoted wife, tried to catch the poison in a bowl but every time she emptied it the venom fell back onto Loki. His writhing makes the earth tremble and there he will remain till Ragnarøkr (**158–161**).

Detail from the Gosforth Cross shows a bound man and a woman with a bowl. They are thought to represent the tortured Loki and his faithful wife Sigyn. (*Photo: Werner Forman Archive.*)

231 This picture of Loki as Baldr's murderer is probably a late one and supported only by the *Lokasenna*, another later work. The *Vǫluspá* and *Baldrs Draumar* both support Saxo's variant account which attributes Baldr's death to Hǫdr alone. The tale of the mistletoe dart may also be a late addition, or derive from Snorri's misunderstanding of his sources, for mistletoe is not native to Iceland. There was however a Norse tradition of a wonderful sword called *Mistillteinn* (*Mistletoe*) and, as we shall see, Saxo says that Baldr was killed with such a magical sword. On the other hand, Snorri's references to the dart may derive from a version in which Baldr was killed by a charmed stick being pointed at him, a well-known feature of the *shaman's* art, referred to several times in association with Ódinn.

232 In his *Gesta Danorum* Saxo describes the warrior Baldr attended by a troop of minor goddesses resembling the Valkyries. They feed him on food steeped in snake's venom, inoculating him against all ills.

233 Baldr's great rival was Hǫdr, with whom he contended for the hand of beautiful Nanna. They fought several battles. Once Baldr's fleet and host were utterly routed, although the gods supported them. On another occasion Baldr proved the victor of the battle but he still failed to win Nanna, whom Hǫdr married.

234 Baldr pined with grief, becoming so weak that he had to be carried in a cart, but Hǫdr knew he could never kill this redoubtable foe unless he could obtain the magical sword guarded by the satyr Mimingus. He therefore set out on the terrible journey through cold and darkness to the Otherworldly land where Mimingus lived. Taking the satyr by surprise he managed to wrest the sword from him.

235 With it Hǫdr succeeded in wounding Baldr. Next day their armies met in a final great battle, though Baldr was already so weak that he had to be carried onto the field. Three days later he died. Determined to avenge him Ódinn fathered Bous (Boe) upon Princess Rinda and when Bous grew up he killed Hǫdr. So Baldr was avenged.

The Hero Sigurdr (Siegfried) and the Dwarf's Treasure
236–246

236 The story of Sigurdr (German Siegfried) is told both in the Norse *Vǫlsunga Saga* and the German *Nibelungenlied (Lay of the Nibelungs)*.

237 Sigurdr, the posthumous son of the great hero Sigmundr, was fostered by the smith Reginn (Mime), who persuaded him to kill the dragon Fáfnir (Reginn's transformed brother) and so win the hoard of dwarf gold upon which the dragon lay.

238 Reginn, Fáfnir and their father Hreidmar (whom they later had

murdered) had compelled the Aesir to steal this gold for them from the dwarf Andvari (q.v.) in recompense for having accidentally killed Hreidmar's third son, Otr.

239 Sigurdr slew Fáfnir and ate his heart. This enabled him to understand the language of birds and from them he learned that Reginn was planning to swindle him of the booty. He therefore killed Reginn too, but was himself destined to sorrow, for included in the treasure was Andvari's magic ring, a curse on all who owned it.

240 Sigurdr came to a hill. Within a circle of fire on its summit he saw the beautiful Valkyrja Brynhildr whom Ódinn had condemned to sleep within the flames until she was wakened by a hero with courage to brave the fiery circle. Sigurdr woke her and gave her the dwarf's ring as a token of his love.

241 He then journeyed on to the land of the Nibelungs, where his courage won him many admirers. Here he was given an enchanted drink which led him to forget his love for Brynhildr and so he married the Nibelung Gudrunn. Later he persuaded her brother Gunnarr to seek Brynhildr's hand.

242 When Gunnarr failed to penetrate the fiery circle, Sigurdr, assuming his likeness, did so in his stead and as 'Gunnarr' pledged his troth with Brynhildr. They exchanged rings, so Sigurdr again received the cursed ring of Andvari. Returning home he passed it on to Gunnarr.

The eleventh-century Ramsundsberg stone, Södermanland, Sweden, illustrates the tale of Sigurdr and Fáfnir. The dragon's body forms the picture's frame. Inside, left to right: the beheaded Reginn lies among his tools; Sigurdr, roasting Fáfnir's heart, sucks a burned thumb; his horse Grani stands tethered beneath the birds who warned Sigurdr of Reginn's treachery. (*Photo: Topograviska Arkivet, Stockholm.*)

The marriage of Kriemhild and Etzel from a fifteenth-century German manuscript of the *Nibelungenlied*. Staatsbibliothek, Berlin, Ms. Germ. fol. 855, 86 v. (*Photo: Bildarchiv Preussischer Kulturbesitz*.)

243 Brynhildr, aware of the trick, yet resolved to play her part. However during the wedding feast the effects of the charmed potion Sigurdr had been given began to wear off and he was once more overwhelmed by love for her. She, driven to fury by Gudrunn's mockery of the way she had been tricked into marriage with Gunnarr, was however determined to avenge herself on her lover. She persuaded her brother-in-law Guttormr to kill Sigurdr while he lay sleeping; then, overcome by remorse, killed herself, sharing Sigurdr's funeral pyre (cf. **225**; 3.3: Signy; vol. 3: 5.2. **160**). By contrast, Gudrunn, Sigurdr's widow, far from expressing any grief, immediately re-married, her second husband being Atli (i.e. Attila, German Etzel) King of the Huns.

244 The hoard of gold which Sigurdr had owned was now taken by Gunnarr and Guttormr, who secretly hid it at the bottom of the Rhine. King Atli killed them for it, but failed to discover its whereabouts. To avenge her brothers' murder, Gudrunn now killed Atli and fled the country.

245 According to the *Nibelungenlied*, Siegfried, having bathed in the dragon Fáfnir's blood was invulnerable, except at a point between his shoulders, which a falling leaf had shielded from the immortalising bath (cf. vol. 1: 2.2. **294, 321**; vol. 3: 5.3: Isfandiār). The furious Brünhilde (Brynhildr) therefore

hubschen mit den frawen das sey m lieb getan
So sprach der starck Seiferid mit herlichen sit
wann ir jagen rettent da wil gerne mit
So sult ir vmc lerhen amen schutz man
Vnd ettlichen pracken so vil ich retten in den tan
Welt ir nicht nemen emen sprach der kunig ze hant
Ich leihe ew welt ir viere den vil wol ist bechant
der walt vnd auch die stone wa die diere hine gaund
die euch nicht verwerse ze den herbergen retten laund
Do rait zu semem weibe der reck vil gemait
schier het hagen den kunig gesait
wie er gewinnen wolte den trewlichen degen
Auff grosser vntrewen solte nimm man gephlegen

Hagen murders Siegfried.
Illustration from a fifteenth-
century manuscript of the
Nibelungenlied.
Staatsbibliothek, Berlin.
Ms. Germ. fol. 855, 58 v.
(*Photo: Bildarchiv
Preussischer Kulturbesitz.*)

persuaded Siegfried's wife Kriemhild (Gudrunn) to make him a shirt marked with a cross which at once covered and indicated the vulnerable spot, as Kriemhild in confidence told Hagen (q.v.). Guided by this, Hagen stabbed Siegfried. Hagen took the dwarf's treasure and hid it.

246 Kriemhild demanded he give it to her, and when he refused to reveal its hiding place she killed him. Shocked by her parricide, her husband King Etzel thereafter spurned her and she eventually met her death at the hand of one Hildebrand.

FINNO–UGRIC MYTHS FROM THE *KALEVALA*

The Creation
247–248

247 Ilmatar Luonnotar (Daughter of the Air, Daughter of Creation) tired of her lonely life among the deserts of the air descended into the sea, floating on its waves. Its winds and waters awakened life within her, so that she became Mother of the Waters; but she bore no child or any perfect offspring. In bodily torment for 700 years she drifted; then a teal appeared, seeking somewhere to nest and seeing Luonnotar's knee above the waters' surface it built its nest in its crook and there laid its eggs, brooding on them for three days. Luonnotar's knee became scorched by the heat from the duck's feathers and at last she gave an involuntary shudder at the pain. The eggs tumbled into the sea and sank into the abyss below, where they were transformed into the substance of the universe.

248 From the lower shells came the earth, from the upper the skies. From the yolks came the sun, from the white the moon, and white spots within the eggs formed stars, dark spots clouds. Now Luonnotar shaped the coastline and the ocean-bed setting rocks as pillars for the sky.

Väinämöinen
249–272

(i) HIS BIRTH

249 Ilmatar Luonnotar's son Väinämöinen gestated for thirty years, musing on how he might exist in this gloomy home. At length he called upon the sun and moon to deliver him from it; to the Great Bear to teach him how he might escape. None replied.

250 Väinämöinen grew bored. With the nameless finger (ring finger) he hammered on the castle gate. With his left big toe he breached its one wall and, on hands and knees, dragged himself across the threshold and fell into the sea, an old man.

(ii) HIS FIGHT WITH JOUKAHAINEN

251 Väinämöinen was the first to clear and till the soil. He was a great magician. When the thin Laplander Joukahainen challenged his power, he chanted such magical songs that the earth trembled, copper mountains rocked and huge boulders shivered into fragments. Väinämöinen changed Joukahainen's sledge into a lake, his whip into a reed on the shore, his horse into a river boulder. He changed Joukahainen's sword into lightning, his bow into a rainbow, his arrows into hawks, his dog into a stone. He transformed Joukahainen's clothes into clouds, stars and water-lilies and then he cast the Laplander up to his waist in a swamp, up to his hips in a meadow and finally up to his armpits in a bog. To escape Joukahainen promised that Väinämöinen should marry his sister Aino, but she jumped into the sea rather than marry such an old man.

(iii) HIS QUEST FOR A WIFE IN THE LAND OF POHJOLA

252 Väinämöinen sought the advice of his aged mother, who stirring on the sea-bed told him to seek a wife in Pohjola (the North Country, sometimes equated with Lapland, but often even further north than that).

253 As he rode north Väinämöinen was ambushed by Joukahainen who shot his horse, sending the aged hero tumbling into the sea. A storm blew him out of sight of land and for eight days he swam before being rescued by the eagle, who carried him to the borders of Pohjola. There abandoned in a strange land where he could find no path, the old man wept.

254 His sobs caught the attention of the Maid of Pohja (Pohjola), young daughter of Louhi, Lady of Pohjola. Louhi promised him that if he would make her a *sampo* (unidentifiable talisman) she would give him her daughter for his wife and lead him back from the snowy wastes to his own fertile land of cornfields and bird song.

255 Confessing himself unable to forge the *sampo* Väinämöinen promised to send Ilmarinen the divine smith to make it for her. Warning him that only the forger of it could have her daughter, Louhi gave him a horse and sledge and, telling him not to look up or stop on his journey, sent him home.

256 As he journeyed Väinämöinen heard the sound of a loom and forgetting the prohibition, raised his eyes and saw the Maid of Pohja seated on the rainbow weaving golden cloth. He invited her to become his wife which she agreed to do on the condition that he fulfilled several tasks: to split a horsehair with a blunt knife, tie an egg in knots, though no knot be apparent in it, peel a stone, cut a pile of ice without splintering any and finally to carve a boat from fragments of her spindle and shuttle.

257 While he was performing this final task the evil spirits Lempo, Paha and Hiisi so directed his axe that he drove it hard into his knee and being unable to think of any binding spell incorporating the words of the origin of iron, which would heal the wound, he went to a nearby village to seek help, and finally after being turned away by some, found an aged man who healed him.

(iv) THE SHIPBUILDING AND JOURNEY TO THE UNDERWORLD

258 The account of the building of Väinämöinen's ship is one of the most interesting episodes in the *Kalevala* both for its references to binding spells and in its account of the hero's underworld adventures.

259 At each stage of his ship-building Väinämöinen sang the appropriate charm to bind the work together, but when he came to join the planks he found that he had forgotten three vital words, and so was unable to finish the boat. He searched everywhere for the missing formula and finding it nowhere on earth set out for Tuonela, the underworld land.

260 The journey took three weeks. During the first he marched through shrubland; during the second through woods; during the third through deep forest. At last he came to the black river which guards the entrance to Tuonela. There he saw the ugly dwarfs, daughters of Tuoni and Tuonetar, the rulers of this kingdom, who were washing their rags in the dark water. Väinämöinen persuaded them to take him across to the island of Manala, the land of the dead. There, warning him he would never be allowed to leave the island, Queen Tuonetar offered him a mug of beer, crawling with worms and frogs.

261 Afterwards, while Väinämöinen was resting from his journey, Tuoni's son cast an iron net and sunk it in the river to prevent the hero from escaping; but Väinämöinen changed himself into a steel serpent and slipped through the meshes to safety.

262 Still seeking the lost formula he now took a shepherd's advice and went to the giant Antero Vipunen, who lay below the earth. A poplar tree grew from his shoulders, a birch from his temples, fir from his forehead, alder from his cheeks, willow from his beard and a wild pine tree from between his teeth.

263 Väinämöinen felled all the trees and then thrust his iron staff into Antero Vipunen's throat. The giant gagged and swallowed the hero, staff and all. However Väinämöinen, ever resourceful, turned his shirt into a forge, his shirt sleeves and coat into bellows, created an anvil from his own knee, a hammer from his elbow and set to work hammering so fiercely that the anvil sank into the giant's heart until at length the unhappy Antero Vipunen promised to repeat the magic words Väinämöinen had forgotten, and so enabled him to finish building his ship.

(v) ILMARINEN AND THE FORGING OF THE *SAMPO*

264 Ilmarinen, the divine smith, Väinämöinen's brother, had been born on a heap of cinders, his destiny to tame the evil iron. When Väinämöinen returned from Pohjola he sent Ilmarinen there to forge the *sampo* for Lady Louhi.

Ilmarinen forges the *sampo*.
Illustration to a Russian
edition of the *Kalevala*. St.
Petersburg, 1881. The
London Library.

265 Taking a swan's feathers, the milk of a barren heifer, a little barley grain and fine sheep's wool, Ilmarinen cast them into his furnace, summoning slaves to stoke the fire. Each day Ilmarinen looked to see what had grown in the flames. Many marvels came from them: a golden bowl, a red copper ship, a golden-horned heifer and a plough with silver-tipped handles, golden share and copper frame. All these Ilmarinen recognised as evil. He broke them up and threw the pieces back into the furnace. At last there emerged among the flames the wonderful *sampo,* with a beautifully decorated cover. One side of it was a corn mill, one side a slate mill and the third a coin mill.

266 The *sampo* was given to Lady Louhi, whose daughter, the Maid of Pohja, said she would prefer to marry Ilmarinen rather than Väinämöinen, so she and the smith were betrothed. Then he returned to Kalevala.

267 Having at last built his ship, Väinämöinen set out for Pohjola intending to woo the Maid, but Ilmarinen, learning of his departure, set out in the same direction on a fast horse. The Lady Louhi advised her daughter to marry Väinämöinen, who managed to arrive first, but the Maiden still preferred Ilmarinen and his rival retired dejected, concluding that old men should not compete with youths for the hands of young women!

(vi) THE THEFT OF THE *SAMPO*

268 On the death of his first wife, Ilmarinen went again to Pohjola hoping to marry her sister. When the Lady Louhi refused her consent he abducted the girl. However she played him false, so he turned her into a seagull.

269 On this visit to Pohjola Ilmarinen realised the true worth of the *sampo* he had forged, for it had brought wonderful prosperity to the whole land. He and Väinämöinen decided to steal it. The hero Lemminkainen (273–279) accompanied them.

270 On the voyage their boat rammed a huge pike, from whose jaw Väinämöinen made a wonderful *kantele* (five-stringed lute). At the sound of its dulcet tones all the people of Pohjola fell asleep. Väinämöinen easily snatched up the *sampo,* but unfortunately Lemminkainen burst into a triumphant song, rousing everyone.

271 Louhi pursued the three heroes with a terrible storm. The *kantele* was washed overboard, the *sampo* smashed to smithereens, but Väinämöinen managed to salvage some fragments and so powerful was their magic that they alone were sufficient to transform Kalevala into a land of plenty, and though Louhi attacked the country with plague and even stole the sun and moon, Väinämöinen's arts were too strong for her and eventually he triumphed.

272 At the end of his life the hero sailed away in a copper boat to the land between earth and heaven.

Väinämöinen plays the *kantele* in Pohjola. Illustration from a Russian edition of the *Kalevala*. St. Petersburg, 1881. The London Library.

Lemminkainen
273–279

273 Lemminkainen, son of Lempi (Love), a lively and mischievous youth, wooed the lady Kylli of Saari (Kronstadt) and eventually he won her. He promised that he would go on no warlike expeditions if in return she promised not to attend village dances. This she promised. However, one day while Lemminkainen was away, she broke her word. Ainikki, her sister-in-law, reported it to Lemminkainen, who divorced Kylli and set out to woo the Maid of Pohja.

274 Arriving in the dark land he drove all men from Louhi's home except for the blind old cowherd Märkhättu, who seemed so wretched that Lemminkainen pitied him, much to Märkhättu's fury.

275 The hero asked Louhi for the hand of her daughter and was set three tasks, the first to catch the Elk of Hiisi (a camel), which he did; then to catch Hiisi's fire-breathing horse, which again he managed to do; third to shoot a swan on Tuonela's river.

276 As he approached the river the cowherd Märkhättu lay in wait for him. He sent a water serpent to attack Lemminkainen and when the hero lay dead threw his corpse into the river, where Tuoni's son hacked it into five pieces, hurling them into a whirlpool.

277 Meanwhile Lemminkainen's mother Kyllikki noticed blood flowing from his hairbrush and realising harm had befallen him she went to Pohjola to discover what was wrong. Louhi told her that Lemminkainen had been sent to shoot a swan of Tuonela and the sun described to her the hero's fate.

278 Kyllikki went to Tuonela and with a long rake collected all the scraps of her son's body. These she rejoined and healed, but the body remained senseless. Kyllikki therefore summoned a bee. She asked it to fetch honey from the woods and Metsola's (the woodlands') meadows, then more from beyond the highest heaven. With this she anointed her son's corpse and Lemminkainen revived. (See also vol. 1: 1.2. **77, 156–157**).

279 We may note that this story combines the traditional tale of the hero's test (cf. the labours of Heracles, vol. 1: 2.2. **173–184**) with a version of the fertility myth in which a youthful god or goddess is lost, trapped in the power of the underworld, but, after a long search, found, released and revived (cf. **88–92**; vol. 1: 1.2. **40–42, 48–52, 105–109**; 2.2. **111–116**).

PART 3
Index and Glossary

The following abbreviations are used:
AS: Anglo-Saxon; B: Baltic; C: Celtic;
G: Germanic; N: Norse; N-G: Norse-
Germanic; F-U: Finno-Ugric; S: Slav.
'British' refers to Celtic Britain and
Wales; 'Britain' to the region after the
Anglo-Saxon dominance.

Aedán mac Gabráin King of Dál Riata **38**

Aegir (N-G) the sea-god, often referred to as 'the Ale-brewer'. He and his consort Ran (q.v.) entertained not only drowned sailors but also the gods at their underwater banquets. Aegir is said to have had nine daughters. These may possibly be the nine giantesses who mothered Heimdallr (q.v.). See also Gymir, Ruadh and Wachilt.

Aesc (AS) traditional founder of the Aescing tribe. This tradition may be related to the story of Askr (q.v.).

Aeschere (AS) counsellor to Hrodgar (q.v.), he was seized by Grendel's mother in vengeance for Grendel's (q.v.) death.

Aesir (N-G) generic term for the group of gods led by Óðinn. See also **143–145, 149, 153–157, 165, 215, 218.**

Aganippus, King of the Franks (British) according to Geoffrey of Monmouth he was husband to Cordelia, youngest daughter of Leir, King of Britain (q.v.).

Ahti (F-U) god of the waters. He lived in the 'black slime' of an undersea cave at the foot of a cloud-wreathed promontory, attended by Tursas, Vetehinen (qq.v.) and all the water spirits. His consort was Vellamo. Ahti, who was also known as Ahto, is possibly to be identified with the hero Lemminkainen (q.v.).

Ahura Mazda 162.

Aífe 53.

Ailill (C, Ireland) according to the *Taín Bó Cuailnge* he was consort to Medhbha, Queen of Connacht (q.v.). See also **42, 73.**

Ailill Aine, King of Leinster see Cobthach Coel

Aillén mac Midhna 64.

Ainikki 273

Ainnle 72.

Aitvaras (B, Lithuanian) a mysterious flying creature, sometimes depicted as a cockerel, at others with the head of the lucky *Žaltys* (grass snake) (q.v.) and a comet's fiery tail.

Akka (F-U) consort of Ukko (q.v.), also called Rauni ('Mountain Ash'). The rowan tree is sacred to her.

Alaisiagae (G) female spirits associated with the war-god. Cf. Valkyries and Idisi and see also Baudihillie.

Alba 38, 53.

Albany (C, British) Scotland, also called Alba (q.v.).

Albion (C, Britain) the name of Britain prior to the arrival of Brutus (q.v.), or so says Geoffrey of Monmouth!

Alcis (N-G) twin gods, said by Tacitus to have been worshipped by the Naharvali tribe. He refers to the extraordinary similarity between this cult and the Roman one of Castor and Pollux (see vol. 1: 2.3.), but concludes that the Naharvali's cult is indigenous rather than imported. The two gods, who would seem to be the Germanic form of the Indo-European twin deities, were worshipped in forest sanctuaries by priests wearing ornate effeminate costume. No other evidence of this Indo-European cult has been found among Norse-Germanic peoples. See also the Ashvins, vol. 3: 5.3. and the Dioscuri, vol. 1: 2.3.

Alfheimr (N-G) the home of the elves of light.

Alisanos (C, Gaulish) deities of rocks.

Alka (B, Lithuanian) sacred groves, springs or fields, which could not respectively be felled, fished, or ploughed. Cremations were performed in or beside them and votive offerings made to the gods there.

Amhairghin 17–18.

Andate see Andraste.

Andraste (C, British) according to Dio Cassius' *Annals XIV*, a goddess of victory to whom human sacrifices were made in a sacred grove. Her name may have been Andate.

Andvari (N-G) a dwarf, owner of a great hoard of gold, which Loki (q.v.) compelled him to give up. Andvari tried to retain one ring from the treasure to help him win new wealth but Loki insisted on having everything. It was this ring that ultimately caused the death of the hero Sigurdr (G: Siegfried). See also **237–246.**

Angrboda (N-G) 'Boder of Grief', giantess, consort to Loki (q.v.) and mother of Fenrir, Midgardsormr and Hel (qq.v.).

Anna (Britain) sister to Arthur, King of Britain (q.v.). According to Geoffrey of Monmouth she married either Loth of Lodonesia (q.v.) or Budicius, King of Brittany.

Annwn (C, Welsh) the Otherworld (q.v.). In the *Preiddeu Annwn (Spoils of Annwn)* which describes King Arthur's (q.v.) expedition to the Otherworld to capture a magic cauldron (q.v.) various aspects of the region are described. At one point Arthur and his men come to a glass fort (Caer Wydyr) and cannot persuade its watchman to speak to them. This suggests the land of the silent dead, also referred to in Nennius's *Historia Brittonum*. However Arthur and his company also visit Caer Feddwid (the Fort of Carousal), also called Caer Siddi, where the fountain runs with wine and no one ever knows illness or old age. In other parts of the poem Annwn seems a shadowy underworld, while in the *Mabinogion* it is described as a recognisable kingdom. See also **76–77, 93** and Nera.

Antero Vipunen 262–263.

Apples, Isle of 129 and cf. **34.**

Apples of Youth (N-G) the golden apples of Idunn (q.v.), which preserved the gods' youth. The giant Thjázi (q.v.) blackmailed Loki (q.v.) into helping him steal them. The Aesir (q.v.) began to age and, Loki's complicity in the theft being discovered, he was threatened with death if he failed to recover Idunn and the apples. Disguised as a falcon he penetrated Thjázi's home while the giant was fishing, turned Idunn into a nut and carried her and the apples safely home.

Aranrhod 103–104.

Arawn, King of Annwn **76–77, 93.**

Arberth 87.

King Arthur stands upon the crowns of his 30 vassal realms. Illustration to the early fourteenth-century *Chronicle of Peter of Langtoft*. British Library Ms. Royal 20, Aii f. 4r. (*Photo: Cooper-Bridgeman Library*.)

son Paschent, and was buried at Salisbury within the Giants' Ring (q.v.). According to the monk Gildas (fl. A.D. 540), Ambrosius was 'the last of the Romans' and led the British Celts' last, unsuccessful stand against the invading Saxons. Later Celtic tradition identifies him with King Arthur (q.v.).

Aurvandill 185.

Aurvandill's Toe 185.

Auseklis see Aušrinė.

Aušrinė (B, Lithuanian) the goddess 'Morning Star', known to the Latvians as Auseklis.

Autrimpas (B, Prussian) god of the sea and lakes.

Avalon, Isle of 128–129

Avranches 28.

Babieça (Spain) the famous horse of El Cid (q.v.).

Badhbh (C, Irish) one of three war goddesses, the others being Macha and the Mórríghan (q.v.), who foretold war and dire slaughter. They were sometimes seen before a battle, or on the battlefield, in the form of carrion birds. Badhbh's name denotes a raven or hooded crow. See also p. 23

Bagpūtys (B. Lithuanian) a sea-god, particularly associated with storms. He rode the waves in a boat with a golden anchor.

Balar 14, 30

Baldr (Balder) 161, 171, 205, 223–235. 223–235.

Baldrs Draumar 231.

Banbha 2, 17.

Bannik (S) the spirit of the bath house. He claimed every fourth bath as his own and woe betide anyone who thought to deprive him of it. Bannik could sometimes be induced to foretell the future: if he caressed the enquirer's bare back, luck was on the way, if he scratched it, there were bad days ahead. See also Domovoi, Dvorovoi and Ovinnik.

Bardoyats (B, Prussian) the god of ships.

barstukai (parstukai) (B, Lithuanian) underworld fairy-men believed to influence the harvest and to perform household tasks for those who made offerings to Puškaitis (q.v.). Tables of food were left in barns where the barstukai were said to gather and feast secretly at midnight.

Bath, Battle of 119.

Baudihillie (G) one of the two Alaisiagae (q.v.) to whom an altar was dedicated at Housesteads on Hadrian's Wall. The other was Friagabi. The goddesses' names may mean 'Ruler of Battle' and 'Giver of Freedom'.

Baugi (N-G) brother to the giant Suttungr, from whom he helped Ódinn to steal the Mead-of-Inspiration (q.v.)

Bayard see Renaud.

Beann Ghulban, the magic boar of 68.

Beaw see Beow.

Bedivere 112.

Bedwyr (Bedivere) 112.

Belenus (C, Gaulish) tutelary god of the Alpine kingdom of Noricum. Probably a solar deity, he was also worshipped in northern Italy, southern Gaul and Britain. His name may be related to Beltene (Beltane) q.v.. In Gaul Belenus was assimilated to the cult of the Romano-Greek Apollo.

Belt-of-Strength, Thórrs 176, 183, 190.

Beltane see Beltene.

Beltene (C) festival of Mayday, which was celebrated with bonfires, the Beltane fires. See also 17.

Bendigeidfran, King of Britain 86, 96–100.

Beow (G) possibly a fertility deity. His name, also spelled Beaw, occurs in some Anglo-Saxon genealogies.

Beowulf (N-G, Britain) hero of the epic of the same name, which probably dates from the eighth century. He sailed to Denmark with fourteen companions and there killed the monster Grendel (q.v.). He also slew Grendel's mother in an underwater duel. (Possibly this episode and that of vol. 3: 5.2. 95–96 derive from a common original for Beowulf's heroic deed is almost certainly a late version of the myth of the god's fight with a monster of drought or chaos. See also vol. 1: 1.2. 198–202; and 21–28, 83–88, 105–110; and 2.2. 133–138. Beowulf succeeded his uncle Hygelac as King of the Geats (q.v.) and ruled for fifty years. A dragon whose treasure had been stolen by a runaway slave then attacked Beowulf's kingdom. The aged monarch went out to fight the monster, but his sword was soon broken and all his companions fled except Wiglaf his kinsman. Between them Beowulf and Wiglaf killed the dragon, but the king received a mortal wound. A huge barrow was raised above the ashes of his funeral pyre, around which the dragon's hoard had been heaped.

Bergelmir 141, 144.

berserkir (N-G) warriors maddened with the fury of battle, i.e. berserk. They are sometimes referred to as berserkers. See also 51 and Horatii vol. 1: 2.3.

Bestla 143.

Beyla (N-G) a minor god, companion to Freyr. His name may mean 'Bee'. See also Byggvir.

Biarki (N-G) also called Bodvar (Bothvar)-

Biarki, he was a legendary warrior, henchman to Hrolf, King of Denmark. His name, 'Little Bear', refers to his ability to assume a bear's form at will.

Bifrǫst (N-G) the rainbow bridge between heaven and earth. See 154, 159.

Bith 2.

Bláthnad 61–62, 101.

Blodeuedd 101–108.

Boann (C, Irish) wife of Nechtan, mother of Oenghus (q.v.).

Boe 235. See also Bous.

Bog People 203

bogatyr (S, Russian) heroes of the byliny (q.v.). They include Ilya-Muromyets, Mikula, Sadko, Svyatogor and Volkh (Volga) (qq.v.).

Bóinn (C, Irish) goddess of the River Boyne.

Borr 143

Bors, Sir (C, Anglo-French) Arthurian knight, companion to Sir Galahad (q.v.) in the Grail Quest. See 135–140.

Borvo (C, Gaul) a deity whose name denotes bubbling water. He was associated with thermal springs and may have been among those gods assimilated to the cult of the Romano-Greek Apollo. His companion was Damona (q.v.).

Boudicca, Queen p. 22

Bous (Boe) (N-G) son of Ódinn and Rinda (qq.v.). He avenged his brother Baldr's (q.v.) death. See 235.

Bragi (N-G) the god of poetry. He may simply be an aspect of Ódinn for one of his names, 'Long-bearded One', is also used of Ódinn. Late sagas depict him welcoming dead heroes to Valhalla. His wife was Idunn (q.v.), whose brother he is said to have killed, but the story of their fight is lost.

Bran (C, Irish) One day while taking a solitary walk Bran heard beautiful music, which lulled him asleep. When he woke he found a spray of white blossom beside him. This he took home and a woman appeared before him singing of the Otherworld (q.v.). Next day with twenty-seven companions Bran set sail to find this realm and eventually arrived at Tír inna mBan, the supernatural Land of Women. Here he and his company were lavishly entertained but eventually the other sailors grew homesick and so the party set sail for Ireland. As they drew near the shore people called out asking who they were, but when told, said the only Bran they knew of was the hero of the old story The Voyages of Bran and when one of the sailors jumped ashore he immediately crumpled into ashes, as if long dead and buried. Bran therefore resumed his wanderings, though where

Third-century Romano-British relief of the goddess Brigantia from Birens, Dumfriesshire. (*Photo: National Museum of Scotland.*)

supply them with ships, bullion and provisions and allow them to leave the country. With them Brutus sailed west. On an island beyond the Pillars of Hercules (vol. 1: 2.2. **182**) he found another group of Trojan exiles, led by Corineus (q.v.). They joined forces and after various adventures in Aquitaine, landed at Totnes. There they were attacked by giants under the leadership of Gogmagog (q.v.) but defeated them. Brutus founded his capital Troia Nova (New Troy i.e. London) on the banks of the Thames. It was later to be called Trinovantum. There Brutus was eventually buried. According to tradition he was the ancestor of the British people and their name derives from his (in fact it is probably a corruption of *Pictish*). Brutus's story is told by Geoffrey of Monmouth.

Brünhilde 245.

Brynhildr 173, 240–245.

Búri 143.

busi-urt (F-U, Votyak people) the soul of the cornfield; cf. Kurke, Rugiu̜ Boba and vol. 4: 7.1: Rice Mother.

Buyan (S) an oceanic island, home of the three winds, North, East and West.

Byelobog (S) the 'White God', epitome of all goodness, light and life. His opposite is Chernobog (q.v.). In Russia he was personified as Byelun, an old man, seen only in the daytime, who rescued the unfortunate and helped peasants with their toil.

Byelun see Byelobog.

Byggvir (N-G) a minor god, attendant on Freyr (q.v.). His name, derived from *bygg*, may mean 'Barley'. See also Beyla.

byliny (S, Russian) epics and heroic poems, divided into two cycles of which the first is the older.

Cadbury, Somerset **129.**

Cador, Duke of Cornwall **128.**

Caedmon (Britain) legendary seventh-century poet and singer who received his musical gift from heaven in a dream.

caer **88–89.**

Caer Feddwid see Annwn.

Caer Lludd 32.

Caer Lundein 32.

Caer Siddi see Annwn.

Caer Wydyr see Annwn.

Caerleon-on-Usk 125.

Cairenn see Níal Noígiallach

Caledon Wood, Battle of (C, Britain) battle fought by King Arthur (q.v.). either in the Scottish Caledonian (Celyddon, see Myrddin) forest or Celidon Wood, near Lincoln. See **119**.

Caliburnus (C, Britain) King Arthur's

Brutus, legendary founder of the British, pictured in Holinshed's *Chronicles*, 1577. The British Library. (*Photo: Ray Gardner.*)

Corineus and Gogmagog depicted as Elizabethan wrestlers in Holinshed's *Chronicles*, 1577. The British Library. (*Photo: Ray Gardner.*)

Relief from a pillar dedicated to Jupiter by the 'sailors of Paris', A.D. 14–37, depicts the horned god Cernunnos. Musée de Cluny, Paris. (*Photo: Photoresources.*)

(q.v.) sword. See also *Excalibur*.

Camlan, Battle of **128.**

Camlan, River **128.**

Cano (C, Irish) an historical figure whose death is recorded as occurring in 688, Cano was the son of the Scottish King Gartnán. Exiled to Ireland he was entertained by the elderly Marcán (little Mark) whose beautiful young wife Créd was daughter of King Guaire of Connacht. Créd had fallen in love with Cano even before she saw him and at a feast drugged the whole company, begging him to take her as his mistress (cf. **66**). Cano refused to do this while he remained an exile but pledged his troth to Créd, giving her a stone which embodied his life. Eventually he was

called home to Scotland and there became king. Each year he and Créd attempted to meet at Inber Colptha (the Boyne estuary) but were always forestalled by her stepson Colcu with a guard of one hundred warriors. At last they decided to meet instead at Lough Créde in the north, but as they came within sight of each other Colcu again appeared and drove Cano away. Distracted with grief, Créd dashed her head against a rock (cf. **74**). In falling she dropped Cano's stone, which smashed to smithereens. Three days later he also died. This tale, together with those of Derdriu and Gráinne (qq.v.), is thought to have been one of the sources of the Tristram (q.v.) story.

cantrefs **86.**

Carmun 29.

Cartimandua, Queen p. 22.

Caswallawn, son of Beli **86.**

Cathbhadh, the *druid* **70, 72.**

cauldron, magic **7, 21, 61, 96, 98, 137–138.** See also Otherworld.

Cei (Sir Kay) **112.**

Celyddon forest see Myrddin, and Caledon Wood, Battle of.

Cernunnos (C) 'the Horned One', the name used as a generic term for all Celtic manifestations of this ancient fertility god. It is taken from the name found on a damaged carving discovered in Paris. The god is commonly shown seated cross-legged. He has animal as well as human ears, and antlers also, from which hang one, or sometimes a pair of torcs. He is accompanied by a ram-headed serpent or a serpent with a ram's horn. Some pictures also show a bull and a stag accompanying him. One of the most splendid images of the god appears on the Gundestrup Cauldron (q.v.) and bears a striking resemblance to the horned god of the Indus city Mohenjo-Daro (vol. 3: 5.1.) Cernunnos appears on artefacts found throughout the Celtic realms. He was associated with material wealth and, like most fertility deities, had a chthonic aspect, indicated particularly by his horned-snake companion. It is possible that both the Irish Conall Cernach (q.v.) and the Keeper of the Forest referred to in the Welsh poem *Owain,* are representations of this god. Recently the English poet Geoffrey Hill has used the image of Cernunnos as one of the unifying symbols in his fine sequence *Mercian Hymns* (1971). See also Ciarán, Saint, of Saighir, and **163.**

Cesair 2.

Charlemagne, the Emperor (France) Charles the Great, eighth-century Emperor of the Franks. His twelve legendary knights or *paladins* included Ganelon, Renaud, Roland and Oliver (qq.v.).

Chernobog (S) the 'Black God', epitome of evil, darkness and death, the opposite of Byelobog (q.v.)

Chrétien de Troyes 130, 138.

Christ see Jesus.

Christian 131, 137, 170.

Ciarán, Saint of Saighir (C, Irish) Celtic saint whose first convert was a boar. The creature at once began vigorously to tear down branches and grass to build the monk a cell. Later they were joined by a fox, badger, wolf and stag. Mac Cana suggests this legend may possibly incorporate elements of the Cernunnos (q.v.) myth.

Cigfa 85, 87, 90–91.

City of the Legions, the **125.**

Clud see Gwawl fab Clud.

Cobthach Coel, King of Brega (C, Irish) This monarch usurped the Irish throne, killing his brother Loegaire Lorc, King of Ireland, and Loegaire's son Aillil Aine, King of Leinster. He drove Aillil's son Labhraidh Loingsech into exile. With the aid of the Munstermen Labhraidh regained his kingdom and made peace with Cobthach, inviting him to his court. Labhraidh had an iron house prepared for the visitor and his thirty vassal kings and when they were all fast lodged within it, he ordered

The horn dancers of Abbot's Bromley, Staffs., c. 1910. (*Photo: Mansell Collection.*)

Cordeilla Queene.

Above: Cordelia, daughter of King Leir, from Holinshed's *Chronicles*, 1577. The British Library. (*Photo: Ray Gardner.*)

Below: Third-century stone found in Coventina's well, Carrawburgh, Northumberland, shows the goddess reclining on a water-lily leaf and supporting her left elbow on an urn of flowing water. In her right hand she holds a plant or flower. Museum of Antiquities, Newcastle-upon-Tyne. (*Photo: Photoresources.*)

fires to be kindled round the walls and roasted Cobthach and his supporters to death. See also p. 20.

Codex Regius p. 26.

cóigedh, the five **6.**

Coirbre 10.

Colcu see Cano.

Cold (F–U) son of Louhi, Lady of Pohjola (q.v.).

Colgrin 118.

Conaire Mór, King **47.**

Conall 53.

Conall Cernach 54, 58–59.

Conchobhar mac Nessa, King of Ulster **48–49, 70, 72–74.**

Condatis (C, Gaulish) deities of river confluences.

Conla (C, Irish) son of Conn Cétchathlach (q.v.). He fell in love with a woman from the Otherworld (q.v.) and went to live with her there. None saw him again.

Conlaí 53–55.

Conn Cétchathlach (C, Irish) Conn of One Hundred Battles, father of Conla and grandfather of Cormac mac Airt (q.v.). One day as he stood on the rampart at Tara with his *druids* and *filidh* (qq.v.) a horseman came out of the dawn mist and invited the company to visit his home. He led them to Mag Mell (q.v.) and there in a house with a golden ridge-pole, built next to a golden tree they found Lugh and the Sovereignty of Ireland. Beside the god and goddess stood a golden bowl and cup and a silver vat and these remained with Conn after the vision faded. See 29 and 36.

Connacht 5, 6, 58, 66. See also Medhbha, Queen of Connacht.

Constans see Aurelius Ambrosius.

Constantine II, King see Aurelius Ambrosius.

Constantine III, King 128.

Conte de Grail, Le 130.

Corbenic Castle 135.

Cordelia (C, Britain) youngest daughter of Leir, King of Britain (q.v.), to whose throne she succeeded. Her husband was Aganippus, King of the Franks.

Corineus (Britain) a Trojan exile leader, renowned as a soldier and giant-killer. He allied with Brutus (q.v.) and received the land of Cornwall, naming it after himself.

Cormac mac Airt (C, Irish) by tradition the King of Ireland A.D. 227–66. See 36.

Cormac mac Cuilennáin 35.

Cormac mac Dubthach 73.

County Longford 42.

Coventina (C, British) goddess of the spring at Brocolitia (Carrawburgh), a fort on Hadrian's Wall, Cf. Sequana.

Craig-y-Dinas 129.

Crann Bethadh (C, Irish) the Tree of Life.

Créd see Cano.

Creiddylad (C. Welsh) daughter of Llud Llaw Ereint (q.v.), and the original of Cordelia (see Leir, King of Britain).

Creidhne see Goibhniu and 11, 13,

Crucifixion, the, of Jesus 135–136.

Crucifixion, the, of Ódinn 170.

Cú Chulainn p. 20 and 48–63.

Cú Roí mac Dáiri, King of Munster 58–62, 101.

Culann the Smith 50.

Culhwch (Kulhwch) 109–115.

Cynddylig the Guide 112.

D'Arcy, Margaretta 130

Daghdha, the, see Donn and 7, 10, 14, 16, 19, 20–27.

Daghdha, the cauldron of the 7, 21. See also cauldron, magic.

Daghdha, the harp of the 14, 21.

Dál nAraidi p. 22 and 38.

Dál Riata p. 22 and 38.

Damona (C, Gaul) goddess possibly associated with a cow cult. See also Borvo.

Danu, the People of the Goddess see Tuatha Dé Danann.

Datan (S, Polish) one of the three gods of the field, the others being Lawkapatim and Tawals.

dausos (B. Lithuanian) mysterious realm of the dead, governed by Dievas (q.v.). It is not simply heaven or paradise but a realm of that kind. It lies beyond the high hill of the sky, which the dead have to climb, and therefore they need strong finger-nails or animal claws to grip the slippery slope. The journey is very long and spirits also travel by horseback, or in the smoke of fires, or by the Birds' Way (Milky Way), or by boat, like the sun at night travelling the darkness.

Day 147.

Dazhbog (S) the sun-god, offspring of Svarog (q.v.). He lives in a golden palace in the eastern land of summer, and daily drives across the sky in a chariot drawn by a pair of white horses, or, according to the Poles, by three horses, one of gold, the second of silver, the third of diamond. He married Myesyats (q.v.) and so fathered the stars. He is also god of justice. See also Zorya, the two, and cf. Dievas.

de Troyes, Chrétien 130, 138.

Deichtine 48.

Deirdre 70–74.

Dennitsa see Zvezda, the two.

Derdriu p. 20 and 70–74.

Devana (S, Czech) goddess of the hunt. Her name is cognate with that of the Roman Diana (vol. 1: 2.**81**). Among the Serbs she was called Diiwica, among the Poles, Dziewona.

d'u-urt (F-U, Votyak people) the corn soul; see also *busi-urt*.

Dian Cécht (C, Ireland) the god of healing and the mythical author of the *Judgements of Dian Cécht,* a tract on the legal responsibilities of one who has caused another's illness. See also 11, 13, 31.

Diarmaid ua Duibhne 66–69.

Dievas (B, Lithuanian) the high god. His name is cognate with the Sanskrit *dyut:* to shine, and *deiuos:* of the sky. The Lithuanians depicted him as a handsome Iron Age king in a silver-coloured robe, with a cap and belt and sword. He lives beyond the sky's hill (see *dausos*) in an enclosed estate entered by three silver gates. Within lie his manor house, farms, sauna bath, garden and the whole is surrounded by forest. Each day Dievas drives very carefully down the sky's hill in a chariot (or sledge) of gold (or copper), taking great care not to make the earth tremble or disturb so much as a dew-

drop, for he is particularly concerned to promote the earth's fertility. He stimulates the corn's growth and tramples weeds underfoot. In association with Laima (q.v.) he also determines men's fate. Although he is the most powerful of the deities he is not their king or governor, but rather *primus inter pares.* By the Letts he was known as Dievs.

Dievs see Dievas.

Diiwica see Devana.

Dinnshenchas (C, Irish) 'the lore of the prominent places', Irish legends concerning the origins of local place-names.

'Dis Pater' (C, Gaulish) according to Julius Caesar, the Celts of Gaul regarded this deity as the divine ancestor of mankind; cf. Donn and see also Yama and Yima (vol. 3: 5.3. and 5.2. **20–26**). Some scholars believe Sucellus (q.v.) may have been equated with 'Dis Pater'.

Dísir (N-G) generic term for goddesses.

Dogoda (S) the gentle god of the west wind.

Doldavius, King of Gotland 122.

Domovikha (Domania) see Domovoi.

Domovoi (S) the house spirit. Although he and other spirits rebelled against the creator and were expelled from heaven, Domovoi and his wife Domovikha are benevolent. He lives beneath the house threshold, or near the stove, she in the cellar.

Dôn, the sons of, see Gwydion and Gilfaethwy.

Donar (Thunor) (G) the thunder god, particularly associated with oak trees. Cf. Thórr and Perkúnas.

Donn (C. Irish) the god of the dead, who lived on the offshore island Tech Duinn. When they died he called the Irish, his descendants, to go to him there. Donn's name means 'Dark One' or 'Brown One'. In modern Irish folklore he is not only the god of the dead but also the ambivalent god of shipwrecks and storms at sea and guardian of the crops and cattle. Some authorities believe him to be identical with the Daghdha (q.v.) but in all extant texts the two are clearly differentiated. Cf. 'Dis Pater' and see also 17.

Donn, the, of Cuailnge (C, Irish) the 'Brown' (Dark) Bull of Cuailnge, adversary of Finnbhennach (q.v.). It is probably to be identified with Tarvos Trigaranus (q.v.). According to the *Taín Bó Cuailnge,* Donn and Finnbhennach were originally divine swineherds of the Otherworld and attained their present form after many reincarnations as other animals.

Bas-relief from a pillar dedicated to Jupiter by the 'sailors of Paris' A.D. 14–17, shows the god Esus cutting branches from a tree and is partnered by the relief of Tarvos Trigaranus, p. 126, with whom Esus was associated in a myth now lost. Musée de Cluny, Paris. (*Photo: Photoresources.*)

Douglas, Battle of the River **118.**

dragons (N-G) usually thought of as huge serpents, rarely either winged or fire-breathing. They are generally referred to as guardians of a grave and its treasures. In some late *sagas* the dragon is said to be a metamorphosed corpse. See also Fáfnir, and Beowulf.

draugr (G) the restless tenant of a grave mound.

Draupnir (N-G) Óðinn's (q.v.) gold ring, from which all others derive. See **207, 225, 228.**

druid pp. 23, 26 and **10, 70.**

Dubthach 73.

Dumézil, Georges p. 19 **16, 157.**

Dumnonii 5.

Dunatis (C, Gaulish) deities of strongholds.

Durandal (France) the famous sword of Roland (q.v.), said once to have been owned by Hector (vol. 1: 2.2. **315.**

Dvorovoi (S) the spirit of the household yard. He was generally benevolent but hostile to all creatures with white fur. White-feathered chickens he tolerated. See also Bannir, Domovoi and Ovinnik.

dwarfs 145, 147, 213, 220, 238–239. See also Mead-of-Inspiration and vol. 3: 5.3: *ribhus.*

Dyfed 76–77, 86, 92.

Dylan Eil Ton 103.

Dylan, Son of the Wave **103.**

Dziewona see Devana.

Édain 42–47.

Édain, daughter of Édar **43–47.**

Édain, daughter of Eochaidh **47.**

Édain Echraidhe (C, Irish) 'Horse-riding Édaín', probably the Irish equivalent of the Welsh Rhiannon, possibly of the Gaulish Epona (qq.v.). See also **42–43.**

Édar 43.

Edda, the **197.**

Edda, the *Prose* p. 26 and **147, 187.**

Efnisien 96, 98.

Egil see Volundr.

Egils Saga ok Ásumndar **171.**

Eiríkr inn Sigrsaeli (Eric the Victorious) (N) famous tenth-century king of Sweden. Before the Battle of Fyris-vellir (A.D. 960), he dedicated himself to Óðinn (q.v.), vowing to sacrifice himself to the god after ten years had passed. A tall, hooded figure appeared and, handing him a stick, told him to shoot it over the army of his enemy Stybjorn. This Eiríkr did. The entire enemy host was struck blind and an avalanche engulfed it.

El Cid (Spain) legendary hero and warrior, historically the mercenary knight Rodrigo Diaz de Bivar (c. 1040–99). His legendary exploits in driving the

The White Horse of Uffington, a prehistoric hill figure possibly sacred to the Celtic goddess Epona. (*Photo: Ashmolean Museum, Oxford.*)

Moors out of Spain, in order to prove himself worthy of the beautiful Ximena (q.v.) are told in the epic *Poema del Cid*.

Elatha 9.

Eliot, T. S. 130.

Elizabeth see Tristram.

Elli 194–195.

Embla 146.

Emer 53, 54.

Emhain Abhlach 34.

Emhain Mhacha (C, Irish) the chief court of Ulaidh (q.v.), situated some 2 miles west of Antrim. See also **49, 50, 73**

Eochaidh Airemh, King of Ireland **44–47.**

Eochaidh Ollathair 21.

Eochu Mugmedón see Níal Noígiallach.

Eoghan mac Durthacht 73–74.

Eopa see Aurelius Ambrosius.

Epona (C, Gaulish) an important goddess possibly to be identified with the Irish Édaín Echraidhe and the Welsh Rhiannon (qq.v.). She may have been connected with a horse cult, but this is not certainly established.

Érainn (C, Irish) the ancient Celtic rulers of Ireland.

Erisvorsh (S) god of storms; see also Vartulis.

Ériu 17.

Esus (C, Gaulish) According to Lucan, Esus was one of the three chief gods of Gaul, the others being Taranis and Teutates. Welsh and Irish evidence suggests that Taranis was the thunder god (Welsh: Taran; Irish: Torann) and Teutates a tribal deity (Welsh: *tud,* Irish: *tuath* = tribe) Lucan says human sacrifices were made to all three deities.

Etna, Mt. 129.

Etzel, King, **243, 246.**

Eucharist, the **137**

Excalibur (C, Anglo-French) the magical sword of King Arthur. When Arthur broke his first sword Merlin took him to a lonely lake and a hand rose from the middle of the water brandishing a sword. The Lady of the Lake (q.v.) approached and told Arthur he might have the sword, so he rowed out and took it. Malory in telling the story does not name the weapon. In the early Welsh story of Culhwch and Olwen the sword is called *Caledvwlch,* which suggests a link with the magical sword *Caladbolg* owned by Cú Chulainn. In Geoffrey of Monmouth the sword has become *Caliburnus* and so derives the *Excalibur* of the romances.

Eyrbyggja Saga **186.**

Eyvindr Kelda (N-G) legendary descendant of Haraldr inn Hárfagri (q.v.). He was a wizard (*shaman*) and Oláfr

Late romanesque pier in the crypt of Freising Cathedral, W. Germany, depicting the wolf-man Fenrir. (*Photo: Bildarchiv Preussischer Kulterbesitz.*)

Tryggvason drowned him.

Eżerinis (B, Lithuanian) god of lakes.

Fáfnir see Hreidmar, Reginn and 237–239

Fáfnisbani (N-G) scourge of Fáfnir, a title of Sigurdr. See 237, 239.

Fál, the stone of 7.

Fedlimid 70.

Fenrir (N-G) wolf-son of Loki and Angrboda (qq.v.). Tyr (q.v.) bound him, but at Ragnarøkr he will escape. See 158, 160.

Fercherdne 62.

Ferghus mac Roich 73.

Fiachna Lurgan, King of Dál nAraidi 38–39.

fian (a), the (C, Irish) roving band(s) of warriors. See 64, 68.

fili (C, Irish) a member of the bardic class or filidh. See p. 26, 17, 18, 70.

filidh see fili.

fimbulvetr 158.

Find (C, Irish) 'the Fairhaired One', possibly a title of Lugh (q.v.). On the Continent he was known as Vindonnus, a name forming the basis of such place-names as Vienna (Uindobona).

Finn mac Cool (C, Irish) Fionn mac Cumhaill (q.v.).

Finnbhennach (C, Irish) 'the White-horned', a bull, adversary of the Donn of Cuailnge (q.v.) in the final battle of the saga Taín Bó Cuailnge.

Fintan 2.

Fionn mac Cumhaill p. 20 and 31, 33, 64–69, 101.

Fir Bholg, the 5–6, 8.

Fir Dhomhnann 5.

fís p. 20.

Fisher Kings, the 135–139.

Fjǫrgynn (N-G) Thórr's (q.v.) mother, believed to be a fertility goddess.

Flateyjarbók 210.

Fled Bricrenn 57.

Flidhais (C, Irish) goddess of the forest animals. The deer were her 'cattle'.

Flood, the 2, 141, 144.

Flowerface (Blodeuedd) 105–108.

Fódla 17.

Fǫlkvang 219.

Fomhoire, the 3–4, 8–16, 24–26, 30–31, 34.

Forgall 53.

Forseti (N-G) a god worshipped particularly by the Frisians, he was said to be the gods' lawgiver and son of Baldr (q.v.).

Franks Casket, the, a walrus ivory box made in seventh-century Northumbria and carved with scenes from Norse, Anglo-Saxon, Classical and Biblical myth and history. The box may be seen in the British Museum, except for one panel, which is in the Bargello, Florence. See below.

Freawaru see Heathobards.

Freyfaxi (N-G) legendary horse referred to in the Hrafnskels and Vatnsdoela Sagas. See 213.

Freyja 153, 178, 179, 182, 204, 218–222.

Freyr 156, 204, 206, 207–217, 218.

Friagabi see Baudihillie.

Frigg 218, 224.

Frija (G) wife of Wodan (q.v.).

Frollo the Tribune 124.

Frost Giants, the 142, 144–145, 150, 153, 178–180, 183, 185, 218. See also Jǫtnar.

Fuamhnach 43.

Fulla (N-G) goddess, servant to Frigg (q.v.).

Gabija (B, Lithuanian) the fire-goddess of the domestic hearth. She is sometimes said to have been brought to earth by Perkúnas (q.v.), at others by a swallow, which was badly burned while carrying her.

Gailioin, the 5

Galahad, Sir (C, Anglo-French) son of Sir Lancelot of the Lake (q.v.) and the Fisher King's (q.v.) daughter. He delivered his grandfather's kingdom of Logres and completed the Grail Quest (q.v.). His companions were Sir Bors and Sir Perceval (q.v.). See also 140.

Ganelon (French) stepfather to Roland (q.v.). Such was his envy of his famous stepson that he betrayed to the Saracens the Frankish army Roland was leading, and so brought about the hero's death.

Panel from the Franks Casket showing, left to right: Weland in his smithy; Weland and the Swan Maidens; the Adoration of the Magi. British Museum. (*Photo: British Museum.*)

Prehistoric temple at Stonehenge, Wiltshire, built, according to legend, by Merlin. (*Photo: The British Tourist Authority*.)

Gangleri (N-G) the Swedish King Gylfi, hero of the *Gylfaginning*, the first section of Snorri's *Prose Edda*. Disguised as the old vagrant Gangleri, Gylfi went to the Aesir's (q.v.) hall to test their wisdom.

Garmr (N-G) the hound of Hel (q.v.). He may have been an alternative form of Fenrir (q.v.). See also **160**.

Gartnán, King of Scotland, see Cano.

Gawain (Sir Gawain) (C, Anglo-French) called Walgainus by Geoffrey of Monmouth. Gawain may, it is thought, derive from an early Celtic sun-hero such as Cú Chulainn. Like such heroes, his strength waxes in the morning, reaching a peak at noon, and then declines. Although in French romances he is presented as promiscuous, in early English stories he is not only King Arthur's chief companion and warrior but also 'a verray, parfit gentil knyght' and the hero of one of the finest of all medieval English poems, the anonymous *Sir Gawain and the Green Knight*. Its opening episode again suggests Gawain's relationship to Chulainn or a similar hero. It describes King Arthur's Christmas feast, which is interrupted by a green giant, who challenges the knights to cut off his head on the condition that he be allowed to retaliate in kind the following year. Only Gawain dare accept the challenge. See also **59**.

Geats (N-G, Britain) the tribe to which Beowulf (q.v.) belonged. They were probably conquered by their foes, the Swedes, sometime during the sixth century.

Gefjun (N-G) the goddess to whom unmarried girls went after death. She may possibly be an aspect of Freyja. See **222**.

Gefn 222.

Geirrødr (Geirrøthr) **182.**

Geoffrey of Monmouth 116.

Gerdr (Gerthr) **207–209.**

Chalk figure on the Gogmagog hills, Cambridge, allegedly depicting a Celtic deity, but, according to some authorities a nineteenth-century work. (*Photo: Director in Aerial Photography, University of Cambridge.*)

gessa **66.**

Gesta Danorum p. 28 and **232.**

Giant, the Chief, see Ysbaddaden.

Giants' Ring, the (C, Britain) Stonehenge, which, according to legend was built by Merlin. With the help of Uther Pendragon and 15,000 men Merlin transported the Ring from Mount Killaraus in Ireland to Salisbury Plain, as a memorial to the British warriors massacred by Hengist. See Aurelius Ambrosius.

Gilfaethwy 102.

Gillingr (N-G) the giant who brewed the Mead-of-Inspiration (q.v.). He was killed by dwarfs.

Gilmaurius, King of Ireland **122.**

Gimli (N-G) the golden-roofed hall in Asgardr (q.v.) to which good men went after death. Forseti (q.v.) is associated with it.

Ginnungagap (N-G) the primordial space, the gap between Múspellheimr and Niflheimr. See **142.**

Giraitis (B, Lithuanian) god of the forests, referred to in seventeenth-century and eighteenth-century manuscripts.

Gjall, River (Resounding River) **226.**

Gjallarbrú (Resounding Bridge) **226.**

Gjallarhorn (*Resounding Horn*) **154, 160.**

Gjǫlp (N-G) 'Howler' one of the nine daughters of Aegir (q.v.).

Glastonbury 129.

Glastonbury Thorn, the (Britain) a thorn tree in the grounds of Glastonbury Abbey, said to have sprung from the staff of Joseph of Arimathea (q.v.).

Glifieu 100.

Glob, P. V. 203.

Glúm (N) legendary Icelandic warrior and poet, hero of the early *Viga-Glúms Saga.*

Glwelwyd 110.

Gna (N-G) goddess, servant to Frigg (q.v.).

Gobbán Saer (C, Irish) Gobbán the Wright, a miraculous builder and mason, an aspect of Goibhniu (q.v.).

Guinevere ill in bed, sends a ring to Sir Lancelot. Illustration from the fourteenth-century French *Roman de Lancelot du Lac*. Bodleian Library Ms. Douce 199 f. 44v. (*Photo: Bodleian Library*.)

Detail from the Gundestrup Cauldron showing a god brandishing two deer. (*Photo: Photoresources.*)

Gunnarr, Brynhildr's husband, in a snake pit, playing his harp with his toes. Twelfth-century carving from Hylestad Church, Setesdal, Norway. University Museum, Oslo. (*Photo: Werner Forman Archive.*)

Gudrunn 241, 243, 245–246.

Guinevere, Queen 121, 127. See also Joyous Gard, and Sir Lancelot of the Lake.

Gullifaxi (N-G) 'Goldenmane', Hrungnir's (q.v.) horse.

Gullinbursti 213.

Gundestrup Cauldron, a silver-plated copper bowl, probably dating from the first century B.C. The outside is decorated with busts of unidentified gods, the inside with mythological scenes. It was found in 1891 in a peat bog at Gundestrup, Denmark, to which it had probably been consigned as a sacrifice. It is now in the National Museum, Copenhagen.

Gungnir 166.

Gunhpar, King of the Orkneys 122.

Gunnarr 241–243.

Gunnarr Helmingr 210–212.

Guttormr 243.

Gwalchmei fab Gwyar 112.

Gwawl fab Clud 79–81, 92.

Gwenddoleu see Arthuret, Battle of.

Gwenhwyfar (C, Welsh) Guinevere, Queen, (q.v.).

Gwent-Is-Coed 84.

Gwrgi see Arthuret, Battle of.

Gwrhyr the Interpreter 112.

Gwri 84.

Gwydion 93–95, 102–105, 108.

Gwynn ap Nudd (C, Welsh) the son of Lludd Llaw Erient (q.v.) and Welsh equivalent of Fionn mac Cumhaill (q.v.).

Gwyn Gohoyw (G. Gloyw) 85.

Gwynned 93.

Gylfi (N-G) See Gangleri and 222.

Gymir (N-G) possibly another name for Aegir (q.v.). See also 207.

Haddingr (N) famous Danish hero, a favourite of Óðinn (q.v.) who taught him the strategy of arranging his troops in wedge formation. During one battle the god descended in the form of an old man and stood behind Haddingr shooting arrows to drive away the magical storm roused by the hero's enemies.

Haedcyn (Haethcyn) (N-G, Britain) son of King Hredel of the Geats (q.v.), a character of *Beowulf*. He killed his brother.

Hafgan 76–77.

Hagen (G) in the *Nibelungenlied* King Gunther of Burgundy's vassal who discovers Siegfried's one vulnerable spot and treacherously slays him. See 245.

Haki (N-G) legendary early king of Norway. As he lay dying he was placed in a boat which was then fired and allowed to drift out to sea on the tide.

Hálfdan Svarti (N-G) Hálfdan the Black, a ninth-century Norwegian king whose body was quartered. Four different districts each kept one piece of it, a proceeding which suggests the ritual dismemberment and scattering of the corpse of the sacrificial victim in a fertility rite.

haltija (F-U) Finnish name for the concept of the spirit or soul with which all things are imbued, cf. *kama* and *mana*, (vol. 3: 6.3. and vol. 4: 7.1.). The Votyak people call it *urt*, the Cheremiss *ort*.

Haraldr inn Hárfagri (N-G) Harald Fairhair, ninth-century king of Norway.

Haraldr Hildiþǫnn (N-G) Harald War-tooth, a legendary king of Denmark. See 167.

Harbardr (Harbarthr) (N-G) the lover of Signy (q.v.), he was killed by her father. Saxo refers to him as Hag-barthus.

Hávamál 170.

Heardred see Hygelac, King of the Geats.

Heathobards (N-G, Britain) a Germanic tribe with whom the Danes had a blood feud. Hrodgar (q.v.) tried to quell it by marrying his daughter Freawaru to the Heathobard leader Ingeld.

Hebrides, the 3.

Hefeydd the Old 78.

Heidrún (N-G) a goat which fed on the Yggdrasill (q.v.) and supplied Valhalla with mead. 166.

Heilyn 100.

Heimdallr (N-G) a complex god whose precise function has eluded scholarly definition, though much ink and effort has been spent on its attainment. He is the sleepless guardian of Asgardr (q.v.) ready to blow his warning *Gjallarhorn* (q.v.) at the hint of danger. He is called 'The White God', which suggests a link with Finnish Yakut stories of the father of mankind, known as 'The White Youth', who was fed by the spirit of the World Tree, and in the *Rígspula* Heimdallr is identified with Ríg (q.v.) the father of men. He was said to have been born of nine giant maidens, usually taken to be marine giantesses, possibly the nine daughters of Aegir (q.v.). He is associated with Freyja and is said to have fought Loki (qq.v.). No evidence exists of any cult in his honour, but the bulk of references to him suggest some association with the Vanir (q.v.). See also 154, 160, 178.

Hel (N-G) daughter of Angrboda and Loki (qq.v.) she is ruler of death's kingdom, which is named after her, Hel. See 171, 227–228 and Niflheimr.

Helgrind (N-G) the gate between the worlds of the living and the dead. It is also called Nágrind or Valgrind. See also 227.

Hengist (C, Britain) a Saxon leader, who, with his brother Horsa, is said to have become the ally of Vortigern (q.v.). Hengist's daughter Renwein became Vortigern's queen and Hengist received Kent as the bride price. Defeated in battle by the noble Vortimer (q.v.) he fled to Germany, but Vortigern recalled him. Hengist returned with 300,000 men and persuaded Vortigern to summon all the British leaders to a parley at Salisbury. There he had them massacred. Hengist was eventually killed by Aurelius Ambrosius (q.v.). His story is told by Bede and Geoffrey of Monmouth.

Henwinus, Duke of Cornwall see Leir, King of Britain.

Heorot (N-G, Britain) hall of the Danish King Hrodgar (q.v.) referred to in the poem *Beowulf*.

Herfjǫturr 173.

Hermódr (Hermóthr) 171, 226–228.

Hermódr (Hermóthr) King of the Danes, (AS) notorious legendary king, miserly and bloodthirsty. He was compared unfavourably with the hero Beowulf (q.v.).

Hern the Hunter (C, Britain) leader of the Wild Hunt, an antlered giant said to live in Windsor Great Park. He is probably a survival of Cernunnos (q.v.). See also 163.

Hiisi 257, 275.

Hiisi, the Elk of 275.

Hildebrand (G) (i) the hero of the *Hildebrandslied*, a poem dating from *c*. 800. Returning home after many years' fighting abroad he is challenged by a young knight and compelled to fight him. The youth proves to be his own son, Hadubrand. The poem only exists in fragments, but it would seem that this episode is a version of an old Indo-European story, since similar tales appear from both Ireland and Iran. Cf. 53–56 and vol. 3: 5.3: Sohrab. (ii) see 246.

Hildigǫltr (N-G) 'Battle Pig', a helmet owned by Athils, King of Sweden. See also *Hildisvín* and *Sviagríss*.

Hildisvín 214. See also *Hildigǫltr* and *Sviagríss*.

Hildr 173.

History of the Kings of Britain, the 116–128.

Hlidskjálf (Hlithskjálf) (N-G) 165, 207.

Hlǫkk 173.

Hǫdr (Hothr) (N-G) legendary Icelandic outlaw, hero of the *Hardar (Harthar) Saga*; also the blind god who killed Baldr; see 224, 231–235.

Hoel, King of Brittany 119–120, 124.

Hoenir 146–147, 156.

Horatii 51.

Horsa (C, Britain) brother to Hengist (q.v.).

Hrafnkell (N–G) hero of the Icelandic *Hrafnskels Saga Freysgoda (Freysgotha)*.

Hredel (Hrethel), King of the Geats (N–G, Britain) grandfather to Beowulf (q.v.).

Hreidmar (N–G) father to Fáfnir and Reginn, by whom he was murdered. See 238.

Hringhorni 225.

Hringr (N–G) a nickname of King Sigurdr of Sweden, according to Saxo, who describes his defeat of the Danish King Haraldr Hilditǫnn (q.v.)

Hrodgar (Hrothgar) King of the Danes (N–G, Britain) legendary monarch descended from Scyld Scefing (q.v.). He built a great hall, the Heorot, but was unable to defend it against the monster Grendel (q.v.). See also Beowulf.

Hrungnir 182–184.

Hugi 194–195.

Huginn 165.

Hvergelmir 150.

Hygelac, King of the Geats (N–G, Britain) uncle to Beowulf (q.v.). He and his son Heardred were killed in a war against the Franks (c. 521). He was an historical figure.

Hymir 199–202.

Hymiskvida 197.

Hyndla (N–G) a giantess, rival of Freyja (q.v.). She revealed the ancestry of Ottarr Heimski (q.v.)

Ialonus (C, Gaulish) the god of cultivated fields.

Ibn Fadlan 175.

Idisi (G) generic term for women who, like the Valkyries (q.v.), controlled the outcome of battles by binding some soldiers and aiding others. Their name seems to be cognated with the Norse *Dísir* (q.v.). Cf. Alaisiagae.

Idunn (Ithunn) (N–G) goddess guardian of the golden Apples of Youth (q.v.). She was wife to Bragi (q.v.).

Ignoge see Brutus.

Ilma (F–U) the air-god, whose daughter is Luonnotar (q.v.).

Ilmarinen 255, 264–271.

Ilmatar Luonnotar see Luonnotar.

Ilya-Muromyets (S, Russian) hero of innumerable heroic poems, this 'peasant's son' spent his first thirty-three years too weak to move, but then two itinerant minstrels gave him a draught of honey, sending strength coursing through his limbs. Blessed by his aged parents Ilya now embarked upon a series of remarkable exploits,

flying through the air on his marvellous horse, splitting oaks and church towers with his arrows and fighting the infidel, for, though some aspects of his character recall the pagan god Pyren (q.v.) Ilya was held to be a faithful Christian. His last act was the building of Kiev cathedral. When it was finished he died and his body immediately turned to stone.

Imbolg (C, Irish) the spring festival, celebrated on 1 February, later St. Brighid's Day. See Brighid, Saint.

Immram Curaig Maíle Dúin p. 20. See also Maíle Dúin.

immrama p. 20.

Indra 163, 176.

Ing (N–G, Britain) hero or god associated with Denmark. He is said to have been the ancestor of the kings of Bernicia.

Ingeld (N–G, Britain) leader of the Heathobards (q.v.).

Invasions, the 1–19.

Ireland, the Sovereignty of, see Ireland, the Spirit of and Medhbha, Queen of Connacht.

Ireland, the Spirit of p. 23, **2**, 17–18, 29, 42. See also **121**.

Irminsul (G) the world pillar; cf. Yggdrasill.

Iseult see Tristram.

Iseult of the White Hands see Tristram.

Island of the Mighty, the 86, 96–100.

Island of the Mighty, The, by Arden and D'Arcy **130**.

Jesus Christ 135–137, 139.

Joseph of Arimathea 135–137. See also Glastonbury Thorn.

Jǫtnar (N–G) the race of giants. See also Frost Giants and 142, 144–145, 150.

Jǫtunheimr 150, 178.

Joukahainen 251, 253.

Joyous Gard (C, Anglo-French) the castle of Sir Lancelot of the Lake, to which he eloped with Queen Guinevere (qq.v.).

Jumala (F–U) the supreme being, possibly an ancient sky deity, for his name is cognate with that for dusk. The oak was sacred to him.

Juras Māte (B, Latvian) 'Mother of the Sea', the sea-goddess.

Kalevala (F–U) the land of Kaleva, the ancestor of the heroes whose exploits are recounted in the *Kalevala* (q.v.). See also **266, 271**.

Kalevala, the p. 29 and 247–279.

Kalma (F–U) the goddess of death, whose name means 'Smell-of-the-Corpse'. Her home was guarded by the monstrous Surma (q.v.).

Kalvaitis (B, Lithuanian) the divine smith. He daily forges the sun anew and makes a ring for the dawn goddess,

a silver belt and golden stirrups for each of Dievas's (q.v.) sons Cf. Hephaestos (vol. 1: 2.2. **46–56**), Ilmarinen and Vǫlundr.

kantele 270–271.

kaukai see Puškaitis.

Kay, Sir 112.

Keeper of the Forest, the, see Cernunnos.

Ketill (N) legendary Norwegian, hero of *Ketils Saga Hoengs*.

Kipu-Tytto (F–U) the goddess of sickness, one of the hideous daughters of Tuoni and Tuonetar. See Kivutar and 260.

Kivutar (F–U) goddess of suffering, sister to Kipu-Tytto (q.v.). See also 260.

Kjalnesinga Saga 186.

Kormák (N) legendary ninth-century Icelandic poet and hero whose story is told in *Kormáks Saga*.

Kremara (S, Polish) the patron spirit of pigs. Cf. Kurwaichin and Walgino.

Kriemhild 245–246.

Krukis (S) patron spirit of blacksmiths. He also watched over domestic animals.

Kullervo (F–U) a powerful but evilly-disposed warrior, a character in the *Kalevala* national epic.

Kulhwch see Culhwch.

Kupala (S) popular fertility goddess whose midsummer worship included ritual river bathing, offerings of wreaths cast upon the waters, jumping over bonfires (cf. Beltene) and the sacrifice of a cock beneath a birch pole which had been stripped of all but its topmost branches and hung with garlands (cf. the traditional British Maypole).

Kurke (S. Russian) the corn spirit depicted as a cockerel (cf. Rugiǫ Boba). A cockerel was sacrificed to it at the harvest festival and a few ears of corn left standing in the field for it.

Kurwaichin (S, Polish) the patron spirit of sheep (cf. Kremara and Walgino).

Kvasir (N–G) 155.

Kvasir's Blood 155.

Kylli of Saari 273.

Kyllikki 277–278.

Labhraidh Loingsech, King of Leinster see Cobthach Coel.

Lady of the Lake, the (C, Anglo-French) abductress of Sir Lancelot (q.v.) she is sometimes identified with Vivien (q.v.), but in Malory remains anonymous. She is a version of Morgan le Fay (q.v.). See also *Excalibur*.

Laighin, the 5.

Laima (B, Lithuanian) goddess of fate. Lime trees were sacred to her. She controlled all life, animal, plant and human. Some stories referred to three

Sir Lancelot (*left*) and his son Sir Galahad in a boat. The anonymous knight in white armour is a divine messenger, summoning Galahad to go forward alone on the last stage of the Grail Quest. Illustration from the fourteenth-century manuscript *Quête du Saint Graal*. The British Library Ms. Royal 14E iii f. 134 v. (*Photo: the British Library*.)

or even seven such goddesses (cf. Norns). Her name is cognate with *laimè* (happiness) and occasionally she is referred to as Laima-Dalia (Happiness-Fate).

Laima-Dalia see Laima.

lamb, the Paschal 135.

lance, the bleeding 136–137.

lance, of Longinus 136.

Lancelot, Sir, of the Lake (C, Anglo-French) one of King Arthur's (q.v.) Knights. He undertook the Grail Quest but his adultery with Guinevere (q.v.) prevented him from accomplishing the quest. See also Joyous Gard, Lady of the Lake, Vivien and **140**.

Land of the Living see Tír inna mBeo.

Land of Promise see Tír Tairngiri and **36, 42, 46**.

Land of Promise, Lord of the **36**.

Land of Women see Tír inna mBan and **37**.

Last Supper, the 135, 137.

Laukpatis (B, Lithuanian) the 'Lord-of-the-Fields', sometimes known as Lauksargis, 'Guardian-of-the-Fields'.

Lauksargis see Laukpatis.

Lawkapatim see Datan.

Leabhar Gabhála Éireann (C, Irish) *The Book of the Conquest of Ireland*, popularly known as *The Book of Invasions*. It is a twelfth-century pseudo-history embodying early traditions. Its emphasis is on the prestige of the late Gaelic ruling class. See p. 20 and 1.

Lebhorcham 71.

Leiden 28.

Leinster 5, 6.

Leir, King of Britain (C, Britain) the prototype of Shakespeare's tragic hero King Lear, Leir was the son of King Bladud. He ruled for sixty years and founded the town of Kaerler (Caerleir, i.e. Castle Leir) or Leicester. His two older daughters, Goneril and Regan, played upon the old man's vanity and induced him to give them each a quarter of his kingdom as their dowries. Cordelia, the youngest daughter, refused to flatter her father and so received nothing. Goneril and Regan's husbands, Maglaurus, Duke of Albany, and Henwinus, Duke of Cornwall, seized the rest of the kingdom. Maglaurus allowed Leir a retinue of 140, but Goneril reduced it to 80, Regan to five and then Goneril reduced it yet further, to a single man. Leir now went to France, where he was honourably received by Cordelia and her husband King Aganippus, who provided him with an army, enabling him to regain his throne. On Leir's death three years later, he was buried downstream from Leicester in a vault dedicated to the Roman god Janus (see vol. 1: 2.3.) and there the town's craftsmen came annually to observe the god's festival.

Leire 222.

Lemminkainen 269–270, 273–278, See also Ahti.

Lempi 273.

Leodegrance, King 134.

Leshy (S) the wood-spirit who teases travellers by leading them astray. He can be foiled if the traveller sits down, removes his clothes and replaces them back to front and his shoes on the wrong feet. The Leshy was particularly lively and troublesome in the spring when he re-emerged after a winter's disappearance. His complexion was blue, his eyes and beard bright green.

Liegnitz 28.

Líf 161.

Lífdrasir 161.

Lincoln, Battle of 119.

Llallawc see Myrddin.

Llallogan Vyrdin see Myrddin.

Lleu Llaw Gyffes 33, 101–108.

Lludd 28–32.

Lludd Llaw Ereint (C, Welsh) 'Lludd of the Silver Hand', Welsh variant of

King Leir from Holinshed's *Chronicles*, 1577. The British Library. (*Photo: Ray Gardner.*)

Nuada Airgedlámh and the British Nodens (qq.v.). His daughter was Creiddylad, the original of Cordelia (see Leir, King of Britain). His son was Gwynn ap Nudd, the Irish Fionn mac Cumhaill (q.v.).

Llwyd fab Cil Coed 92.

Llŷr, King of Britain (C, Welsh) father of Bendigeidfran, Branwen and Manawydan (qq.v.).

Loch Lomond 119.

Lódurr (Lóthurr) 146–147.

Loeg (C, Irish) charioteer to Cú Chulainn (q.v.).

Loeghaire Buadhach 58–59.

Loeghaire Lorc, King of Ireland see Cobthach Coel.

Logi 194–195.

Lohengrin 130.

Lokasenna 231.

Loki 159, 160, 178–179, 188–196, 224, 230–231.

London 32, 99, 118. See also Brutus.

Lot, King of Orkney (C, Anglo-French) in Malory the father of Gawain (q.v.).

Loth of Lodonesia (C, Britain) brother-in-law to King Arthur (q.v.). His two sons were Gawain and Mordred (qq.v.). See also 120, 124.

Lough Neagh 41.

Louhi, Lady of Pohjola 254–255, 264, 266–268, 271, 274–275.

Loviatar (F-U) the source of all evil, the most dreadful of all Tuoni and Tuonetar's terrible daughters. See 260. On her the wind fathered nine monsters: Pleurisy, Colic, Gout, Tuberculosis, Ulcer, Scabies, Cancer, Plague and a nameless monster of envy.

Luchta see Goibhniu and 13.

Lucius Hiberius 126.

Lug see 'Mercury' and 28.

Lugh (C, Irish) a god often associated with the Roman Mercury (vol. 1: 2.3.) See also Lleu Llaw Gyffes, 'Mercury' and 12–16, 24, 28–33.

Lugh, the spear of 7.

Lughnasadh, the 29.

Lundein 32.

Luonnotar 247–249.

Lwndrys 32.

Lŷtir (N) Swedish god referred to in the *Flateyjarbók.* His name may have been a title of Freyr (q.v.), for, like that god he was taken round in a wagon. King Eiríkr inn Sigrsaeli (q.v.) led the wagon to a particular spot and waited till it became heavy, a sign that Lŷtir had entered it. The king then drove the wagon to his royal hall and there welcomed the god and consulted with him.

Lytuvonis (B, Lithuanian) the rain-god.

Mabinogion, The 75–115.

Mabon (i) (C, Welsh) the son of Modron, he was stolen from his mother at the age of three nights and taken to Caer Loyw (Gloucester) which here symbolises the Otherworld (q.v.). Rescued by Culhwch (q.v.) he hunted the magic boar Twrch Trwyth (q.v.) and took from between its ears the razor which Culhwch needed.

(ii) (C, French) the name of Maponos (q.v.), in the French Arthurian cycle.

Mabonagrain see Maponos.

Mabuz see Maponos

Mac Cécht 17–18.

Mac Cuill 17–18.

Mac Da Thó 57–58.

Mac Gréine 17–18.

Mac ind Óg see Oenghus.

Macha see Badhbh.

Macha, Grey of 48.

Mader Akka see Mader Atcha.

Mader Atcha (F-U, Lapp) the divine creator. He formed the soul of man while his wife Mader Akka was responsible for the body.

Maen Tyriawg (Maentwrog) 95.

Maeve a variant of Medhbha Queen of Connacht (q.v.). See also 58.

Mag Mell (C, Irish) 'The Delightful Plain', a supernatural world. Cf. Tír na nOc, Tír inna mBan and Tír Tairngiri. See also the Otherworld.

Magh Tuiredh, First Battle of 8–11.

Magh Tuiredh, Second Battle of 12–16, 23–26, 30–31.

Magh Tuiredh, the Battle of p. 20.

Maglaurus, Duke of Albany see Leir, King of Britain.

Magni (N-G) son of Thórr (q.v.), by the giantess Járnsaxa. He owns part of his father's hammer and will be one of those who survive Ragnarǫkr, see 161.

Maíl Dúin (C, Irish) a story probably dating from the eighth century, though the text is from the tenth, tells how Maíl, the son of a nun, set out on a voyage to find the murderer of his father who was said to have been a Arran Islander. After a long odyssey Maíl and his companions meet a hermit who tells them that although they will find the murderer they should spare his life in gratitude to God, who has spared them from so many perils in the course of their long voyage. Eventually, guided by an Irish falcon, the sailors find their way home. See also p. 20.

Maíl Fohartaig (C, Irish) handsome, lively son of Rónán, King of Leinster. His stepmother, the young and beautiful daughter of Echaid, fell in love with Maíl and tried to seduce him.

Repulsed she accused him of violating her. Rónán at first refused to believe it, but later, convinced of Maíl's guilt, had him killed.

Mājas Kungs see Žemėpatis.

Malory, Sir Thomas 130.

Man, Isle of 3, 34, 35.

Manala (F-U) the land of Mana, an alternative name for Tuonela. See 260.

Manannán mac Lir 30, 34–40, 42.

Manawydan fab Llŷr 35, 86–92, 100.

Mannu, Mother of (F-U) the earth spirit.

Manu 141.

Maponos (C, Gaulish and British) the Divine Youth, worshipped in Gaul and northern Britain, where he was thought of especially as a hunter. His mother seems to have been Matrona (q.v.). In Welsh stories he appears as Mabon (q.v.), in French Arthurian tales as Mabon, Mabuz or Mabonagrain. See also Mac ind Óg.

Marcán see Cano.

Mark, King of Cornwall see Tristram.

Märkhättu 274, 275.

Marzanna (S, Polish) the fruit-goddess.

Math fab Mathonwy, Lord of Gwynned 93–95, 102–103, 105.

Matholwch, King of Ireland 86, 96–98.

Mati-Syra-Zemlya (S) the earth-goddess 'Moist-Mother-Earth'. Cf. Žemyna.

Matrona (C, Gaulish) the Divine Mother, goddess of the River Marne. See also Maponos.

Mead-of-Inspiration, the (N-G) a drink brewed from the blood of Kvasir, whom the dwarfs had murdered. Whoever drank of it was inspired to wisdom and poetical utterance. Eventually, to save their own lives, the dwarfs were compelled to give the Mead to Suttungr (q.v.), son of the giant Gillingr, from whom they had stolen it, after killing him. It was later stolen from Suttungr's daughter by Óðinn, who took it to Asgardr. See also 155.

Meath 6, 45.

Medeine (B. Lithuanian) goddess of the forest referred to in thirteenth-century texts.

Medhbha (Medbh) Queen of Connacht (C, Irish) also called Maeve. According to the early *Tain Bo Cuailnge* Medhbha was ruler of Connacht (Connaught). Her name means 'Intoxication' and she seems originally to have been a personification of sovereignty, imagined as a goddess whom the king must marry. Possibly the idea derives from the primitive concept of the tribal god's union with the earth-goddess, or the king's ritual marriage with her (cf. Sumerian ritual marriages of the king and high priestess). The concept may also be related to the Hindu idea of the *shakti* (vol. 3: 5.2.). Medhbha is said to have been the wife of nine Irish kings and only her mate could hold the throne. See also Ireland, Spirit of, and p. 23 and **58, 73**.

Meliodas, King of Lyonesse see Tristram.

Meness see Mėnuo.

Menglǫd (Mengloth) (N-G) a divine maiden wooed by the hero Svipdagr.

Mėnuo (B. Lithuanian) the moon-god, in Latvian Meness. He wore a starry robe and travelled the sky in a chariot drawn by grey horses. He married Saule (q.v.), but later fell in love with Aušrinė (q.v.) and was punished by Perkūnas, who broke him in halves. In Latvian myth he is said finally to have married the Weaver of the Stars.

Menw fab Teirgwaedd 112.

'Mercury' (C, Gaulish) according to Caesar, the chief Gaulish deity. He was credited with the invention of all the arts and honoured as the patron of commerce and travel. He was also the war-god. Place-name evidence and his similarity to the Irish Lugh (q.v.), make it almost a certainty that this god was commonly known as Lug or Lugus. His consort was Rosmerta (q.v.). See also **28.**

Merlin (C, Britain) legendary wizard, sage and prophet associated with King Arthur. He derives from the Welsh Myrddinn (q.v.). According to Geoffrey of Monmouth, he was the son of an incubus and a nun. He foretold the overthrow and death of Vortigern (q.v.), the victory of Aurelius Ambrosius (q.v.) and transported the Giants' Ring (q.v.) from Ireland. In later Arthurian legends he appears as Arthur's mentor. See **117, 134** and also Vivien.

Merseburg Charms, the (G) two ninth-century pagan spells naming various deities.

Metsola 278.

Metsola, Mother of (G-U) the frost-spirit.

Midgardr (Midgarthr) (N-G) **145, 153.**

Midgardsormr (Mithgarthsormr) **159, 160, 194–195, 197–202.**

Midhir 42–47.

Mikula (S, Russian) one of the *bogatyr* (q.v.), a farmer of superhuman strength greatly favoured by Mati-Syra-Zemlya (q.v.).

Mil Éspáine, the sons of **1, 17–19.**

Mil the Black (C, Welsh) an opponent of King Arthur, who killed him.

Mime 237.

Mimingus (N-G) according to Saxo, he was the old man who furnished Hothergus (Hodr) with the sword he used to kill Baldr. See **234.**

Merlin teaching his magic arts to the Lady of the Lake. Illustration to the early fourteenth-century *Lestoire de Merlin*, from Bologna. The Bodleian Library Ms. Douce 178 f. 249. (*Photo: the Bodleian Library*.)

Merlin astride a black horse brings together King Arthur's army. Illustration to the early fourteenth-century *Lestoire de Merlin* from Bologna. The Bodleian Library Ms. Douce 178 f. 195. (*Photo: the Bodleian Library*.)

Mímir (N-G) He may originally have been thought of as a giant, possibly the same one who made the marvellous sword *Mimming*. If so, he is perhaps to be identified with Mimingus (q.v.). He was also referred to as Mímr and Mími and associated with the Yggdrasill and the Well of Urdr, although this is differentiated from the Spring of Mímir in Snorri's account. See also p. 28 and 150, 156, 165.

Mímir, the Spring of 150, 165.

'Minerva' (C, Gaulish) a goddess referred to by Caesar as Minerva is probably the one known in Ireland as Brighid, in Britain as Briganti (Brigantia) (qq.v.).

Mistillteinn (N-G) 'Mistletoe' a wonderful sword owned by various heroes including Hromund Greipson. See also 231.

Mitra-Varuna 28.

Mjǫllnir (N-G) Thórr's hammer, made for him by the dwarfs. See 176–178, 179, 183–184, 188, 191–192, 201.

Moccos (C, Gaulish) the boar-god.

Modeina (S, Polish) one of the two forest deities. The other was Siliniets.

Modgudr (Mothguthr) (N-G) the girl who guarded the bridge to Hel. See 226.

Modron (C, Welsh) the 'divine Mother' of Mabon (q.v.).

Mǫkkurkalfi 183.

Mongán, King of Dál nAraidi 38–41.

Moon 147, 158.

Moraunt, King of Ireland see Tristram.

Moray 119.

Mordred 127–128.

Morgan le Fay (C, Anglo-French) Morgan is first referred to by Geoffrey of Monmouth in his *Vita Merlini* as the chief of nine 'fays' living in the Otherworldly realm of Avalon (q.v.). In Layamon's *Brut* (132) she appears as Avalon's Queen (M)Argante and when King Arthur lays dying arrives in a boat and carries him away to her supernatural kingdom (cf. 128). In later romances she is presented as a fiercesome witch queen, possibly as a result of Christian hostility. Her later character may also have been influenced by memories of the ancient Irish goddess, the Mórríghan (q.v.). In medieval romance Morgan is Arthur's illegitimate half-sister, educated in a convent where she perversely spent her days studying the powers of evil. The ambivalent Lady of the Lake (q.v.) is another version of the same figure.

Morholt, Sir see Tristram.

Mórríghan, the p. 23 and 23, 63. See also Badhbh. Although generally spoken of as terrible, the Mórríghan was also a fertility goddess, commemorated in low hills known as the Paps of the Mórríghan.

Morrigu variant of the Mórríghan (q.v.).

Morte Darthur, Le 130.

Mothers, the (C and N-G) goddesses of plenty, worshipped in the Roman period by Germans and Celts. The three goddesses represent triple aspects of the earth mother. They are commemorated in Wales in the Y Foel Famau, Hall of the Mothers. See also Nehalennia and Brighids, the Three and 96.

Moylinny 41.

Moytura, Battle of see *Magh Tuiredh, the Battle of*.

Mughain, Queen of Ulster 52.

Mumu (C, Irish) one of the four Irish provinces referred to in the *Táin Bó Cuailnge*. Its capital was in West Kerry. Later it became known as Munster.

Muninn 165.

Munster 6, 58.

Murkwood see Swan Maidens.

Múspell, the sons of the host of Surtr. See 159.

Múspellheimr 142, 159

Myesyats (S) the moon-deity. The name is masculine in form, but the deity is usually spoken of as a goddess, the wife of Dazhbog (q.v.) and mother of the stars. In the Ukraine however, Myesyats is a god, husband to the sun-goddess.

Myrddin (C, Welsh) according to early Welsh poems Myrddin, later called Merlin (q.v.), fought at the Battle of Arhuret (q.v.) where his lord Gwenddoleu was killed. Grief for his lord drove Myrddin distracted. He spent the remainder of his life as a hermit living wild in the Scottish forest of Celyddon (Caledonia) lamenting Gwenddoleu's death. In his frenzy he acquired the gift of prophecy. This story relates Myrddin to the Irish King Suibne Geilt (q.v.) from whose legend the tale may be derived, although Myrddin is first referred to in the tenth-century poem *Armes Prydain* (q.v.) while the *Buile Suibne,* which recounts the Irish legend is probably two centuries older. It is therefore difficult to be certain which tale influenced the other, or if both derive from some independent source. It is thought that Myrddin's name derives from a mistaken analysis of Caerfyrddin (Carmarthen). In other poems he is called Llallawc or Llallogan Vyrdin.

Naglfar 159.

Nanna 225, 233

Nantosvelta (C, Gaulish) water-goddess associated with Sucellus (q.v.).

Naoise 71–73.

Navigatio, Brendan, p. 20. See also Brendan, Saint.

Nechta Scéne, the three sons of 51.

Nechtan (C, Irish) river-god, husband of Boann (q.v.).

Nehalennia (N-G) goddess of plenty, worshipped on Walcheren Island in Roman times. Cf. The Mothers.

Nemhedh 4.

Nera (C, Irish) At the feast of *samhain* Nera left the court of Aillil and Medhbha (qq.v.) and went outside. A corpse hanging from the gallows complained of thirst, so he stopped to take it down and give it a drink. When he returned to the court he found his people killed by a *sídh* (q.v.) host which he pursued into the underworld. There he was kindly received by the king who gave him a wife and home. In return he was commanded to collect the monarch's firewood. Warned by his wife in a vision that the *sídh* hosts would attack the court of Connacht again on the next *samhain*, he went aloft to warn Aillil and Medhbha, taking primroses, wild garlic and fern to prove he had been in the underworld. Medhbha's people destroyed the *sídh*, but Nera was trapped within it and so will never now escape until Doomsday.

Nerthus (N-G) according to Tacitus a Danish fertility goddess. See also 203–204.

Níal Noígiallach (C, Irish) 'Nial of the Nine Hostages', founder of the fifth Irish province formed by the division of the ancient Ulaidh (q.v.). His capital was at Tara. His descendants, the Uí Néill, gained control over all central and northern Ireland. They are believed to have been a new group of invading Celts, referred to in legends as the Sons of Míl Éspáine (q.v.). Níal himself was said to have been the foster-son of the poet Torna Éices of Munster. His father was Eochu Mugmedón, his mother Cairenn, a Saxon from Britain.

Nibelungenlied 236, 244–246.

Nibelungs, the 236, 241.

Nidhad, King (N-G, Britain) the Old English equivalent of King Nidudr. See Vǫlundr.

Nidhǫggr (Nithhǫggr) (N-G) 'Corpsetearer' a flying dragon who stole corpses; also the serpent that gnaws the roots of Yggdrasill. See 151.

Niflheimr 142, 150.

Night 147.

Nimiane see Vivien.

Nimue see Vivien.

Njál (N) tragic hero of the Icelandic *Njáls Saga* or *Brennu-Njáls Saga (The Saga of Niall's Burning)*.

Njǫrdr (Njǫrthr) 156, 203–206, 215.

Noah 2.

Nodens (Nodons) (C, British) tutelary god of the sanctuary at Lydney, Gloucs., a temple of healing. He is to be identified with the Irish Nuada Airgedlámh and Welsh Llud Llaw Ereint (qq.v.).

Norns, the three 149. See also Wyrd.

Nuadha 9, 11–12, 16, 31.

Nuadha Airgedlámh (N. Argetlám) 11.

Nuadha of the Silver Hand see Nuadha Airgedlámh.

Nuadha, the sword of 7.

Odd (N-G) legendary hero and traveller whose story appears in the *Ǫrvar-Odds Saga*.

Óðinn (Óthinn) p. 28 and 143–147, 155, 160, 162–173, 175, 218, 222, 223, 225, 226, 228, 231, 235.

Óðr (Óthr) (N-G) Husband to Freyja (q.v.) whom he abandoned.

Oenghus (C, Irish) also known as Mac ind Óg, Oenghus was a clever trickster and quibbled possession of Bruigh na Boinee (q.v.) from his father the Daghdha (q.v.), or, some say from Elcmhaire. The *Aislinge Oenguso (Oenghus's Dream)* tells of his lovesick quest for the girl of his dreams and eventual discovery of her. See also 42, 67–68.

Oenghus Mac ind Óg see Oenghus.

Offa (Britain) legendary builder of Offa's Dyke (A.D. 757–796), an earthwork on the English-Welsh border.

Ogham script see Oghma.

Oghma (C, Irish) a 'strong man', inventor of the Ogham, a fourth-century script probably resulting from the combination of an earlier form of magical writing and the Latin alphabet. Some authorities feel that he and the Gaulish Ogmios (q.v.) represent the Celtic type of the Indo-European god of magical powers whose other forms include the Vedic Varuna (vol. 3: 5.3.). See also 10, 14, 16.

Ogmios (C, Gaulish) god of eloquence, according to the second-century Greek Lucian. He is possibly to be identified with Oghma (q.v.). Lucian describes him as an old man wearing a lion's skin and leading a group of followers whose ears are chained to his tongue. Lucian says he is shown wearing the lion's skin because the Celts believed eloquence more powerful than brute force and it grew stronger with age, hence the man's elderly appearance. Lucian identifies the god with Hercules (vol. 1: 2.3.), although he remarks that Ogmios's characteristics are not entirely Herculean.

Qku-Thórr (N-G) Thórr the Charioteer, a title of Thórr (q.v.) in his rôle as thunder-god, driving a chariot drawn by goats. See also Perkūnas.

Olaf the Holy (N-G) Saint Olaf, a Norwegian king (A.D. 1016–30).

Oláfr Geírstadaálfr (O. Geírstathaálfr) (N-G) Olaf, Elf of Geirstad, an early Norwegian king at whose tomb sacrifices were offered.

Oláfr Tryggvasson, King 210, 212.

Oliver (French) friend and comrade-in-arms of Roland (q.v.). They were once drawn against each other in single combat to settle a dispute between their lord Charlemagne (q.v.) and his vassal de Montglave but after five days' fighting in which neither had the advantage they suddenly recognised each other and both simultaneously conceded the victory.

Olwen 109–115.

ort see *haltija*.

Otava (F-U) the Spirit of the Great Bear (q.v.) (Ursa Major).

Otherworld, the (C) although sometimes given a single name, such as Annwn or later Avalon (q.v.), the Otherworld is often conceived of as comprising several realms. In Irish stories like that of the voyages of Bran these are various islands or foreign countries. The region is not simply or even primarily the world of the dead, but more a paradisal fairyland, whose ruler(s) feasts guests from a magic cauldron. Several heroes, including Cú Chulainn and King Arthur sought to steal such a cauldron. See also Donn, Nera, Ghoibhniu, 17, 19, 21, 34, 36–37, 40, 42, 46–47, 61, 76, 234.

Otr (N-G) Otter, son of Hreidmar (q.v.). He was slain by Loki, see 238.

Otso (F-U) a woodland spirit invoked by Ilmarinen's (q.v.) wife.

Ottarr Heimski (N-G) Ottar the Simple, a devotee of Freyja (q.v.) who helped him discover from Hyndla (q.v.) the secret of his ancestry.

Ovinnik (S) the spirit of the barn. He looked like a black cat with fiery eyes, but had a fierce bark.

Paha 257.

Paiva (F-U) the sun-god.

Pandrasus, King of Greece, see Brutus.

Paris, Battle of 124.

Parsifal 130.

Partholán 3–4.

Parzival 130.

Paschent (C, Britain) third son of Vortigern (q.v.). See also Aurelius Ambrosius.

Patrimpas (S) god of rivers and springs.

Pellervoiene (F-U) the god of vegetation, guardian of crops.

Pendaran Dyfed 85.

Perceval, Sir (C, Anglo-French) Arthurian knight, companion to Sir Galahad (q.v.) in the Grail Quest (135–140). In German stories he is Parsifal or Parzival. See 130 and 140.

Peredur see Arthuret. Battle of.

Perkonis see Perkūnas and 186.

Perkons see Perkūnas.

Perkūnas (B. Lithuanian) the thunder-god, in Latvian Pērkons, in Prussian: Perkonis; Czech: Perun; Russian: Pyerun. He resembles the Norse-Germanic Thórr (q.v.) and is a vigorous red-bearded man brandishing an axe. He rattles across the sky in a chariot drawn by his sacred animal the billy goat (cf. Qku-Thórr). Like Thórr also he is just, but irascible and impatient. He lives in a castle on the hilltop in the sky (see *dausos*). As the agent of justice and goodness he attacks the devil with lightning. At evil men he hurls his thunderbolt, or strikes their homes with lightning. In Baltic as in Norse-Germanic and Indian mythology, the thunderbolt is a fertility symbol and in spring Perkūnas's thunder is held to purify the earth of winter's evil spirits and stir it to new life. Cf. 22.

Perun see Perkūnas and Varpulis.

Phol (N-G) possibly should be Vol. He was a companion of Volla and is referred to in the second *Merseberg Charm* (q.v.). He may have been a fertility god.

Picts, the 118, 119.

Pohja 256.

Pohja, Maid of 256, 266–267, 273.

Pohjola 252–256, 264.

Pohjola, Lady of see Louhi, Lady of Pohjola.

Polevoi (Polevik) (S, Russian) the field-spirit, whose hair was green as grass. See also Poludnitsa.

Poludnitsa (S, Russian) in northern Russia the field-goddess, depicted as a beautiful woman dressed in white. She punishes those who work at midday and sometimes lures children into the cornfields and loses them there. See also Polevoi.

Preiddeu Annwn see Annwn.

Pryderi 85–95, 100, 101, 102.

Puškaitis (B, Latvian) a god who ruled

Reginn mends Sigurdr's sword; twelfth-century carving from Hylestad church, Setesdal, Norway. University Museum, Oslo. (*Photo: Werner Forman Archive.*)

over the *barstukai* (q.v.) and *kaukai* (subterranean spirits) and himself lived beneath an elder bush. He rewarded offerings by sending his subjects with corn as a gift to his worshippers.

Pwyll, Lord of Dyfed **75–84.**

Pwyll Head of Annwn 77.

Pyerun (S, Russian) the thunder-god (cf. Perkūnas) and also the god of war, combining characteristics of Óðinn and Thórr (qq.v.).

Radigast see Svantovit.

Ragnarøkr 158–161, 202.

Ragnarr Lodbrókr (R. Lothbrókr) (N-G) heroic dragon-slayer whose story is told in *Ragnars Saga Lodbrókr (Lothbrók)*. His sons are said to have conquered England.

Ran (N-G) sea-goddess, wife of Aegir (q.v.). She nets drowned sailors and entertains them in her deep sea hall.

Ratatoskr 151.

Rauni see Akka.

Ravens, Óðinn's see Huginn, Muninn.

Regan see Leir, King of Britain.

Reginn (N-G) a smith, the son of Hreidmar and brother to Fáfnir. After Fáfnir had commandeered the golden hoard of Andvari (q.v.) Reginn asked Sigurdr the Volsung to kill his brother, intending himself to double-cross the hero. However Sigurdr killed him first. See **237–239.**

Renaud (French) one of Charlemagne's (q.v.) knights, also known as Rinaldo. He caught and tamed the famous wild horse Bayard.

Rhiannon (C, Welsh) probably the Welsh equivalent of Édain Echraidhe and possibly of Epona (qq.v.). See also **78–86, 89, 92.**

Rhine, River **244.**

Richborough, Battle of see Auguselus and **128**

Rig (N-G) hero of the *Rigspula* (a poem in the *Edda*): He journeyed over the earth visiting the three classes of men: earl, farmer and thrall, spending a night in the house of each and sleeping between the husband and wife. The three children born as a result of his visits became the ancestors of these social groups. The preface to the poem identifies Rig with Heimdallr (q.v.) and the whole work suggests there is some relation to or influence from the Celtic Irish tradition. Cf. Manannán mac Lir and Mongán.

Rinda, Princess **235.**

Ringr, King **167.**

Rognvaldra (N-G) Rognvald of Orkney, heroic earl and poet who lived A.D. 1135–58.

Roland (French) legendary Count of Brittany and knight of Charlemagne (q.v.). According to legend he was Charlemagne's nephew. In A.D. 778 as his army was returning from a Spanish expedition it was attacked at Roncesvalles by the Basques (in the legend it was by the Saracens), who, forewarned by the treacherous Ganelon (q.v.) annihilated the unsuspecting Franks. Roland refused to blow his horn to summon the emperor's aid until it was too late and then died in the act of blowing it. See also Oliver.

Ronan, King of Leinster see Maíl Fothartaig.

Roquepertuse p. 24.

Rǫskva 188.

Rosmerta (C, Gaulish) goddess associated with the Gallic 'Mercury', she represents material wealth.

Rouland, King of Erminia see Tristram.

Round Table, the **131–134.**

Ruadh (C, Irish) the son of Rigdonn. While sailing to Norway his three vessels were suddenly arrested in midcourse. Diving to discover why, Ruadh found three giantesses were holding the ship. They bore him off to the seabed and he slept with each one before being released. The women told him they would bear his son and he said he would return to visit them on his way home. This he failed to do. When the giantesses realised that he had broken his word they chased after him with the child, but he had too big a start and, realising they would never catch him they cut off his son's head and threw it after him. See also Aegir and Wachilt.

Ruadh Rofhessa 21.

Rugavit see Svantovit.

Rugių Boba (B, Lithuanian) the 'Old One of the Rye', a female figure made from the last sheaf of the harvest. She is honoured at the harvest festival feast and kept for a year. Cf. Rice Mother vol. 4: 7.1.

rusalka (S) the spirit of a drowned girl. During the winter such *rusalka* spirits live in rivers, during the summer in the forest. In some areas they were regarded as malevolent, in others as kindly.

Sabines the **16.**

Sadko (S, Russian) legendary merchant of Novgorod. Once when sailing the sea he found his ship suddenly becalmed. Realising that although he had been voyaging for twelve years he had never paid any tribute to the Tsar of the Sea, Sadko therefore took three fine cups and, filling them with silver, gold and pearls, placed them upon the water on a plank. Instead of sinking the plank floated. The merchant realised that the Tsar wanted not riches but a human sacrifice. Lots were drawn and the cast fell upon Sadko himself. Taking a holy icon of Saint Nicholas and his lute the merchant stepped out onto the plank and fell asleep, to wake in the Tsar of the Sea's underwater palace. After his equally miraculous return to the upper world Sadko plied his trade on the waters of the Volga for a further twelve years, offering the river-god a tribute of bread and salt, which so pleased him that he entrusted Sadko with a message for his brother, the spirit of Lake Ilmen, who repaid the merchant with silver fish, making his fortune.

sagas p. 26.

Saingliu, Black of **48.**

Saint Michel, Mt. **127.**

Saint Patrick's Purgatory p. 20.

Salmon of Wisdom, the **65.**

Samhain 4, 23, 62, 64.

samildánach **31.**

sampo **254, 264–266, 269–271.**

Saule (B, Lithuanian) the sun-goddess. She and her daughters live in a castle said to be either beyond the hill of the sky (see *dausos*) or at the far end of the sea. She rides across the hill in a copper-wheeled chariot drawn by tireless fiery horses. As evening approaches she stops and washes her steeds in the sea and then sits on the hill's summit, or drives down to her apple orchard in nine chariots drawn by 100 horses. Sometimes she is spoken of as sailing the sea in a golden boat. The setting sun is a red apple falling from Saule's orchard into the sea. The goddess weeps to see it fall and her tears form red berries on the hilltop. The sun itself is also spoken of as a jug or spoon from which light is poured. At evening Saule's daughters rinse it in the sea. Closely associated with this goddess is the moon-god Mėnuo (q.v.) or Meness and the sons of Dievas (Dievo suneliai) (q.v.).

Saussy, Battle of.

Saxnot (G) called by the Anglo-Saxons Seaxneat, he was an old Saxon war-god and ancestor of the Kings of Essex. His name may mean 'Sword companion'.

Saxo p. 28 and **223, 231–232.**

Saxons, the p. 20, 22, 26, **38, 118, 119.**

Scáthach 53, 54.

Sceaf (N-G, Britain) the child who drifted onto the Danish coast in an open boat with his head resting on a

Sigurdr kills the dragon Fáfnir; twelfth-century carving from Hylestad church, Setesdal, Norway. University Museum, Oslo. (*Photo: Werner Forman Archive.*)

She killed him with her necklace, possibly a ritual execution by Skiálf as priestess of Freyja (q.v.).

Skídbladnir (Skíthblathnir) 215–216.

Skírnir (N-G) Freyr's (q.v.) servant and go-between in his courtship of Gerdr. See 207–208.

Skjǫldr (N-G) Óđinn's (q.v.) son, ruler of Denmark and ancestor of the Danish royal house. His wife was Gefjun. See 222, 223, and cf. Scyld Scefing.

Skrymir 190–192.

Skuldr 149.

Slagfidr see Vǫlundr.

Sleipnir 165, 171, 226–227.

Snorri Sturluson p. 26 and 141, 187, 205, 223, 231.

Snowdon, Mt. 129.

Sohrāb 56.

Souconna (C, Gaulish) goddess of the River Saône.

Southampton 119.

Sovereignty of Ireland the goddess see Ireland, Spirit of, Medhbha Queen of Connacht.

Spain 17.

Starkadr (Starkathr) (N-G) legendary hero referred to both in *sagas* and in Saxo's *Prose Edda*. See Vikarr.

Stribog (S) the wind-god. See also Varpulis and Dogoda.

Styrbjorn (N-G) opponent of Eiríkr inn Sigrsaeli (q.v.).

Suaixtis (B, Prussian) god of light. His name probably means 'Star'.

Sucellus (C, Gaulish) god depicted with a mallet, wine cask or flagon and accompanied by a dog. His consort seems to have been Nantosvelta (q.v.). Sucellus may have been a chthonic fertility god and although he is usually assimilated to Silvanus (vol. 1: 2.3.) some scholars feel he should rather be identified with 'Dis Pater' (q.v.).

Suibne Geilt, King (C, Irish) Sweeney the Mad, King of Dal nAraidi, who is said to have lost his wits at the Battle of Moira (A.D. 637). He became a 'wild man' roaming the forest. His life as a hermit is recounted in the *Buile Suibne (Sweeney's Frenzy)*. His story may have provided the basis for that of Myrddinn (q.v.).

Sun 147, 153, 158.

Surma (F-U) a monster whose maw was ever open to catch the unwary. Guardian of Kalma's (q.v.) home, he personified sudden death.

Surtr (N-G) the fire-giant of Múspell-heimr (q.v.). He burns heaven and earth at Ragnarøkr. See 159, 160.

Sutton Hoo 216.

Suttungr (N-G) son of Gillingr. See Mead-of-Inspiration.

Svadilfari (Svathilfari) (N-G) the sire of Sleipnir (q.v.). See also 153.

Svantovit (S, Baltic coast) the principal deity of these people, whose chief temple was at Arcona, where Svantovit was depicted in four aspects on a carved pillar. The god held a bull's horn cup in his right hand. This was annually filled with wine and the amount remaining at the year's end was held to signify the degree of prosperity to which the people could look forward in the coming months. A white horse sacred to the god was kept in the temple precinct and beside Svantovit's statue hung its saddle and bridle, together with a sword and a war banner. The god's rites were described by Saxo and other early chroniclers, who also describe similar deities named Rugevit, Yarovit and Radigast. Their accoutrements differ slightly from Svantovit's but their characters and attributes seem similar to his.

Svarog (S) the sky-father. His children were Dazhbog and Svarogich (qq.v.).

Svarogich (S) the fire-god, offspring of Svarog (q.v.).

Sviagríss (N-G) 'Piglet of the Swedes', a torc owned by Athlis King of the Swedes. See also *Hildisvín* and *Hildigǫltr.*

Svipdagr (N-G) hero who wooed the divine maiden Menglod.

Svyatogor (S, Russian) one of the chief *bogatyr* (q.v.). He was so proud of his great strength that he boasted he could lift the earth, but then, one day while out riding, he came upon a small bag lying in the way. Unable to shift it with his staff he dismounted and with a tremendous effort raised the bag as high as his knees, but in doing so he sweated blood and found himself sunk deep into the earth, unable to escape. So he died.

Swan Maidens, the (N-G) wives of Vǫlundr (q.v.) and his two brothers, the maidens were named Allwise, Swanwhite and Olrun. They flew from their home in Murkwood to the shores of a lake in Wolfdales, where the three brothers came upon them. After living seven years in Wolfdales they suddenly flew home again. See also vol. 4: 7.2. 15–18, 132–134.

swastika 176.

Sweeney the Mad see Suibne Geilt.

—————————————————

Tailtiu 29.

Tailtiu, Battle of 18.

Taín Bó Cuailnge (C, Irish) *The Cattle Raid of Cooley,* a great prose saga

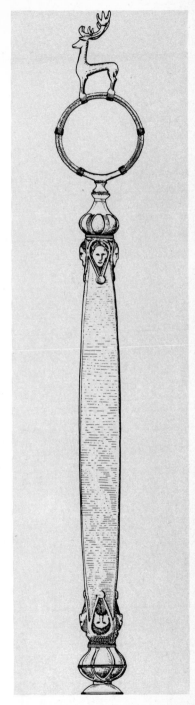

Whetstone-sceptre from the Sutton Hoo ship burial, decorated at either end with typical Celtic heads. Illustration from British Museum's *The Sutton Hoo Ship Burial,* 1970. (*Photo: British Museum.*)

Bas-relief from a pillar dedicated to Jupiter by the 'sailors of Paris', A.D. 14–37, shows the bull Tarvos Trigaranus and three cranes. It is a companion-piece to that of Esus, p. 106. Musée de Cluny, Paris. (*Photo: Photoresources.*)

preserving a picture of the Iron Age traditions of Ireland.

Taliesin 100.

Tanaros (C) the thunder-god.

Tapio (F-U) a woodland spirit who, with his wife Mielkki and their children Nyyrikki and Tuulikki, was invoked by huntsmen.

Tara 17–18, 36, 45–46, 64.

Taranis see Esus.

Tarvos Trigaranus (C) the Three-Horned Bull whose images have been found in both Gaul and Britain. See Donn, the, of Cuailnge.

Tawals see Datan.

Tech Duinn see Donn and 17.

Teiwa (N-W) linguists postulate this as the archaic form of Tîwaz.

Tennyson, Alfred, Lord 130.

Tethra 34.

Teutates see Esus.

Teyrnon Twryf Liant, Lord of Gwent Is-Coed 84.

Thjálfi 188–196.

Thjázi (N-G) see the Apples of Youth. When Thjázi discovered that Loki had recovered the Apples he set out in pursuit in eagle's form, but the Aesir fired a heap of woodshavings and singed his wings, so he fell and was easily overcome and killed.

Thokk 229–230.

Thord Freysgodi (T. Freysgothi) (N-G) a priest of Freyr.

Thorgerdr Holgarbrudr (Thorgerthr Holgarbruthr) (N-G) 'Bride of Helgi', a fertility goddess associated with Freyr and worshipped particularly in Halogaland (northern Norway). Jarl Harkon was her devotee and referred to her as his wife. Saxo says she was a wife of one of Freyr's relatives and with all her companions became a prostitute. In the later *sagas* she is associated with trolls and other fiends.

Thorgrímr Thorsteinsson (N-G) a priest of Freyr. He was slain by his brother-in-law, the outlaw Gisli.

Thorhallr Veidimadr (T. Veithimathr) (N-G) 'The Hunter', a devotee of Thórr. He journeyed to Vinland (q.v.).

Thorólfr Mostrarksegg (N-G) 'Beard of Most', legendary Norwegian from the Island of Most, who was one of the first Icelandic colonists.

Thórr 22, 27, 160, 176–202.

Thrymr 178–181.

Thunor (N-G, Britain) the Anglo-Saxon form of Donar (q.v.).

Tig (N-G, Britain) a name of Tîwaz, whom the Anglo-Saxons also called Tiw.

Tintagel 117.

Tír inna mBan (C, Irish) the super-natural Land of Women, 37.

Tír inna mBeo (C, Irish) the supernatural Land of the Living where sickness and age are unknown.

Tír na nÓc (C, Irish) the supernatural Land of the Young.

Tir Tairngiri (C, Irish) the supernatural Land of Promise, 36, 42, 46.

Tiw see Tig.

Tîwaz 162, 164, 167.

tjetajat (F-U) wizards, that is *shamans* (q.v.).

Torna Eices see Nial Noígiallach.

Trí Dé Dana (C, Irish) the three gods of craftsmanship: Creidhne, Goibniu and Luchta (qq.v.). See also 13, 31.

Trinovantum see Brutus.

Tristan see Tristram.

Tristan 130.

Tristram (c, Irish, British and Anglo-French) also called Tristrem or Tristan. In medieval romances, he is said to be the son of King Rouland of Erminia and Blanchefleur, sister to Mark, King of Cornwall. According to another version of the story, his parents were King Meliodas of Lyonesse and King Mark's sister Elizabeth. While fighting the Irish King Moraunt and his ally the giant Sir Morholt, who had demanded tribute from King Mark his uncle, Tristram received poisoned wounds. They were healed by the Irish lady Iseult. On his return to King Mark's court Tristram's praise of Iseult was so enthusiastic that the king decided to marry her. Tristram was sent to woo her on his uncle's behalf but fell hopelessly in love with her himself. Eventually their liaison was discovered and Tristram fled to Brittany. After some time, mistakenly believing that Iseult had forgotten him, he married the Breton lady Iseult of the White Hands, but their union was never consummated. Later, when grievously wounded, Tristram asked that Iseult of Cornwall be asked to come and heal him. Some stories say that his jealous wife pretended that the plea was refused and Tristram died of a broken heart. Other versions have it that he was killed by King Mark in jealous rage while playing the harp to his mistress. The story is thought to be Irish in origin. Cf. 61–62, 66–69, 70–74, 105–108 and Cano. See also 130.

Tristrem see Tristram.

Troia Nova see Brutus.

Trojans see Brutus.

Tuatha Dé Danann 7–19, 23, 26, 30–31.

Tuonela 259–261, 275–278.

Tuonetar 260.

Tuoni 260–261, 276.

Tursas (F-U) hideous water-fiend, who rose from the sea's depths and fired the hay cut by the Virgins of the Waves (sea nymphs). He is an attendant upon Ahti (q.v.).

Twrch Trwyth 114.

Tyr (N) Danish god reputed to affect the outcome of battles. He succeeded in catching and imprisoning the wolf Fenrir (q.v.) which bit off one of his hands. He is possibly a late develop-ment of the sky-father Tîwaz (q.v.), See also 160.

Uí Néill (C, Irish) the descendants of Níal Noígiallah (q.v.).

Uisnech, the Sons of 70–73.

Ukko (F-U) the 'Ancient Father who Rules the Heavens', a god who seems to have supplanted Jumula as head of the Finno-Ugric pantheon. He supported the world and controlled its weather. He was invoked when all other gods failed to help. His wife was Akka (q.v.).

Ulaidh (C, Irish) one of the four early Irish kingdoms, Ulaidh (Ulster) covered the whole of northern Ireland, including Donegal. Its capital was Emhain Mhacha (q.v.). It was later conquered and divided by Níal Noígiallagh (q.v.). See also Ulster.

Ulaidh, the (C, Irish) the Ulstermen, heroes of a legendary cycle.

Ullr (N-G) famous archer and skier, an inhabitant of Asgardr (q.v.).

Ulster 1, 6, 48, 52, 56, 58, 59, 70.

Ulster Cycle, the p. 20.

underworld, the (C): see Otherworld; N-G: Hel or Niflheimr; F-U: Tuonola or Manala. See also 19, 150, 171, 181, 207, 215, 219, 226–228, 258–261, 276–278 and also Nera.

Unius, River 23.

Upinis (B, Lithuanian) god of rivers. White sucking pigs were sacrificed to him to ensure that the waters remained pure.

Urdr (Urthr) 149.

Urdr (Urthr) the Well of 149.

Urian (Britain) the Lord of Moray, which King Arthur (q.v.) restored to him after he had lost it to the Saxons. His son was Ywain. See 120.

urt see *haltija*.

Utgardar-loki 193–196, 202.

Utgardr (N-G) 177, 187, 193.

Uther Pendragon, King of Britain 117–118. See also Aurelius Ambrosius.

Väinämöinen 249–264, 266–272.

Valaskjálf 165.

Valhalla (Valhǫll) 159, 166, 219.

Váli (N–G) son of Óðinn and Rind (qq.v.) he will be one of those who survive the Ragnarøkr. See **161**.

Valkyries, the (Valkyrja) (N–G) 'Choosers of the Slaughtered', see **173–175, 232, 240**. They included Brynhildr (q.v.), Hildr, Hlǫkk, Gudr, Sigrdrifa, Sigrun, Svafa.

Vammatar (F–U) goddess of illness, one of the terrible hags, daughters of Tuoni and Tuonetar. See **260**.

Vanir (N–G) a race of deities particularly associated with fertility. They included Njǫrðr, Freyr and Freyja (**203–221**). See also **155–157**.

Varpulis (S, Czech) god of the storm wind, attendant upon the thunder god Perun (q.v.). See also Stribog and Erisvorsh.

Varuna 162.

Vé 143–145.

vèlè (s) (B) generic term for spirits of the dead. They are believed to live in families and villages in sandy hills. The concept is roughly comparable to that of the Greek *psyche*. See also *siela, velnias.*

Vellamo (F–U) the consort of Ahti (q.v.).

velnias (B) dangerous spirit of the dead.

Veraldargód (Veraldargóth) (N–G) a name used by Snorri for Freyr (q.v.).

Verdandi (Verthandi) **149.**

Vetehinen (F–U) evil water-spirit attendant upon Ahti (q.v.). See also Tursas.

Vídar (N–G) Óðinn's (q.v.) son, whose death the god avenged by killing Fenrir (q.v.).

Vígrídr (Vígríthr) **159.**

Vikarr, King (N) The late *Gautreks Saga* tells how the Viking King Vikarr prayed to Óðinn (q.v.) for a good wind. The king and his men then drew lots to see whom should be sacrificed to the god in payment. The lot fell upon Vikarr. It was decided to stage a symbolic hanging but as the king stood with intestines hung round his neck like a noose and the man Starkadr, uttering the ritual dedication, struck him with a stick, a true sacrifice took place, for the stick turned into a sword, the intestines into a rope, and gashed, the king hung dangling from the tree and died.

Viking 174.

Vili 143–145.

Vimir, River (N–G) the river in which Thórr was nearly drowned when the giant Geirroðr's daughter stood astride the water making it flood. Thórr hurled a rock at her and, pulling on a rowan tree which overhung the water, hauled himself to safety.

Vinland (N–G) a settlement on the NE American coast, made by Icelanders from Greenland.

Vision of Fursa p. 20.

'Vision' tales p. 20.

Vivien (C, Anglo-French) the Lady of the Lake (q.v.). She seduced Merlin (q.v.) and having learned his spells imprisoned him in an oak tree. She also kidnapped the baby Lancelot (q.v.) and when he had reached the age of eighteen took him to the court of King Arthur to be made a knight. Although Tennyson calls her Vivien in early stories as Merlin's mistress she is named Nimiane or Nimue.

vodyanoi (S) a malevolent water-spirit which particularly haunted millponds. Its appearance varied and it might assume the form of a log, fish, aged man or beautiful woman. Though immortal, *vodyani* aged and were rejuvenated according to the phases of the moon. Human sacrifices were offered to them until comparatively recent times.

Vol see Phol.

Volkh (Volga) (S, Russian) a famous *bogatyr* (q.v.) of Kiev. His name derives from *volkhv*, signifying a *shaman* (q.v.) and Volkh has the *shaman's* characteristic power of shape-changing, taking now the form of a falcon, now that of an ant, now a golden-horned bull, now an aged grey wolf. In the *bylina* (epic) describing his career, these pagan elements are given Christian overtones and Volkh deploys his magical gifts to save Kiev from the hands of the infidel Tsar of India—presumably a Mohammedan, since his aim was to burn down all the churches in Kiev.

Volla see Phol.

Volos (Vyeles) (S, Russian) god of animals. He was associated with the war and thunder-god Pyerun (q.v.).

Volsunga Saga **236.**

Vǫlsungr (N–G) founder of the Volsung family, father of Sigmundr (q.v.).

Vǫlundr (N–G) one of the sons of Wada, King of the Finns. Their story is told in the epic *Vǫlundr*. The hero was known to the Anglo-Saxons as Weland, later as Wayland (q.v.). He and his brothers Egil and Slagfidr took the three Swan Maidens (q.v.) as their wives. After the Maidens had flown away again Egil and Slagfidr went to seek them, but Vǫlundr remained at home in Wolf-dales, working as a smith. While asleep he was captured by King Nidudr's men. The king commandeered his sword and gave Vǫlundr's ring to his daughter Princess Bodvildr. Vǫlundr was hamstrung and marooned on the island of Saevarstod. There Nidudr's two sons secretly visited him, curious to see his treasure. Vǫlundr tricked them and murdered them, burying their corpses in a dunghill, but their heads he mounted in silver, made jewels from their eyes and breast ornaments from their teeth. The skulls he sent to their father, the jewels to their mother, the breast ornaments to their sister Bodvildr. The princess's curiosity was aroused and she also visited Vǫlundr in secret. Making her drunk he raped her; then, shouting that he was avenged he rose into the air on wings he had made himself. Parts of his story are illustrated on the Franks Casket (q.v.).

Vǫluspá **141, 231.**

vǫlva **185, 221.**

von Eschenbach, Wolfram **130.**

Vortigern, King of Britain (C, Britain) after the assassination of King Constantine II, which he had arranged, Vortigern first made Constantine's son Constans a puppet king and later had him murdered, usurping the throne himself, with Pictish aid. He allied with the Saxons Hengist (q.v.) and Horsa, which led to his deposition in favour of his son Vortimer. Vortimer was poisoned by his stepmother and Vortigern regained the throne, but fled to Wales after Hengist's massacre of the British princes at Salisbury. He tried to build himself a tower on Mount Erith in north Wales, but each night its stones disappeared. Merlin (q.v.) ascribed this to the presence of an underground spring, confounding Vortigern's own seers. Vortigern's end was foreseen by Merlin and the king was eventually burned to death in the tower by Constantine II's son Aurelius Ambrosius (q.v.). His story is told by Geoffrey of Monmouth and

Scene from a recent production of Wagner's *Tristan and Isolde* at the Royal Opera House, Covent Garden, London. (*Photo: Houston Rogers.*)

Wayland's Smithy, a prehistoric stone circle near Uffington, Berks. (*Photo: A. F. Kersting.*)

by the Venerable Bede.
Vortimer see Vortigern.
'Voyage' tales p. 20.

Wace 132, 133

Wachilt (N-G) goddess who met King
Vilcinus in the forest and subsequently
rose from the sea, arresting his ship
(cf. Ruadh). She told him she was to
bear his child. Vilcinus took her home
with him and she gave birth to the
giant Wade (see Wada) and then
disappeared. Later she again rose from
the sea to rescue her grandson
Wittich (Widia) (q.v.) and took him to
the seabed out of the reach of those
who were intending to kill him.

Wada (Wade) (N-G) the giant son of
Wachilt (q.v.) father of Vǫlundr (q.v.).
He was especially connected with great
stones and the sea and honoured
particularly by the Danes and Anglo-
Saxons, to whom he was known as
Wade.

Wade see Wada.

Waelcyrge (N-G, Britain) eighth-century
and ninth-century term meaning
'Chooser of the Slain,' used of the
Erinnyes (vol. 1: 2.3.).

Wagner 130, 158.

Walgino (S, Polish) patron god of cattle.
Cf. Kurwaichin and Kremara.

Waste Land, The **130.**

Wayland (N-G, Britain) an Anglo-Saxon
variant of the name Vǫlundr (q.v.).
It survives in several place-names such
as Wayland Wood, near Watton in
Norfolk, traditionally associated also
with the story of the Babes in the
Wood, possibly as a result of the
assimilation of this later folk tale to the
story of the death of Nidudr's sons.

Wealtheow, Queen of the Danes (N-G,
Britain) wife to Hrodgar (q.v.).

Weland the Smith (N-G, Britain) a
variant of Vǫlundr (q.v.). See also
Wayland.

Weohstan (N-G, Britain) father of
Wiglaf, kinsman to Beowulf (q.v.).

White Mount of London, the 99.

Widia see Wittich and Wachilt.

Wiglaf see Beowulf.

Winchester, Battle of **128.**

Wisdom, the Salmon of **65.**

Wittich (N-G) the son of Vǫlundr,
grandson of Wada (qq.v.). The Anglo-
Saxons called him Widia. See also
Wachilt.

Wodan 162–164, 167, 223.

Woden (N-G, Britain) variant of the
name Wodan (q.v.). He was also known
in Britain as Grim, which denotes
someone wearing a hood covering his
face, and is cognate with the Old

Twelfth-century figure of Wotan supporting a vault in the crypt of
Königslutter church, Brunswick, W. Germany. (*Photo: Bildarchiv Preussischer
Kulturbesitz.*)

'The three weird sisters' beneath a tree. Illustration to Holinshed's *Chronicles*, 1577. The sisters probably represent a folk memory of Wyrd and her sister Fates. The British Library. (*Photo: Ray Gardner.*)

Norse Grimr (q.v.) a title of Ódinn. It survives in such place-names as Grim's Dyke.

Wolfdales see Vǫlundr.

Women, Land of (Tír inna mBan) 37.

Wotan (G) a variant of Wodan (q.v.).

Wyrd (N-G, Britain) 'Fate', the Old English equivalent of Urðr (q.v.). The names of her two sisters are unknown, but it is thought that the memory of the three persisted at least until Shakespeare's day and the 'three weird sisters' of *Macbeth* may well represent them. An illustration in the first edition of Holinshed's *Chronicles* (A.D. 1577) (Shakespeare's source) shows the sisters standing beneath a tree, and we know from Norse-Germanic stories that they were associated with the Tree of Life.

Ximena (Spain) daughter of Don Gomez, wife to El Cid (qq.v.).

Yarilo (S) god of fertility and erotic love, depicted as a barefoot youth in a white cloak and crowned with wild flowers, riding a white horse. In his left hand he carries a bundle of wheat. Ceremonies in his honour were held well into the eighteenth century.

Yarovit see Svantovit.

Ygerna 117.

Yggdrasill 148–152, 161, 170, 171.

Ymir 142–145.

Ynawag 100.

Ynglinga Saga 171.

York, the siege of 118, 120.

Ysbaddaden, the Chief Giant 110–111, 114–115.

žaltys (B, Lithuanian) the grass snake, known as the 'gods' watchman'. It was believed to bring fertility and prosperity and it was particularly lucky to have a žaltys in the house. The death of one caused the sun to weep.

Žemėpatis (Žemininkas) (B, Lithuanian) the brother of Žemyna (q.v.), he is the god of the home and sometimes called Dimstipatis (*dimstis:* home; *patis:* father). His Latvian equivalent is Mājas Kungs (q.v.).

Zemes Māte (B, Lett) Mother Earth.

Žemyna (B, Lithuanian) Mother Earth. She is also known as Mother-of-the-Fields, –of Springs, –of Forests, and as the Blossomer and the Bud-Raiser. See also Žemėpatis.

Zeus 172, 176.

Zorya (Zarya), the two (S) the daughters of Dazhbog (q.v.), named Zorya Utrennyaya and Zorya Vechernyaya. The first is goddess of dawn and opens her father's palace gates each morning so that he may ride forth. The second is goddess of dusk and closes the gates in the evening after he has returned home. Zorya Utrennyaya is sometimes also associated with Pyerun (q.v.) and then has the character of an Amazonian warrior goddess (cf. Anath, vol. 1: 1.2. 111–113). See also Zorya, the three, and Zvezda, the two.

Zorya (Zarya), the three (S) Zorya Utrennyaya, Zorya Vechernyaya and their sister the goddess of midnight. They are the three guardians of the world who watch the god who is chained to Ursa Major. If he breaks free the world will end.

Zvezda, the two (S) Zvezda Dennitsa, the Morning Star, and Vechernyaya Zvezda, the Evening Star, companions to the two Zorya (q.v.). They groom the horses of the sun, their father Dazhbog (q.v.). Vechernyaya Zvezda is sometimes described as the wife of Myesyats (q.v.).

PART 4

Bibliography

The standard work on Norse-Germanic religion and mythology is de VRIES, JAN *Altgermanische Religiongeschichte.* Berlin: *Walter de Gruyter.* 2 vols. 2nd ed. 1956.

ALEXANDER, MICHAEL (trans.) *The Earliest English Poems.* Penguin Books. 1966.

ANDERSON, R. B. *Viking Tales of the North.* Chicago, Ill.: Scott. 1889.

*BARBER, R. W. *Arthur of Albion.* Barrie & Rockcliff with the Pall Mall Press. 1961.

BEDE, *A History of the English Church and People.* Translated by Leo Shirley-Price. Penguin Books. 1955.

BRANSTON, BRIAN *The Lost Gods of England.* Thames & Hudson. 1957.

BRØNSTEAD, J. *The Vikings.* Penguin Books. 1964.

CHADWICK, N. K. *Russian Heroic Poetry.* Cambridge University Press. 1932.

——*The Celts.* Penguin Books. 1970.

D'ARBOIS DE JUBAINVILLE, H. *The Irish Mythological Cycle.* Translated from the French by R. I. Best. Dublin: Hodges & Figgis. 1903.

DILLON, MYLES and CHADWICK, NORAH *The Celts.* Weidenfeld & Nicolson. 1967.

DOWNING, C. *Russian Tales and Legends.* Oxford University Press. 1956.

ELIADE, MIRCEA *Shamanism: Archaic Techniques of Ecstasy.* N. York: Bollingen Series LXXVI. 1964.

*ELLIS DAVIDSON, H. R. *Gods and Myths of Northern Europe.* Penguin Books. 1964.

FEDRICK, ALAN S. (trans.) *'The Romance of Tristan' by Beroul and 'The Tale of Tristan's Madness'.* Penguin Books, 1970.

FILIP, JAN *Celtic Civilization and Its Heritage.* Prague: The Czechoslovak Academy of Sciences and Arts. 1960.

GIMBUTAS, MARIJA *The Balts.* Thames & Hudson. 1963.

GLOB, P. V. *The Bog People.* Translated from the Danish by Rupert Bruce-Mitford. Faber & Faber. 1969.

GORDON, R. K. *Anglo-Saxon Poetry.* J. M. Dent; 1927.

HATTO, A. C. (trans.) Gottfried von Strassburg: *Tristan;* Thomas: *Tristan.* Penguin Books. 1960.

*JACKSON, KENNETH HURLSTONE (trans.) *A Celtic Miscellany.* Penguin Books. rev. ed. 1971.

——*The Oldest Irish Tradition.* Cambridge University Press. 1964.

JONES, GWYN and JONES, THOMAS (trans.) *The Mabinogion.* J. M. Dent. 1949/63.

KERSHAW, N. (trans.) *Stories and Ballads of the Far Past.* Cambridge University Press. 1921.

——*Anglo-Saxon and Norse Poems.* Cambridge University Press. 1922.

KIRBY, W. F. (trans.) *Kalevala: The Land of Heroes.* J. M. Dent. 2. vols. 1907.

*LEWIS, I. M. *Ecstatic Religion: An Anthropological Study of Spirit Possession and Shamanism.* Penguin Books. 1971/75.

LOOMIS, R. S. (trans.) *'The Romance of Tristram and Ysolt' by Thomas of Britain.* N. York: Columbia University Press. 1951.

*LOOMIS, R. S. (ed.) *Arthurian Literature in the Middle Ages.* Oxford University Press. 1959.

LOOMIS, R. S. *Wales and the Arthurian Legend.* University of Wales. 1956.

LUQUIENS, FREDERICK BLISS (trans.) *The Song of Roland.* New York: Macmillan & Co. 1952.

*MAC CANA, PROINSIAS *Celtic Mythology.* Paul Hamlyn. 1970.

MAC CULLOCH, JOHN ARNOTT *Celtic Mythology.* Boston: Gray and Moore. 1918.

MAGNUSSON, MAGNUS and PALSSON, HERMAN (trans.) *Njal's Saga.* Penguin Books. 1969.

MATARASSO, P. M. (trans.) *The Quest of the Holy Grail* [*Quest Saint Graal*] Penguin Books. 1969.

MERWIN, W. S. (trans.) *Poem of the Cid (El Poema del Mio Cid).* J. M. Dent & Sons. 1959.

MEYER, KUNO and NUTT, ALFRED (trans.) *The Voyage of Bran.* David Nutt. 2 vols. 1895.

MONMOUTH, GEOFFREY of *The History of the Kings of Britain.* Translated by Lewis Thorpe. Penguin Books. 1966.

MURPHY, GERARD *Saga and Myth in Ancient Ireland.* Dublin: Three Candles Press. 1955.

——(trans) *Duanaire Finn: The Book of the Lays of Fionn.* Dublin: The Educational Company of Ireland. 1953.

O'RAHILHY, CECILE (ed.) *'Tain Bo Cuailnge' from the 'Book of Leinster'.*

Dublin: Institute of Advanced Studies. 1967.

PATON, LUCY ALLEN (ed.) *Morte Arthur: Two Early English Romances Morte Arthure* and *Le Morte Arthur* J. M. Dent. 1912/36.

Arthurian Chronicles represented by Wace and Layamon. J. M. Dent. 1912.

*REES, ALWYN and REES, BRINLEY *Celtic Heritage.* Thames & Hudson. 1961.

RHYS, JOHN *Celtic Folklore, Welsh and Manx.* Oxford University Press. 1901.

ROBINSON, J. ARMITAGE *Two Glastonbury Legends.* Cambridge University Press. 1926.

*ROSS, ANNIE *Pagan Celtic Britain.* Routledge & Kegan Paul. 1967.

SARGANT, WILLIAM *The Mind Possessed: A Physiology of Possession, Mysticism and Faith Healing.* Heinemann. 1973.

SJOESTEDT, MARIE-LOUISE *Gods and Heroes of the Celts.* Translated from the French by Myles Dillon. Methuen. 1949.

STONE, B. (trans.) *Sir Gawain and the Green Knight.* Penguin Books. 1959.

*TATLOCK, J. P. S. *The Legendary History of Britain.* University of California Press. 1950.

TOLKIEN, J. R. R. and GORDON, E. V. (eds) *Sir Gawain and the Green Knight* [the medieval text] Oxford University Press corrected ed. 1930/55.

VINAVER, E. (ed.) *The Works of Sir Thomas Malory.* Oxford: The Clarendon Press. 3 vols. 1947.

WEBB, J. F. (trans.) *Lives of the Saints* [Brendan, Columba and Wilfred]. Penguin Books. 1965.

WESTON, JESSIE L. *From Ritual to Romance.* Garden City N. York: Doubleday Anchor Books. 1955.

——(trans.) *'Parzival', A Knightly Epic by Wolfram von Eschenbach.* David Nutt. 1894.

WRIGHT, DAVID (trans.) *Beowulf.* Penguin Books. 1957/66.

YOUNG, JEAN I. (trans.) *The Prose Edda of Snorri Sturluson: Tales from Norse Mythology.* Introduced by Sigurdur Nordal. Cambridge: Bowes & Bowes. 1954.

*These books contain detailed bibliographies.

133

CHAPTER 4

Southern and Central Africa

PART 1

Introduction

The first three chapters of this series have dealt with myths and legends known to us primarily from written records and the patient work of the linguist and archaeologist. Almost all our knowledge of central and southern African myths and legends derives from travellers and missionaries, anthropologists, ethnographers and students of comparative religion, who have collected and recorded oral traditions.

    Ancient African writings survive only from the Sudan and, rather later, from Ethiopia. The great Sudanese empire of Kush, centred at Meroë, (see map, vol. 1: p. 20), from the 6th century B.C. to A.D. 325 left a number of records but the Meroitic script still baffles scholars. Most early Ethiopian writing, apart from the chronicle of kings, is predominantly Christian in inspiration.

Royal pyramids dating from the third century B.C. to the fourth century A.D. in the North Cemetery of Meroë, second city of that name and capital of Kush. (*Photo: Werner Forman Archive.*)

አዘዘረ፡ወ፡ክ፡ልሳን፡ሦስ፡እን
ጋድ፡ቀንብ፡ኑ፡ልቁ፡ሰብአ፡ወ
ክልኤ፡እምታስ፡ዕብራን፡ዋህ
ድ፡ሰበ፡እምድሳሪ፡አይሳ፡ወጠ

ኑ፡ሐኒጸ፡ልዑል፡ወሃነፉ፡ድ፡
ዝርምሙ፡ስእጰራርየ፡ከመ፡
ሐሠረ፡ክል፡እምዓዋ፡ድ፡
ወከሙ፡በነፉ፡ኃያል፡ይዘረወ፡ሐመ፡

Illustration from an eighteenth-century Ethiopian manuscript shows God in a cloud watching the building of the Tower of Babel. British Library Oriental Ms. 590 f. 10 r. (*Photo: the British Library.*)

The men of the highly sophisticated civilisations which flourished in western and central Africa between the sixth and twelfth centuries of our era must surely have been literate, but so far as we know they left no written records at all. Our sketchy ideas of their mythology therefore derive from surviving artefacts and the occasional notes of medieval Arab travellers.

It will be evident that most of our information on African myths and legends derives from very recent material. However, as the legend of the Fall of Kush (**129–135**) illustrates, the oral traditions of a people may be preserved over many hundreds of years. African stories still show traces of the impingement of ancient civilisations to the north and east, as well as of the more recent impact of Europe, for Africa has never been entirely an isolated continent.

Long before 500 B.C. traders were crossing the Sahara between north Africa and the Niger. A second great trade route ran from the Nile to the region of Lake Chad. Ocean-going merchants came from as far away as Indonesia. It was probably they who introduced two of East Africa's staple food crops, the banana and the yam, whose importance to the African economy may be guessed from the Bugandan myth which says these were the two plants men first brought down from heaven (126). Some scholars, notably A. M. Jones, believe that Malay traders even established colonies in central and western Africa. Evidence for this theory derives mainly from the study of particular musical instruments and techniques of cloth-making found only in Indonesia and these regions of Africa. We may note possible supporting evidence in the very close similarity between the Ashanti myth (82), and the Indonesian myth (vol. 4: 7.2. 12).

Perhaps the most marked influence upon African civilisation however came from much nearer home. It was that of Islam, whose importance to our study is twofold. Its fierce monotheism is antipathetic to the promulgation of many kinds of religious myths, but the mythology of African peoples on the fringes of Islam has nonetheless been influenced by its concepts, as, for example in the myth 91–92. The Arabs also introduced a new literate culture, which enabled many legends to be preserved, particularly in the Swahili-speaking regions of eastern Africa, where the intermarriage of Arab settlers and indigenous peoples gave rise to a civilisation whose splendour is only now beginning to be appreciated with the excavation of such ancient cities as Tanzanian Kilwa, which traded as far afield as China.

Ruins of the great mosque at Kilwa, Tanzania. (*Photo: Werner Forman Archive.*)

Prehistoric rock carvings of antelopes, Tassili, Algeria. Similar carvings and paintings of ritual significance are found in many parts of Africa and have been made until modern times by the Bushmen. Musée de Préhistoire et d'Ethnographie de Bardo, El Djezair (Algiers). (*Photo: Werner Forman Archive.*)

COMMON CONCEPTS

In Africa, as in India, groups of widely differing levels of culture and sophistication have long lived side by side, and although there are roughly one thousand different peoples in central and southern Africa, we may nevertheless distinguish a number of common concepts which are reflected in their different myths and legends.

Spiritual Categories

THE SUPREME BEING AND LESSER DIVINITIES

Virtually all African peoples conceive of a supreme being whose name may be translated 'God'. In many cases he is felt to have become somewhat remote from man—usually through man's fault. He is often thought to dwell in the sky, but also permeates the universe as the source and sustenance of all things. He is particularly associated with rain and in some African languages his name also connotes 'rain', but the people conceive of it as expressing his nature—God is the rain in the rain—not as completely embodying him.

Although God is unquestionably ruler of all things, he is often held to delegate specific functions to lesser divinities and heroes. Again these gods are felt to be particular expressions of the supreme being and are worshipped as such. While God himself is beyond man's ken and therefore no images can be made of him, the lesser divinities are depicted in metal pottery and painting, the famous Ifé and Benin bronzes being among the most splendid examples of this religious art.

Lesser divinities fall into two classes; those, who like God himself, have always been divine spirits and those deified ancestors who once were men. The Yoruba gods Jakuta and Shango are a case in point: Jakuta, the ancient god of storms, is a god *per se,* Shango a legendary king who later assumed divine characteristics. Many tribal ancestors occupy the intermediary position of demi-gods.

Spirits

Spirits also form two classes of beings; the first includes those whom God created as spirits, the second the spirits of the dead. Virtually all African peoples believe in the second, not all in the first.

Spirits, of whatever origin, may be either good or evil. They have a shadowy form of their own, which is sometimes visible to man, and also possess the power of assuming human or animal shape. They inhabit all kinds of natural phenomena. Sometimes they may be referred to as *Its,* expressing the sense that they have in some ways less individuality than men. On the other hand they have direct access to God and are far more powerful than most human beings.

Spirits of the recently dead and of particularly memorable ancestors are generally thought of as still intimately concerned with their descendants' daily lives, acting as personal, family and tribal guardians. As in the West it is customary to place flowers on a grave, and burn candles before images of saints, so in Africa it is usual to offer food or other tributes expressing the esteem in which the dead are held. It is generally mistaken to suppose that such tributes signify ancestor worship.

Female ancestor figure of
the *Bambara* people, Mali.
Museum of Mankind, the
British Museum. (*Photo:
British Museum.*)

Medicine-men

Medicine-men or 'doctors'—the witch-doctors of Western tales—are gifted with powers of healing and spiritual insight. They are highly-trained specialists whose work includes protecting the community from evil spirits, witches and sorcerers. Like the *shaman* (see 3.1.) they combine the rôles of doctor and priest-seer and have the power to command spirits. They are often diviners and may be trance mediums. They may also function as rain-makers, but among some peoples this highly important rôle is assigned to a separate specialist. The work of the 'doctor' is not usually a masculine prerogative and women also practise.

Divining bowl used for detecting witches, *Bavenda* people, N. Transvaal, S. Africa. Museum of Mankind, British Museum. (*Photo: British Museum.*)

Witches and sorcerers

The moral antitheses of the medicine men, witches and sorcerers are greatly feared. Like the 'doctors' they can control spirits, but they exploit this power to harm their fellow men. They can change their shape and assume animal forms at will.

PRINCIPLES OF SELECTION AND ARRANGEMENT

To outline the entire body of myths from even one people such as the Dogon, Baganda or Yoruba would take more space than is here available. Therefore, in order to give as varied and representative a selection as possible within the present compass, stories have been chosen from many parts of central and southern Africa and arranged under headings according to their general subject-matter, rather than their provenance. It is hoped that this will enable readers to draw comparisons and contrasts between the myths and legends of different African peoples. While it is possible here to outline only a few representative stories, brief details of many other myths and legends will be found in Part 3 of this chapter.

SPELLING AND PRONUNCIATION

African languages contain many sounds foreign to European tongues and European attempts to render these sounds by phonetic spelling have resulted in variants such as Mukasa, Mugasha. There are few generally-agreed forms and those adopted here are those used by the authorities quoted in the Bibliography.

As a general rule names should be pronounced phonetically and vowels occurring at the ends of words sounded as independent syllables, e.g. Lebé, Chirubé. The initial Ng should be pronounced as ŋ, as in si*ng*.

Figure of a *Bena Lulwa* man from Zaïre, with a knife and 'medicine' bowl, *c.* 1800. Collection of Mr & Mrs J. W. Gillon, New York. *(Photo: Werner Forman Archive.)*

Cave paintings of scenes from *Dogon* myths, Mali. The white figure on the left may possibly represent Amma Sérou (26) falling from heaven. *(Photo: Werner Forman Archive.)*

Carved and painted granary door of the *Dogon* people, Mali, depicting mythological figures. Fuhrman Collection, New York. *(Photo: Werner Forman Archive.)*

PART 2

Narrative Outlines

THE SUPREME BEING AND LESSER DIVINITIES 1–36

1 Some peoples conceive of only one or two secondary gods, but others in both west and east Africa have worshipped a pantheon, led by one or more great gods, sons and deputies of God himself. It is probable that in both eastern and western parts of the continent men's conceptions of such pantheons have been influenced by Middle Eastern ideas carried by migrating peoples and traders. The Nigerian stories which follow illustrate the relation between the supreme being and lesser divinities and the rôle of these secondary gods in creation.

(i) Osanobwe and Olokun

2 Olokun, ruler of the sea and son of the supreme being Osanobwe, challenged his father to a competitive display. An open market was chosen for the contest and on the appointed day Osanobwe sent his messenger Chameleon to tell his son that he was ready. Olokun should come at once.

3 Olokun had arrayed himself splendidly but discovered Osanobwe's messenger was dressed exactly like him. Hurriedly Olokun went and put on even more magnificent garments and additional coral necklaces, but again he found Chameleon dressed exactly as he was. Seven times this happened. In the end Olokun admitted defeat. He could not possibly go out and compete with his father when he could not even outdo the messenger. (*Edo* myth, west-central Nigeria).

(ii) Olodumare and the Orisha (gods)

4 All 1700 Orisha hatched a plot against the supreme being Olodumare. Deciding he must abdicate they went to him and asked him to relinquish all power to them, at least for a trial period of sixteen years. Olodumare

Olokun, the *Yoruba* sea-
god, Nigeria. Rijksmuseum
voor Volkenkunde, Leiden.
(*Photo: Rijksmuseum voor
Volkenkunde.*)

suggested that it might be better for them to make a trial run of sixteen days for a start. They agreed to this proposal and set to work. By the end of the eighth day the universe had come to a complete standstill. The Orisha asked the advice of the oracle divinity Orunmila, but his oracle gave no reply. There remained nothing for them to do but return to Olodumare, admit their foolhardiness and ask his pardon. Somewhat amused, Olodumare forgave them, and restored the universe to order. The Orisha went away hymning his praises. (*Yoruba* myth, western Nigeria).

(iii) Olorun and Orishanla

5 In the beginning the world was a desolate swamp. Olorun, the supreme being, and other gods lived in 'skyey heaven' but from time to time the lesser divinities descended by great spider-web bridges and disported themselves in the swamp.

6 One day Olorun summoned Orishanla, the chief Orisha, and giving him three things—a snail shell containing a little earth, a pigeon and a five-toed hen—commanded him to go and create some firm ground in the swamp. So Orishanla descended and shook the earth out of the snail shell. He put down the pigeon and the hen, who scratched about, scattering the earth until almost the whole swamp was covered and then Orishanla returned to Olorun and said he had completed his task.

7 Olorun sent Chameleon to inspect the work. Chameleon walked slowly all over the world and returned saying that although the ground was wide it was far too damp. After a while Olorun asked him to go and look again. This time Chameleon reported that the ground was dry.

8 Olorun now sent Orishanla back to earth to plant trees. He gave him four trees, including the precious oil-palm and when they were planted he sent rain to water them.

9 When the earth was tidily organised Olorun commanded Orishanla to make sixteen human beings. Like a potter Orishanla moulded them from clay. Olorun allowed him to make them in any colour and shape he pleased, so men are of various colours and sizes and sometimes their bodies are misshapen.

10 Although Orishanla formed men and women, only Olorun himself could give them life. Orishanla envied him this power and longed to discover its secret. One night, when he had finished making the first set of human forms he hid himself behind a pile of them so that he might watch and learn how Olorun brought them to life; but Olorun, who knows everything, knew where he was hiding and cast him into a deep sleep, so Orishanla never discovered the secret of life. (*Yoruba* myths, western Nigeria).

Wood carving of a figure
used in rain-making
ceremonies by the *Dogon*
people of Mali. At other
times such figures are
stored in the *Dogon's*
granaries. (*Photo: Werner
Forman Archive.*)

(iv) Amma, the Nummo and the Eight Ancestors

11 The myths of the *Dogon* people of Mali are some of the most striking and poetic in all Africa. The following stories concern the relation of the supreme being Amma and a pantheon headed by a pair of twin divinities, the Nummo. The other gods are the deified Eight Ancestors. Incorporated in the stories are poetic accounts of the origin of a number of tribal practices, including female circumcision.

12 Amma first created the sun and moon, making them from clay, like a potter. The sun he made white hot and surrounded it with eight rings of red copper. Round the moon he placed eight rings of white copper. To make the stars he kneaded scraps of clay and threw them into space. Earth he made by the same means.

13 Earth spread out flat with the north at its top and its various parts branching out in different directions like the limbs of a supine body.

14 Feeling lonely Amma approached Earth and attempted to have intercourse with her but was frustrated by a small red anthill. This he cut down and was then able to unite with Earth, but the hiatus had damaged their union and instead of the twins it would have been natural for her to bear, Earth's first child was the Jackal. However, a further union with Amma was more fruitful and Earth bore the twin Nummo, one male the other female.

Twin Ancestor figures of the *Dogon* of Mali. Schindler Collection, N. York. (*Photo: Werner Forman Archive.*)

15 The Nummo had red eyes and forked tongues. Their bodies were covered with brilliant green hair glittering like water. The tops of their bodies resembled human beings' but their lower parts were flexible as a snake's. Created from the life-giving power of Amma, they are an embodiment of this power, which animates all things. It is the power of water and of light. The Nummo are the essence of water. They embody light.

16 The Nummo went to skyey heaven to ask their father Amma what he wished them to do, but when they looked down and realised that their mother, Earth, was both naked and dishevelled they descended again bringing bundles of plant fibres, which they arranged in bunches before and behind her, making a woman's skirt. This skirt was permeated with the Nummo's life-giving essence and it gave Earth the power of primitive utterance.

17 Jackal envied his mother's possession of this First Word and tried to tear off the skirt in which it was hidden. Seeking to evade him Earth turned herself into an ant and hid in an anthill, but Jackal pursued her deep into the ground, tore off her skirt and stole the Word from her. He is therefore now able to reveal Amma's secrets to diviners, who can understand his primitive cry.

18 Since Earth had been defiled by this incestuous rape, Amma decided to create other living beings without her help. While he was forming them the Nummo realised that there was a danger of no more twin births occurring, for the new creatures would have but one parent. To avert this catastrophe the Nummo drew the outlines of two bodies on the ground, one male, the other female, one above the other. At first therefore all people now have twin souls and are bisexual until puberty when they are circumcised and become wholly men or women.

19 The first man and woman drawn by the Nummo bore four pairs of twins, the Eight Ancestors. Four were male, four female.

20 After some time the first ancestor, Amma Sérou, disappeared into an anthill, the womb of Mother Earth. Behind him he left his sun hat, a wooden bowl. By studying this bowl and the anthill into which he had vanished men discovered how to build themselves houses. Previously they had sheltered in caves.

21 The male Nummo led Amma Sérou far into the earth. He condensed like water into the shape of a seed. Then he rose up into skyey heaven. After a time, one by one each of the ancestors followed him, being transformed into pure essence and ascending into heaven where the Nummo were their rulers.

22 For the sake of peace the Nummo ordered each ancestor to live alone, but Amma the supreme being, had given each of them eight kinds of food grains and when all but the last of these had been eaten Amma Sérou and Lebé Sérou, the eighth ancestor, joined together to consume it. By disobeying the Nummo they thus defiled themselves and so had to leave heaven and return to earth. The other six ancestors agreed to accompany them. Amma helped them, giving them useful tools and equipment.

A *Dogon* granary door carved with mythical figures. Musée de L'Homme, Paris. (*Photo: Giraudon.*)

23 According to some versions, the two Nummo were different in character, one was evil and it was he who raped Mother Earth and was transformed into the Jackal. His good twin was the saviour of the world and protects it from Jackal's evil. He brought the Eight Ancestors to earth in a model granary, which also contained specimens of all the plants and animals.

24 This Granary of the Master of Pure Earth was made of clay on a basket-work frame. It had a circular base, symbolising the sun. Its square top represented the sky and contained a circular hole for the moon. On each side was a flight of ten steps. Some say these symbolise the Nummo and the Eight Ancestors, others that they represent the ancestors' children and all other living creatures. Like a *Dogon* granary, the model had eight divisions. In them were arranged the different kinds of seed Amma gave man. These seeds also signify the organs of the human body.

25 Some stories say that Amma Sérou brought the granary to earth on his return.

26 Amma Sérou also decided to bring fire to earth and decided to steal a piece of the sun from the Nummo's smithy. From strong leather he made a pair of bellows in which to hide the stolen fire. As he crept away from the smithy the female Nummo threw a flash of lightning at him, but Amma Sérou shielded himself with the bellows, which the lightning failed to pierce. Then the male Nummo hurled a thunderbolt at him. Amma Sérou slid down the rainbow, dropping the Granary of the Master of Pure Earth, which he was also carrying. Buffeted by thunder and lightning, the granary whizzed earthwards. As it landed men, animals and seeds were flung all over the face of the earth. Amma Sérou himself made such a hard crash-landing that he broke all his arms and legs. Ever since the limbs of mankind have been jointed at the elbows and knees.

27 When the Eight Ancestors returned to earth men became grouped into eight families. The most important was the eighth for it was descended from Lebé Sérou and had speech.

28 Lebé embodied language. He did not die, for Death had not yet come to earth, but for the sake of men he had to seem to die. Lying supine, with his head to the north, he was buried and Binou Sérou, the seventh ancestor, who had changed himself into a snake, ate him.

29 The snake regurgitated a stream of stones in the pattern of a body. There was a stone at its head and eight large stones, one for each ancestor, indicated the main joints. Pebbles outlined the other bones. So, by allowing himself to be swallowed and transformed into stones Lebé enabled the Word to be purified and given to all men. All its goodness was now incorporated in the stones and their arrangement showed man that the life force of the Eight Ancestors had been transmitted to the bodies of their descendants. The pattern of the stones also showed man how to organise his society, for the design of the eight principal stones established a pattern alternating between left and right, upper and lower, which is the pattern of life. (*Dogon* myths, Mali).

Carved and painted *Yoruba* bowl depicts the world serpent above a human couple. Museum of Mankind, British Museum. (*Photo: British Museum.*)

(v) Dan Ayido Hwedo, the Divine Python

30 The snake, shedding its skin and emerging 'newly born', appears immortal and in west Africa the design of a snake coiled with its tail in its mouth symbolises eternity. It is thought of as supporting the world.

31 It is said that the earth resulted from the co-operative efforts of Mawu, the supreme being, and Dan Ayido Hwedo, the divine python or Rainbow Snake. Dan Ayido Hwedo was the first created thing and carried Mawu in his mouth all over the world. Everywhere they stopped for the night mountains were formed of the snake's excrement. It contained treasures men may still find if they excavate the mountains.

32 When Mawu had finished his journey he realised that he and Dan Ayido Hwedo had overburdened the earth with mountains, trees and large animals. To stop the world from sinking under their weight and drowning in the sea, Mawu asked the python to support the earth, by coiling himself into a circular carrying pad, with his tail in his mouth. This the snake did and, although for most of the time he has lain very still, occasionally he wriggles. This causes an earthquake.

33 The sea keeps him cool and he is fed by the red monkeys who live in it. Mawu ordered them to make iron bars for the snake to eat whenever he feels hungry. If they should ever forget or refuse to feed him, Dan Ayido Hwedo would have to eat his tail. Should that happen, the earth, now even more burdened than at first—since men and animals have multiplied and built houses—would sink into the sea and the world would end.

34 Another myth speaks of the snake as holding the earth between his coils. There are 3500 coils above the earth and the same number below it. If they were loosened the world would fall apart.

35 In another myth he symbolises life's constant pulsating movement. It is said that in the beginning all the earth's water was stagnant and dead. The python travelled over the world gouging out channels for rivers and streams and so brought life to the earth. He may still be glimpsed moving in the current of a river, in the waves of the sea. His coils, revolving above the earth, keep the planets and stars in motion. He arches in the rainbow and flashes in the lightning.

36 One story says that the python built four pillars at the corners of the earth to support the skyey heaven and twisted himself round them to keep them up. At night he is clothed in black, during the day in white and at twilight he wears red. These colours therefore encircle the pillars of heaven. (Myths of the *Fon* (Dahomey and Togo) and of other west coast peoples).

THE CREATION OF MAN 37–42

37 In some areas of Africa man is imagined to have appeared from below the earth. *Ashanti* peoples (Ghana and Ivory Coast) say he came up through a large wormhole. The *Herero* (Namibia) record that he emerged from the tree Omumborombonga, the *Zulus* (S. Africa) that he burst out of an exploding reed, called Uh Panga Lwe Zizwe, the Reed of All Nations. The *Yao* (Mozambique) declare he was discovered by the chameleon who found the first pair of human beings caught in his fish trap.

38 In myths of this kind there is no account of man's creation. He simply appears. Other stories, as we have seen, say that God shared the work of creating man with one or more deputies. Examples follow of myths in which the supreme being alone acts as man's creator.

(i) The Creator Juok

39 Juok created all men from earth. In the lands of the white man he made them from sand or clay. In Egypt he formed them from the Nile mud, so they were brown. From the black earth of Shilluk he made black men.

40 Juok decided to give man two legs like flamingoes', so that he could walk and run. He made him two arms so that he might till the soil, one arm to hoe with, the other to pick up weeds. He gave man two eyes so that he might see, a mouth so that he could eat what he had grown and lastly he made him a tongue so that he could speak, shout and sing and two ears that he might hear. (*Shilluk* myth, Sudan).

(ii) A Panhouin creation myth

41 God formed man from clay. Originally he gave him the shape of a lizard and put him in a pond, where he left him seven days. At the end of that time instead of a lizard a man came out of the pond. (*Panhouin* myth, Gabon).

(iii) The Creator Wâga

42 The first man was born with all the limbs and organs we have but, although he could see, he was in other ways completely paralysed, unable even to breathe. Wâga's wife asked him if he could give the man some medicine to make him speak. God replied that he had none, but he would bring the man some breath, which he did. Now the man began to move, speak and till the soil. When he died Wâga took his breath back again. (*Konso* myth, Ethiopia).

MYTHS CONCERNING NATURAL PHENOMENA 43–56

43 Many African myths are concerned to account for natural phenomena and in most of these stories—though not all—animals, real or imagined, play a leading part.

(i) Darkness

44 At first the world was never dark or cold, for the sun shone by day, the moon by night; then God called Bat and asked him to take a covered basket of darkness to the moon. God said he himself would follow later and tell the moon what to do with it.

45 Bat set off with the basket on his back. After some while, feeling tired, he broke his journey, put the basket down and went off to search for something to eat. In his absence some animals found the basket by the roadside. Imagining it contained food they raised its lid and Bat returned just too late to prevent the darkness from escaping.

46 Now Bat sleeps all day, but when dusk falls he begins to fly hither and thither trying to recapture the darkness so that he may return it to its basket and obey God's order to take it to the moon. Always however, day returns before he has succeeded. (*Kono* myth, Sierra Leone).

(ii) Lightning

47 Many African peoples conceive of lightning as caused by some bird. The *Baziba* (Tanzania) believe it comes from the glittering plumage of small scarlet birds that breed among the rocks south of Lake Victoria. They say that the birds are sent by the storm-god Kayura and that the beating of their wings causes thunder. The *Ndebele* (Rhodesia) identify lightning with the white-necked fish eagle, while the *Baronga* (S. Africa) say it is a hawk. These people believe that in striking the earth the lightning bird lays eggs, and these must be found and destroyed at once, lest the bird return to fetch them, bringing disaster in its wake. The myths which follow give other accounts of lightning.

TSETSE BUMBA

48 The creator, Bumba, made nine creatures and then man. He ordered each to observe particular taboos, but one creature, Tsetse Bumba, refused to. Bumba therefore expelled her from earth. She took refuge in the sky, where she has lived ever since, but Bumba allows her to make occasional visits to earth to bring fire, for otherwise men would have none. Her descents are a mixed blessing, for every one brings some disaster, but men have been able to light fires from the trees Tsetse Bumba has struck. (*Bushongo* myth, Kasai province, Zaïre).

THE LIGHTNING MONSTER

49 Lightning is caused by an animal which is let down from heaven on a strong cobweb. The creature has the head and body of a goat, but its hindquarters are those of a crocodile. It is usually hauled back to heaven, but should its rope break men must search out the animal and kill it and bury it. Such a task involves great danger and the hunter must be protected with very strong magic. (*Lamba* myth, Zambia).

(iii) Rainbows

50 The *Zulus* (S. Africa) call the rainbow Utingo Lwenkosikasi—Arch of the Queen—believing it to form part of the frame of the Queen of Heaven's hut, and to the *Baganda* (Uganda) the rainbow god Musoke is a wholly benevolent divinity, patron of fishermen. However many African peoples believe the rainbow a sign of great ill omen, probably because they associate it with the end of a rainstorm and rain is very precious to them.

THE RAINBOW SNAKE, MBUMBA LUANGU

51 When he wants to stop rain falling Mbumba Luangu, an enormous snake, rises out of the water and slithers up the nearest tall tree. The rainbow is his reflection. (Myth of various peoples on the Congo-Gabon borders).

A RAINBOW MONSTER

52 The rainbow is a terrible animal that lives in water and comes out under the cover of darkness to devour animals and even people. One such monster lived in Lake Naivasha and swallowed many Masai cattle before young men managed to catch and destroy it. The rainbows we see in the sky and in the spray from a waterfall are not the monster itself but reflections of it. (*Gikuyu* myth, Kenya).

MALE AND FEMALE RAINBOWS

53 Nyambe created rain, from which came all water. To control its fall he also made two rainbows, one male, the other female. The narrow, male rainbow appears first. Alone it cannot halt the rain, but if it is followed by the broad, female rainbow, then the rain ceases. (*Luyi* myth, Kenya).

(iv) Fire

54 Two accounts of the origin of fire have been given already in paragraphs **26** and **48**. The following story comes from Gabon.

55 God had a fire and in front of it sat his old mother trying to warm herself. One day, while God was swinging on his liana swing a man who had lost himself in the forest came upon the fire with the old woman fast asleep before it. The man quietly stole the fire, but feeling chilly the old woman awoke and called loudly for her son. Once he had soothed her God leapt onto his swing, glided to the man and took the fire from him. When the fellow told his friends what had happened one of them came and tried to steal the fire, again without success. Then a third man made himself wings of feathers and succeeded in flying away with the fire.

56 God chased the thief over hill and valley but at last, confessing himself beaten, he called the man his brother and said he might keep the fire, but when he returned home God found that his old mother had died of cold, so he decreed that men too should die as a punishment. (*Panhouin* myth, Gabon).

DEATH MYTHS 57–72

57 Africans ascribe death's inevitability to a number of causes, one of which is quoted in the previous story. Some other examples of their varied myths about death now follow.

(i) Nyambe and Nasilele

58 Nyambe (God) had a wife Nasilele. She wanted man to die once and for all time, but God wanted him to live again. When his dog died and Nyambe wanted to restore its life Nasilele objected, for she had disliked the animal. Sometime later when her aged mother died Nasilele asked her husband to restore the old woman's life. He refused to.

59 According to some stories Nyambe eventually conceded Nasilele's request, but his impatient wife disastrously interrupted him *in medias res*. (*Luyi* myth, Zambia).

(ii) Ndriananahary and Ataokoloinona

60 At first men and all creatures lived in the sky with God. Then Ndriananahary, the supreme being, sent his son Ataokoloinona to earth to investigate the possibility of making living creatures there; but Ataokoloinona found the earth so unbearably hot that after a while he dived into the ground in search of coolness and has never been seen or heard of from that day to this.

61 After some time Ndriananahary, growing anxious, sent for men and told them to go and look for his son. Descending to earth the seekers separated, each taking a different route, but none found the lost god and the men themselves suffered cruelly from the heat and the hard earth, so parched that not a single thing grew on it.

62 Every so often the seekers sent one of their number back to heaven to report and ask Ndriananahary for new orders, but none of these messengers has returned. They are the dead. The seekers meanwhile have multiplied, for they have been on earth a very long time; but, despite their growing numbers they have not yet found Ataokoloinona. Every so often therefore they still send someone up to heaven to ask Ndriananahary how they should proceed and having as yet no reply they are puzzled whether to continue their search or to abandon it. (*Malagasy* myth, Malagasy).

(iii) The Giant Death

63 In the beginning was a famine. Walking through the forest in search of food a young man came to an unfamiliar spot and there saw a great hillock. Drawing closer he realised it was a giant clothed in silky hair so long that it would have reached from one village to the next. As the youth tried to steal away the giant noticed him and asked what he wanted. The lad complained of hunger and the giant said he would feed him if, in return, the lad became his servant. Happily the young man agreed and learned his master's name, which was Death.

64 For a long time the youth was contented in his service, for Death's food tasted delicious, but at length growing homesick, he asked permission to leave. It was granted on condition he bring another youth to replace him. So the young man brought Death his brother and he himself went home.

65 As famine still raged, before long the youth again felt its pinch and returned to the giant, who again agreed to feed him on the condition he resumed his service. The youth again remained a long time, but never saw his brother, whom Death said had been sent away on business. When at length the youth again asked for a holiday the giant said he could go if he brought him a wife. The young man brought his sister.

66 Still famine raged and before long the youth once more came to Death asking for food. Annoyed at being troubled so often the giant told him to go into an inner room of his hut and help himself, which the youth did. With horror he recognised one of the meat bones as that of his sister; then he realised that all the meat in the room came from her and her maidservant's bodies. Fleeing home he brought his relatives to kill the giant.

67 At their first sight of Death, who lay sleeping in the forest, the villagers were afraid, but his hair stretched far and wide and they could reach that without approaching him. Stealthily they set it alight. At last the flames reached Death's head and he grew still.

68 Approaching the body, the youth noticed a packet of magic powder in the roots of Death's hair. An elder suggested they sprinkle some of the powder on the bones in the hut. When that was done the missing boy and his sister and the maidservant all sprang to life.

69 Now the youth wanted to sprinkle Death with the powder. The villagers tried to dissuade him, fearing Death's power would be restored. Nevertheless the persistent youth put a little powder in the giant's eye. Immediately it opened. Everyone fled in terror, but ever since then Death has come among men, for every time the giant blinks a man dies. (*Krachi* myth, Togo).

(iv) Unkulunkulu and the Chameleon

70 Unkulunkulu told the chameleon to take men the message that they would never die. However, the chameleon always walks slowly and this time he stopped en route to eat, so when Unkulunkulu changed his mind and asked the lizard to carry another message telling men they would die, the lizard not only overtook the chameleon and delivered the message, but had returned to Unkulunkulu before the chameleon even reached man. As man had accepted the lizard's message it was too late for him to take the chameleon's. (*Zulu* myth, S. Africa).

71 The previous story is a version of one found in many parts of the continent, in which the creator or his deputy gives a sheep, dog or chameleon a message to carry to man, but the messenger wanders by the way and a faster toad, hare or lizard overtakes it with a contradictory announcement. No reason is given for the despatch of the second messenger. In some versions man sends the two messengers to God, in others, there is only one messenger, but he delivers the wrong message, as in the following myth.

(v) Wâga and the Turtle

72 In the beginning Wâga told the turtle to go and tell man that although he dies he will return while the moon dies for all time. The turtle however delivered the message as, 'Man will die and be lost for ever but the moon will return'. When Wâga learned of this mistake he was extremely angry. He refused to allow the turtle to return with the correct message but, cursing it, cut it in halves, which is why turtles are now so short. (*Konso* myth, Ethiopia).

THE UNDERWORLD 73–79

73 Africans in all regions believe that the dead continue to exist as spirits. Many believe them to make their homes in the bush or mountains, etc., but some people hold that they ascend to the sky, while others, among them the Igbo of Nigeria and the Banyarwanda of Rwanda believe the dead live in an underground world. The following story concerns such an underground kingdom called Kalunga.

74 When his head wife Muhongo died chief Kitambe not only mourned her excessively but, deaf to all protests, insisted that his people should neither speak nor eat until she was restored to him.

75 In desperation his headmen called in a 'doctor', who said his fee would be a cow and a gun. Having received them, he made a herbal infusion and ordered Kitambe and all his people to wash themselves with it. Next he asked for men to dig a grave in the fireplace of his house. Accompanied by his small son the medicine-man descended into the pit. Adjuring his wife to put on mourning and to pour water on the grave every day, he told the men to entomb him.

76 At the bottom of the grave the 'doctor' saw a road. Walking along it he and his son eventually reached a village. Here they came upon Muhongo, who sat weaving a basket. When the 'doctor' had explained his presence, Muhongo indicated a man sitting at some little distance. She said he was Kalungangombe, lord of the underworld, who continually swallows man-

Right: Fetish figures from Zaïre. Anspach Collection, New York. *(Photo: Werner Forman Archive.)*

Left: Janiform mask of the Ekpe society, *Ikoi* people, Nigeria; the white face represents the female, the black, the male aspects of character. Private collection. *(Photo: Werner Forman Archive.)*

Far left: Ivory figure of a horseman, used in the *Yoruba* Ogboni cult. Museum of Mankind, British Museum. *(Photo: Photoresources.)*

Left: Staff topped by a woman wearing the double-headed axe insignium of Shango, the *Yoruba* thunder god. Private collection. *(Photo: Werner Forman Archive.)*

Below: Cult figures at a shrine of Shango in the home of the Temi of Ede. *(Photo: Werner Forman Archive by courtesy of H. H. Oba Laoye XI, Temi of Ede.)*

kind. Then she pointed to a second, more shadowy figure, this time in chains. In it the 'doctor' recognised a likeness to chief Kitambe. Muhongo said it was indeed her husband's spirit. Soon he would die also.

77 Giving the medicine-man a bracelet as proof he had fulfilled his task, Muhongo commanded him to return and tell her husband that none who came to Kalunga could ever return. The 'doctor' must be careful not to mention having seen Kitambe's spirit in the underworld and he and his son must take great care not to eat anything while they remained within its bounds, otherwise they too would have to stay there for ever.

78 Meanwhile the 'doctor's' wife obediently poured water onto his grave every day. One day she saw the earth begin to crack. Gradually her husband's head appeared and then the rest of him emerged, pulling their son after him.

79 Next day the medicine-man reported to his employers. The headmen presented him with two slaves and then going to Kitambe they gave him Muhongo's bracelet and told him all that the doctor had said. Kitambe recognised the bracelet as indeed his wife's. He died a few years later. (*Mbundu* myth, Angola).

MYTHS OF ESTRANGEMENT 80–84

80 African myths generally agree that man was at first in close contact with God and with heaven—usually thought of as being in the sky—but at some point he became separated from them.

(i) A Barundi myth

81 Once God lived among men, going about talking to people and making them children, but there came a day when he made a crippled child and its furious parents decided to creep up on God and stab him in the back. God, who knows everything, knew of their plan. He decided that if men were going to behave as badly as this he would go back to skyey heaven, where he could create things in whatever shape he pleased without being troubled by any complaints. (*Barundi* myth, Burundi).

(ii) Nyame and the Woman

82 At first the sky in which Nyame lives was within man's reach, but such familiarity bred contempt. Children cleaned their hands on the sky. Women used it as a condiment, breaking off a piece and dropping it in their cooking pots to vary the flavour of a dish, and when they pounded corn the women

constantly hit the sky with their pestles. One day a woman with an extra long pestle hit Nyame himself. He moved the sky a little higher, but, raising her pestle so as to pound even more vigorously, the woman hit him in the eye. Nyame was so angry that he moved far away and has remained there ever since. (*Ashanti* myth, Ghana).

(iii) Dorobo and Masai

83 The first man, who was Dorobo, a pygmy, somehow managed to obtain a cow before anyone else on earth had one. However God took the cattle away from him and gave them to Masai, sending them down to him via the leather thong which joined earth and heaven. Dorobo drew his bow and severed the thong with an arrow. (*Masai* myth, Kenya).

(iv) Akongo and the Woman

84 Men once lived in the sky, but one woman was so troublesome that at last Akongo put her and her children into a basket, together with enough seed for them to grow food, and lowered them all down to earth. (*Ngombe* myth, Zaïre).

MYTHS OF THE ORACLES 85–90

(i) Ifa

85 The Ifa method of divination, practised in Nigeria, involves making patterns of four and sixteen palm kernels on a board after tossing them from one hand to another. Ifa is sometimes said to be another name for the oracle god Orunmila and sometimes referred to as a separate individual. His parents were Oroko and Alajeru. He was a man, though born in heaven. Olorun the supreme being sent him to earth to teach mankind medicine and help them to resolve their general problems. He stopped first at Usi and there set up an advice centre. After a while he moved on to Ado and later to Ilesha, establishing centres in each town. Eventually he arrived in Ilé Ifé, a place he liked so much that he decided to make it his home. (*Yoruba* myth, Nigeria).

(ii) Fa

86 The Fa divination practised in Dahomey is similar to the Ifa in that it also

Carved pedestal bowl for the kola nuts used in Ifa divination by the *Yoruba*, Nigeria.
Museum of Mankind, British Museum. (*Photo: British Museum*.)

Carved and painted divination board for the Ifa cult of the *Yoruba* people, Nigeria. The face at the top is that of the messenger god Eshu. Anspach Collection, N. York. (*Photo: Werner Forman Archive.*)

involves making patterns after passing nuts from one hand to the other. One myth says that Mawu (God) sent two messengers to men telling them that everyone should know his own *fa*, that is, the saying Mawu composes at the same time as he creates an individual. Knowledge of his *fa* would enable a man to discern Mawu's will for him and to know which of the lesser divinities the supreme being wished him to worship.

87 The divine messengers chose one man and taught him to divine *fa* by throwing sixteen kola nuts from one hand to the other and tracing the patterns formed when they fall to the ground.

88 In another myth Fa is personified as a god. He lived at the summit of a palm tree, in the sky, and had sixteen eyes. Every morning Legba the gods' messenger and servant climbed the tree to ask Fa how many eyes he would like to have opened. Preferring not to speak, Fa signified his wishes by dropping nuts into Legba's hand, two nuts if he wanted one eye opened, one nut if he wanted two opened. Later, Mawu gave Fa the keys of the sixteen doors of the future and if his diviners use the nuts aright they open Fa's eyes and reveal the correct door for the inquirer. (*Fon* myths, Dahomey).

(iii) Mukasa

89 A different kind of story is told of Mukasa, oracle god of the *Baganda*, who is also associated with fertility and rules the lakes and seas. It is said his father was Wanema, who formed Lake Wanema and his chief wife was Ndwanga, a python evoked especially by barren women.

90 As a boy Mukasa refused to eat the food his parents offered and ran away from home. Coming to an island he sat down under a great tree. A man who found him there picked him up and carried him to a garden where he sat Mukasa on a rock. Believing he was a spirit the local people dared not take him into their homes and so built him a hut on the rock. They were puzzled as to how they should feed him since he refused all their usual food, but when they happened to slaughter an ox he asked if he could have its blood, liver and heart to eat. At once the people recognised him as a god and from thenceforth sought his aid whenever they were in trouble. He was cared for by the local priests and eventually married three wives. One day, without warning, he disappeared. (*Baganda* myth, Uganda).

MYTHS OF THE SPIRITS 91–97

(i) Faran and Zin-Kibaru

91 In the Niger lived a malicious spirit Zin-Kibaru who controlled all the river creatures by the magical music of his guitar. Each night he played the guitar in the rice fields of a man named Faran, inducing fish to come and eat all the plants. When Faran went fishing Zin-Kibaru prevented him from catching anything but two hippopotami. At length the man resolved to challenge the spirit, sought him out and found him on an island at the junction of seven rivers. Zin-Kibaru was playing his guitar and surrounded by musicians and dancers.

92 He agreed to fight Faran for possession of the guitar, but said that if he won he would take the man's canoe. At first Faran seemed likely to prove the victor but then the spirit uttered a spell which cast the man helpless to the ground. However, Faran's mother taught him a stronger charm and he challenged Zin-Kibaru a second time, defeated him and won not only the guitar, but all the spirit's goods and slaves. (*Songhay* myth, upper Niger area).

(ii) Untombinde and Usiququmadevu

93 In the River Ilunange lived the gross monster Usiququmadevu, hump-

Songhay dance mask,
symbolising the heroic
Faran (**91**). Musée de
L'Homme, Paris. (*Photo:*
Hamlyn Picture Library.)

backed and bearded. Untombinde, a chief's daughter, bathed in the river with her companions. When they came to dress the girls found their clothes stolen. Politely each in turn asked the monster to restore her garments, which Usiququmadevu did; but Untombinde refused thus to demean herself, so the angry monster swallowed her. When Untombinde's father sent warriors to her rescue the monster ate them all and then descended on the village and swallowed all the animals and every human being but one man.

94 Vowing revenge on the creature who had swallowed his children—a pair of twins—this man sought Usiququmadevu. First some leopards and then an elephant directed him. Eventually he reached the monster, who hoping to deceive him told him to continue along his road. However he recognised her and, stabbing her in the hump, killed her. Out of her mouth poured all the people and animals she had swallowed. Last of all came Untombinde.

95 Part of the hero's fury derives from the fact that the children Usiququ-madevu had swallowed were twins, who in this part of Africa are considered a great blessing and sign of God's favour.

96 Other versions of the story say that a boy whom the monster had swallowed caused her such discomfort that she begged to be cut open and so all her victims escaped. (*Zulu* myth, S. Africa).

97 A similar tale is told by the *Efé* pygmies of Zaïre, whose deified ancestor, Efé, immediately after his miraculous birth pursued and killed the monster that had swallowed his father and brother.

MYTHS OF THE SECRET SOCIETIES 98–103

98 Few myths are known about the origins of the ritual secret societies, which have an important rôle in African life. It is probable that all such societies have their own stories but these are usually only revealed to initiates. Parrinder however recorded two stories in Sierra Leone.

(i) A Mende myth

99 At a time of great scarcity market women asked exhorbitant prices. Some desperate men decided to frighten the avaricious traders and steal their provisions. They carved themselves grotesque wooden masks and practised making hideous noises, such as had never been uttered by man or beast. Masked, they then went to the market. Some made the ghastly noises, others acted as their interpreters. The market women fled. The disguised men beat all the other men they met and cut scars on their bodies, saying these would protect them from the spirits.

100 The story accounts for the origins of the Poro, a famous secret society also found among other west African peoples, and concerned with the initiation of youths into tribal customs and secrets, the initiates being marked with patterns of scars. At great festivals masked Poro spirits appear in public, wearing long rafia skirts. (*Mende* myth, Sierra Leone).

(ii) A Kono myth

101 An old woman potter took her daughter and went to the river bank to dig for clay. Suddenly she dug up an Object. Although surprised, she put it with the clay, beside her daughter, and continued digging. Then she came upon a second Object. The first had been male. This second was female. Neither spoke although the old woman nipped them sharply.

102 Her daughter fetched other women and they decided to take both Objects home. Reaching their village they shut the men in their huts, all but the medicine-man, whom they asked how to make the Objects speak. He suggested they be placed in a hut and pepper burned there. This was done.

103 After a while the women, listening outside the hut, heard the male Object growl, 'Shake your rattles.' Terrified the women fled, shrieking to their menfolk to save them. The men emerged from their huts, but all they could hear was the female Object, which was singing most beautifully. Unafraid they therefore took charge of both Objects and have kept their secrets ever since. (*Kono* myth, Sierra Leone).

TRIBAL ANCESTORS AND HEROES 104–126

(i) Gikuyu and Moombi

104 Murungu (God) took Gikuyu to the top of the mountain Kere Nyanga and showed him all he had created. In the middle of the whole land Gikuyu saw a grove of fig trees. There Murungu told him to build his home and there he left Gikuyu a wife, Moombi.

105 All their nine children were daughters, so Gikuyu went again to the mountain and prayed for Murungu's help. God told him to return home and sacrifice a lamb and a kid under the largest of the fig trees near his home. The animals' blood should be poured on the tree-trunk and then the whole

Poro society mask of the *Dan* people, Liberia. Museum of Fine Arts, Dallas, Texas. (*Photo: Werner Forman Archive.*)

family should offer the flesh to God. This they did and so mankind learned how to sacrifice to Murungu.

106 Returning home after the ceremony, Gikuyu and his family found nine youths awaiting them. That night they made a feast and next morning Gikuyu offered his daughters to the youths on the condition that if they accepted them as wives they must remain in his house and agree to matrilinear inheritance. This they did, so this became the family of Moombi.

107 Eventually Gikuyu and Moombi died and their daughters shared their inheritance, but at length the family grew so large that each daughter decided to form her own household. So were founded the nine clans of the Moombi tribe. (*Gikuyu* myth, Kenya).

(ii) Aiwel and the Spear Masters

108 The story of Aiwel probably preserves the memory of a tribal migration. It accounts for the authority of the Dinka people's priestly and warrior castes.

109 Aiwel was the son of a woman and a water-spirit. His great gifts were obvious from the first, for he was born with a complete set of teeth. While still apparently a baby, if left alone he would rise from the floor, where his mother had laid him, and fetch and drink whole gourd-fuls of milk. When his mother discovered it was he who had taken the milk she was very angry, but Aiwel warned her to keep the matter secret lest she die. However the woman chattered, and so died.

110 Aiwel spent the rest of his childhood living in the river with his father. On reaching manhood he returned to his mother's village, bringing with him a parti-coloured ox named Longar. Thenceforward Aiwel was known as Aiwel Longar.

111 He remained in the village, herding the cattle he had inherited from his mother. Then a drought decimated all the herds but his, which remained fit and plump. Village youths tracked him and discovered he took his cattle to a spot where deep-rooted grass still grew. Pulling up clumps of the grass he watered his beasts in a pool beneath. Aiwel knew he had been spied on and when the young men told of what they had seen, like his mother, they died.

112 Aiwel told the elders he would lead the people to a deathless land rich in water and good pasture, but they were incredulous, so he set out alone. Some people had second thoughts and tried to follow him but God put huge mountains and rivers in their way.

113 As they tried to ford one such river they saw Aiwel standing on its further bank. He speared each man who crossed until a cunning fellow called Agothyathik conceived a stratagem. He stuck an ox bone on a long stick and holding it before him pushed his way through the reeds on the far side of the river. Aiwel mistook the bone for a human head and while he was taking aim at it Agothyathik leaped on him from behind.

114 They wrestled long but at last Aiwel cried a halt. He told Agothyathik to summon the other people. Not all came, being afraid. To those who were brave enough to obey at once Aiwel gave fishing spears, which he told them to carry when they prayed. Others who followed received war spears and to them all Aiwel gave a bull coloured like the sky. Its thigh bone was to be sacred. Aiwel Longar made the spear masters rulers of the people but promised to help them if they were in trouble or need. (*Dinka* myth, eastern Sudan).

(iii) The Story of Khambageu

115 It is possible that this tale, which is unique in African mythology, preserves an ancient memory of the Middle Eastern Adonis stories, or of very early Christian influence from Nubia, but no hard evidence exists to support such conjectures. Scholars are sure that the myth was not affected by more recent Christian teaching in Africa.

116 Khambageu came among people many years ago. He performed miracles of healing, made good crops grow and resolved men's quarrels; but always after a while people grew tired of him. They began to denigrate him, even tried to murder him, so he moved on to yet another village.

117 When the time of his death approached Khambageu asked the people among whom he then lived to carry his body to another village for burial or otherwise to expose it on a rock. Then he went into his house and died. The people failed to comply with his last request and buried him elsewhere. When the inhabitants of his chosen village heard of this they came to claim his body, but the grave was found to be empty. It was said by some that Khambageu had risen from it and flown to the sun. (*Sonjo* myth, Tanzania).

(iv) Kintu and Nambi

118 The delightful myth of Kintu and Nambi is part of a long series of stories about the Baganda's tribal ancestors and early kings. It has parallels in many languages and concerns the hero's successful completion of a number of apparently impossible tests.

119 Kintu, the first man, lived on earth alone but for a single cow, on whose milk he fed. One day, Nambi, daughter of Gulu, ruler of the sky, came to earth and fell in love with the man, but her relatives despised Kintu for his poverty and ignorance and opposed her marrying him.

120 *The first test*: To test the man's worthiness Gulu stole his cow. Kintu therefore lived on leaves. Then Nambi came and told him that she had seen his beast in heaven. She suggested he fetch it.

121 Arriving in heaven Kintu was astonished by the number of its houses and animals. Before he could track his cow Nambi's brothers Kaizuku and Walumbe had told their father of Kintu's arrival. Gulu arranged a second test for the man.

122 *The second test*: Food enough for one hundred people was placed in a hut in which Kintu was imprisoned and told that if he did not eat every scrap he would be killed. Having eaten as much as he could, Kintu concealed the remainder of the food in a hole in the floor; then he called for servants to come and take away the empty baskets.

123 *The third test*: Convinced that Kintu had tricked him Gulu gave him a copper axe and ordered him to split rocks for firewood. Kintu discovered a cracked rock and broke off slivers from it.

124 *The fourth test*: Now Gulu gave him a water-pot and said it must be filled with dew. Setting the pot on the ground Kintu pondered his task. When, disconsolate, he went to pick the pot up he found it brimming with dew.

125 *The fifth test*: Impressed by the man's cleverness, Gulu said he could marry Nambi. He told Kintu to go and find his stolen cow, which was pastured with Gulu's own cattle. This was another test, for many of Gulu's cows looked exactly like Kintu's. However a large bumble bee buzzed in Kintu's ear that he should choose the animal on whose horns she settled. Next morning when the cows were herded before him Kintu watched the bee. While the first herd passed the insect stayed in a nearby tree, so Kintu said none of these cows was his. The same thing happened when the second herd was brought; but as the third was driven past the bee flew out of the tree and settled on the horns of a large cow. Kintu claimed it as his. Now the bee flew off and alighted on the horns of three calves. Kintu claimed them also, saying his cow had borne them while in heaven. Delighted by Kintu's sagacity Gulu welcomed him as his son-in-law.

126 Now Kintu and Nambi began their journey back to earth. With them they took their cows, a sheep, a goat, a hen, a yam and a banana. (*Baganda* myth, Uganda).

TWO EAST AFRICAN LEGENDS 127–135

(i) The Legend of the Founding of Kilwa

127 The Arabic chronicle of Kilwa, written *c.* A.D. 1520, tells of the foundation of this port, off the Tanzanian coast, which had been one of the greatest Swahili cities. The anonymous historian is sceptical of the tale's veracity, remarking that only God knows if it is true.

128 A father and his six sons left Shiraz in Iran in seven ships. The first landed at Mandakha, the next at Shaugu, the third at Yanbu, the fourth at Mombasa. The fifth ship berthed at the Green Island (Pemba) and the sixth stopped at Kilwa. The seventh ship, captained by the father, continued to Hanzuan.

(ii) The Legend of the Fall of Kush

129 In 1912 an Arab camelman in El Obeid (Sudan) told the anthropologist Frobenius a story which is a remarkable example of a legend passed on by word of mouth for some two thousand years. Some elements of the tale in its present form resemble the stories of Shehrzad, but the legend's core condenses memories of two historical events. The first is the overthrow of the priests of the Golden Temple of Meroë, centre of a religion apparently based on ritual regicide. In *c.* 430 B.C. Herodotus reported that the people of Kush were said to worship Zeus and Dionysus. Diodorus the Sicilian, writing some four hundred years later, says the Golden Temple was overthrown in the third century B.C. by King Ergamenes, who had been given a Greek education. Both historians were relying on hearsay. More certainty attends the date of the second event recorded in the legend, the destruction of the Meroitic empire of Kush by King Ezana of Axum. This happened in *c.* A.D. 325.

130 The legend: Long ago four kings ruled an empire, one in Nubia, one in Ethiopia, one in Darfu, but the Nap of Napata, ruler of Kordofan, was richer than all. He owned all the gold and copper of the whole empire and men came to his court from all over the world. However, each Nap of Napata ruled only a few years; then, when the priests saw in the stars that his time had come, he was slain.

131 Akaf became Nap of Napata. Following the custom he had first to choose the leader of those who would die with him. Akaf choose Far-li-mas, a wonderful story-teller, whom the Nap had been sent by a ruler beyond the Red Sea (Hadramaut in S. Arabia?). Far-li-mas accepted his fate philosophically but when the king's youngest sister Sali-fu-Hamr learned that she was to be the vestal guardian of the sacred fire, who also died with the king, she was horrified. She planned to elude her fate.

132 Sali had heard of Far-li-mas's wonderful stories and asked if she might hear one. She and Far-li-mas fell in love at first sight. Only she resisted the enchanting power of his story-telling, which affected men like a drug.

133 Discovering that the priests had to watch the stars every night to discover the correct day for the king to die, Sali told the Chief Priest that God had given Far-li-mas a greater gift of language than any in the stars. She challenged him to prove her wrong. So the priests also came to the court and listened to the tales, which they found so enchanting that they came every night, until it was discovered that no-one had kept watch on the sky, so the day of the king's death could not be forecast.

134 The Chief Priest asked Akaf to condemn Far-li-mas for destroying their religion. The king put the matter to the people and Far-li-mas was commanded to tell them a story. Soon all were enchanted by it. Far-li-mas spoke all night; as dawn approached his voice grew louder and louder. As the sun came up he ended his tale. All the priests lay dead.

135 King Akaf unveiled himself and showed himself to the people. He was the first Nap of Napata whose face they had seen. Akaf performed the priestly rites and rekindled the sacred fire. He became the first Nap of Napata to live to old age. Far-li-mas succeeded him but Far-li-mas was the last king, for when he died enemies came and Napata was destroyed.

PART 3

Index and Glossary

Abasi Ibom (*Efik* people, Nigeria) name of supreme being. It means 'God Above'.

Abosom (*Akan* and *Ashanti* peoples, Ghana) name for pantheon of lesser divinities.

Abuk (*Dinka,* Sudan) divinity of women's work. She is said once to have been a woman. She and Garang (q.v.) were formed from clay by the creator, Nhialic, and placed in a large pot. When this was later uncovered they grew to normal human size. Abuk is associated with streams. Her emblem is a small snake.

Ado (*Lugbara,* Sudan) supreme being.

Adu Ogyinae (*Ashanti,* Ghana and Ivory Coast) the intrepid hero and leader of the first people, who came to earth through holes in the ground, some stories say through a single wormhole. At first the people were very frightened but on the morning after their arrival Abu Ogyinae laid his hands on them and calmed their fears. The next day he was killed by a falling tree as he and his company were building houses.

Agothyathik 113–114.

Agwatana (*Basa,* Nigeria) supreme being. The word also connotes the sun.

Aiwel Longar 108–114.

Akaf 131–135.

Akongo (*Ngombe,* Zaïre) The *Ngombe* say he is and always has been their people's chief god. They believe all people know him under different names. He is the everlasting, omnipotent and incomprehensible creator of all things. Although not formally worshipped he is easily accessible to man and the guardian spirit of every human being, determining his individual fortune. See also **84.**

Akuj (*Turkana,* Kenya; *Dodo, Iteso, Jine* peoples, Uganda) name of supreme being. It means 'up above'.

Ala (*Igbo,* Nigeria) fertility goddess, Mother Earth. She reigns over mankind and is Queen of the Underworld, receiving the dead into her pocket. Sometimes known as **Ana** or **Ani**, she is the wife—according to some stories the daughter—of the supreme being, Chukwu (q.v.).

Clay pyramids built in honour of the Nigerian Earth Mother, Ala. (*Photo: Mansell Collection.*)

A *Mende* mask from Sierra Leone. Called *Bundu* it represents protective ancestors who preside over the rites of the Sande female initiation society. Museum of Mankind, the British Museum. (*Photo: British Museum*.)

Alajeru 85.
Amadi Oha (*Igbo*, Nigeria) storm-god.
Amma 11–12, 14–18, 22, 24.
Amma Sérou 20–21, 25–26.
Ana see Ala.
Ani see Ala.
Anotchi (*Ashanti*, Ghana and Ivory Coast) legendary medicine-man. He is said to have sought refuge with the Ashanti after quarrelling with his kinsman, to whom they were subject. He enabled them to win their independence by bringing down from the sky a magic golden stool, said to contain the spirit of the *Ashanti* people. On ceremonial occasions it was carried under a splendid umbrella. Not even the king might sit on it although on certain occasions he made ceremonial pretence of doing so. The stool is now in the royal palace at Kumasi.
Are'bati (*Efé*, Zaïre) the moon-spirit who created all God's 'goats' (i.e. animals) by sending a single goat to earth.
Asase Yaa (*Ashanti,* Ghana and Ivory Coast) earth-goddess. The fifth day of the week is sacred to her, hence her name, which may be translated 'Earth Thursday'.
Ashila (*Kambari* and *Dakakari* peoples, Nigeria) supreme being.
Asia (*Agni*, Guinea) earth-goddess. Her son was Pan.
Asia Bussu (*Agni*, Guinea) divinity of the bush.
Asis (*Nande* and *Keyo* peoples, Nigeria) supreme being.
Asisia (*Dorobo,* Kenya) supreme being.
Astar (*Axum,* ancient Ethiopia) ancient moon divinity, mentioned in fourth-century inscription of King Ezana.
Ataokoloinona 60–62.
Atero (*Kafa,* Ethiopia) feast day in honour of Mariam (q.v.).
Ayagba see Enekpe.

Babinga (*Banyarwanda,* Rwanda) king of the *imandwa* spirits and father of Ryang'ombe (qq.v.).
Bakongo (*Teke,* Congo) supreme being. Also known as Manikongo.
Balubare (*Baganda,* Uganda) pantheon of divinities.
balungwana (*Baronga,* S. Africa) little people who live in the sky with Tilo, the supreme being (q.v.). The sight of them falling to earth portends disaster.
Bat 44–46.
Bawai (*Chawai,* Nigeria) supreme being.
Beher (*Axum,* ancient Ethiopia) divinity of rural areas, mentioned in fourth-century inscription of King Ezana.
Bia (various peoples in Ghana and Togo) river-god and oldest son of the supreme

being. Because he was a good amenable son God intended to make him ruler of all fertile land but his brother Tano tricked him out of this heritage so only the poor land was left for Bia.

Biel (*Nuer*, Ethiopia) spirit.

Binego (*Banyarwanda*, Rwanda) a vicious divinity, one of the *imandwa* spirits (q.v.) he is thought to cause dangerous illnesses. The son of Ryang'ombe (q.v.).

Binou Sérou 28.

Bomazi (*Bushongo*, Zaïre) a lord who came down from heaven and married the daughter of the first people. He fathered five sons who became chiefs of the five *Bushongo* tribes.

Borebore (*Akan,* Ghana) a title of the supreme being. It means 'Hewer', 'Carver' etc.

Buk (*Nuer*, Ethiopia) river-spirit and god of fishing.

Bumba (*Bushongo*, Zaïre) the creator god who vomited the universe and eight species of animals, from which all others are derived. See also **48.**

Bundu (*Mende*, Sierra Leone) ceremonial ancestral mask.

Cagn (*Bushmen*, Botswana) supreme being. Only antelopes know his home. His power lies in one of his teeth. He uses birds as messengers and turns his sandals into hounds to chase his enemies. Thorns, once people, attacked and killed him. Ants devoured his corpse; but his bones came together again and he was restored to life.

calabash Among various west coast people, including the *Fon* (Dahomey and Togo) the calabash is an image of the universe. The horizon comes where the upper and lower edges of the cut gourd meet. Here sky and sea intermingle. The earth is flat and floats on the water inside the great calabash. The planets move in the gourd's upper half. Stories differ as to the abode of the dead. Some say it is above the earth, others in the waters beneath it.

Chameleon 7, 37, 70–71.

Chi-wara (*Bambara*, Sudan) fertility god symbolised by the antelope, which is said to have introduced men to agriculture.

Chilube see Sikulokobuzuka.

Chiruwi (various peoples, Malawi) a monster with one human arm, leg and eye, the remainder of his body being formed from wax. He frequents lonely forest glades carrying an axe and challenges any man he meets to wrestle with him. If thrown the man dies. Cf. Kollo, Sechobochobo, Sikulokobuzuka.

Chiuta (*Yumbuka*, Malawi) supreme being.

Ekpe society mask of the *Igbo* people, Nigeria. Museum of Archaeology and Ethnography, Cambridge. (*Photo: Museum of Archaeology and Ethnography.*)

Chukwu (*Igbo*, Nigeria) supreme being. Also spelled Chukuru.

Cogaz son of Cagn (q.v.).

Coti (*Bushmen*, Botswana) mother of the antelope. Wife of Cagn (q.v.).

Dan Ayido Hwedo 30–33.

Darkness 44–46.

Death 57–72.

Deng (i) (*Dinka*, Sudan) a divinity associated with thunderstorms. Rain and human birth are seen as his manifestations. His name also connotes rain. He is at times referred to as the people's first ancestor and son of the earth and sky.

(ii) (*Nuer*, Ethiopia) god of rain and fertility.

Do (*Bobo*, Upper Volta) the god of rain and fertility, symbolised by the butterfly which appears in great numbers at the beginning of the rainy season.

Doche (*Kafa*, Ethiopia) in ancient times a great god. Now a cult figure of spirit

worship and king of the *ek'k'o* spirits (q.v.).

doctor, witch see medicine-man.

Dorobo 83.

Dungu (*Baganda*, Uganda) god of hunting. He carried a magic drum containing pieces of every kind of animal and bird man hunts.

---

earth, creation of **6–7, 12, 31–32.**

Earth, Mother **14, 16–18, 20, 23.** See also Ala, Asia, Nyame.

Ebutokpabi (*Nkum*, Nigeria) supreme being: also called Oshowo.

Efé (*Efé* pygmies, Zaïre) deified ancestor. He came from heaven but after some time God summoned him to return. Efé cut a long stem of liana creeper and pulled himself up to the sky. God gave him three spears and ordered him to go hunting. Efé caused much joy in heaven by killing an enormous elephant with very valuable tusks. After some time he returned to earth

Yoruba Egungun society mask from Abeokuta, Nigeria. Museum of Mankind, the British Museum. (*Photo: British Museum.*)

with the three God-given spears and many other gifts. See also **97**.

Egbo (*Igbo,* Nigeria) a secret society concerned with fertility rites and the invocation of ancestors. Also known as Ekpe.

Egungun (*Yoruba,* Nigeria) robed and masked figures signifying tribal ancestors. They parade during the annual yam festival.

Eight Ancestors, the 11, 14–16, 18–29.

Eji (*Egede,* Nigeria) divinity of the earth.

Ek'k'o (*Kafa,* Ethiopia) spirit of the dead which possesses a man depriving him of responsibility for his actions. He becomes a holy man and must observe rigid rules of conduct.

Ekpe see Egbo.

Enekpe (*Igala,* Nigeria) the heroine, guardian of the tribe's destiny. When the tribe, led by her father, chief Ayagba, was facing defeat in battle Enekpe had herself buried alive as a sacrifice to save the people. An annual festival is held in her honour.

Engai (*Kamba,* Kenya) supreme being.

Enkai (*Masai,* Kenya and Tanzania) supreme being. The same word is used to denote sky and rain.

Ergamenes, King 129.

Eshu (*Yoruba,* Nigeria) a feared god, agent of supreme being's anger at man's sins. He has an unpredictable temper and all the other divinities are wary of him for he is stronger than all but God himself; also called Legba (q.v.).

Evua (*Agni,* Guinea) sun-god.

Ezana of Axum 129.

Fa 86–88.

fa **86–87.**

Faran 91–92.

Far-li-mas 131–135.

fetish a statue or other man-made object worshipped in its own right, not as an emblem or symbol of any divinity. It is usually personal to its owner. The term 'fetish' is often used incorrectly and is best avoided, the synonym 'idol' being less open to misinterpretation.

Fire 26, 48, 54–56.

Gabriel (*Kafa,* Ethiopia) the Archangel Gabriel. The nominally Christian *Kafa* regard Gabriel and the other two archangels, Giyorgis and Mikael as extremely dangerous spirits who must be placated lest they kill men.

Garang (*Dinka,* Sudan) a creative divinity sometimes said to be one of the tribe's first ancestors. He is particularly associated with the Men of Garang, in whom he is said to infuse himself.

Wooden staff depicting the *Yoruba* god Eshu. Museum of Mankind, the British Museum. (*Photo: British Museum.*)

179

These men often dress in leopard skins and are believed to be powerful medicine-men. Garang is sometimes associated with the red and white snake. His other symbols are animals whose fur or hide is patterned in red and white or brown and white, such as the giraffe.

Gborogboro (*Lugbara*, Zaïre, Angola and Uganda) one of the people's first ancestors. The other was Meme.

Gewi (*Bushmen*, Botswana) son of the supreme being, Cagn (q.v.).

Gikuyu (*Gikuyu*, Kenya) son of Murungu the supreme being. See also **104–107.**

Gindri (*Lendu*, Zaïre) supreme being.

Giyorgis see Gabriel.

God's messenger The *Didinga* (Sudan) say fish are the messengers of the supreme being. They fall to earth in the lightning and must not be eaten. The *Suk* (Kenya) say rain is God's messenger. His duty is to carry water and when he spills any, men see it as rain. See also **2, 70–72, 86, 88** and Legba.

Golden Stool see Anotchi.

Golden Temple 129.

Granary of the Master of Pure Earth 23–26.

Green Island (Pemba) **128.**

Gu (*Fon*, Dahomey) the war-god.

Gulu 119–121, 123–125.

Hanzuan 128.

Ha'o (*Janjero*, Ethiopia) supreme being.

Heitsi-Eibib (*Hottentot*, S. Africa) a divinity with characteristics of a tribal hero or sorcerer and, like all sorcerers, he can assume the shape of any animal. One story says his mother was a cow, another that she was a virgin impregnated by eating a potent herb. Although Heitsi-Eibib did not create animals he gave each its peculiar character by cursing it!

Hinegba (*Igbira*, Nigeria) supreme being.

Huveane (*Bapedi* and *Bavendu* peoples, Lesotho) supreme being, creator of sky and earth. When they were completed he mounted into the sky by driving pegs to give him footholds. He pulled out each behind him to prevent man from ascending after him. He still lives in the sky. Some stories make him the first man, according to others he was a practical joker with magical gifts.

Ifa 85.

Ihinegba variant of Hinegba (q.v.).

Ilaansi (*Fipa*, Tanzania-Zambia border) supreme being. See also Indaaka, Indeesa.

Ilat (*Suk*, Kenya-Uganda border) some authorities say the son of the supreme being Tororut. Others have found Ilat regarded as the supreme being. His name connotes rain.

Ilé Ifé (*Yoruba*, Nigeria) holy city in western Nigeria. Said to be the meeting place of the dead who, immediately they enter the next life, must go there to receive their instructions. Ilé Ifé is the place where Orishanla began the creation of the world (see **6–8**). Its name means 'wide', signifying the wideness of the world Orishanla made. See also **85.**

Ilunange, River **93.**

Imana (*Banyarwanda*, Rwanda) supreme being.

imandwa (*Banyarwanda*, Rwanda) a group of socially superior ghosts. They are generally ill-disposed and most are related to Ryang'ombe (q.v.).

Incwala (*Swazi*, Swaziland) a festival aimed at strengthening the throne. Ceremonies include offerings of first-fruits and end with a day of ritual purification in which all garments and utensils used during the year are sacrificed as burnt offerings to ancestral spirits, who are expected to respond by sending rain. Their failure to reply is taken as a very bad omen.

Indaaka (*Fipa*, Tanzania-Zambia border) name of supreme being. See also Ilaansi and Indeesa.

Indeesa (*Fipa*, Tanzania-Zambia border) supreme being. See also Indaaka, Ilaansi.

Iruva (*Meru*, Kenya) supreme being.

Ishila variant of Ashila (q.v.).

Jackal 14, 17, 23.

Jakuta (*Yoruba*, Nigeria) god of thunderstorms. He expresses God's anger at man's sins. Unlike Shango (q.v.) to whom he tends to be assimilated, Jakuta is not a deified man but has always been a god. He is an earlier conception than Shango.

Juok 39–40.

Kabundungulu (*Mbundu*, Angola) twin brother of Sudika-Mbambi (q.v.).

Kaizuku 121. See also Walumbe.

Kaka-Guia (*Agni*, Guinea) bull-headed god who brings dead souls to Nyamia (q.v.) and communicates with the living via spirits.

Kalimulore (*Banyarwanda*, Rwanda) mother of Ryang'ombe (q.v.). Also referred to as Nyiraryang'ombe. As a young women she had a penchant for turning herself into a lioness.

Kalunga (i) (*Ndonga*, Namibia and *Kwanyama*, Angola) supreme being.
   (ii) (*Mbundu*, Angola) the underworld. See **73–77.**

Kalungangombe 76.

Kalwanga (*Ovamo*, Namibia) supreme being.

Kamba (*Kamba*, Kenya) son of Murungu (q.v.) and founder of the *Kamba* people.

Kammapa see Khodumodumo.

Kapirimtiya (*Anyanja*, Malawi) the place where the first people came up out of the ground. It is said their foot-prints and those of their beasts are still visible somewhere to the west of Lake Malawi.

Katonda (*Baganda*, Uganda) a name of the supreme being and creator.

Kayura 47.

Kazooba (*Ankore*, Uganda) supreme being. The word also connotes the sun.

Kere Nyaga (*Gikuyu*, Kenya) name of Mt. Kenya. It means 'Mountain of Brightness'. The earthly home of the supreme being, Murungu.

Khambageu 116–117.

Khodumodumo (*Basuto*, Lesotho) a huge, shapeless creature that swallowed everything in its path until, gorged with prey, it stuck between the walls of a mountain pass and was killed by a hero. Cf. Usiququmadevu (**93–95**).

Khuzwane (*Lovedu*, Transvaal) supreme being and creator of all things.

Kibuka (*Baganda*, Uganda) war-god and god of storms. Brother of Mukasa (**89–90**). He is said to have been killed in a battle against the Banyoro people. His emblems were always carried in tribal wars by his priest and medium.

Kibwebanduka (*Zaramo*, Tanzania) a legendary tribal hero who led the people from Khutu, probably in *c.* 1700, and brought them to their present home, driving out the Akamba who were then, it is said, cannibals. Kibwebanduka's footprints and those of his dog are reputed still to be seen in the north of the tribal area.

Kiir (*Nuer*, Ethiopia) god of origin and god of the Nile. It is said he arose from a green gourd floating down the river.

Kilwa page 139 and **127–128.**

Kimbuji (*Mbundu*, Angola) a giant underworld fish which swallowed the hero Sudika-Mbambi (q.v.) but was killed by his brother Kabundungulu.

Kimera (*Baganda*, Uganda) legendary king of the Baganda. Grandson of Kintu (**118–126**).

Kintu 118–126.

Kinyoko (*Mbundu*, Angola) a five-headed serpent of the underworld. Killed by the hero Sudika-Mbambi (q.v.).

Kipalende see Sudika-Mbambi.

Kirabira (*Baganda*, Uganda) son of Mukasa (**89–90**) and brother of Nende and, like Nende, a war-god of inferior status to their uncle Kibuka (q.v.).

Kitambe 74–79.

Koito (*Kafa*, Ethiopia) an annual feast to placate the lightning, thought of as a kind of *kollo* (q.v.) spirit.

kollo (*Kafa*, Ethiopia) spirits who must be placated. They are divided into two groups. The first inhabit specific trees, wells and other natural phenomena. They are usually given individual names. The second kind of *kollo* is a man-like creature living in the woods. He is a very tall, white, one-legged man and owns all vegetation. It is unsafe to be seen by him before having first caught sight of him. Cf. Chiruwi, Sechobochobo, Sikulokobuzuka.

Kungwa (*Kamuku*, Nigeria) supreme being.

Kunu (*Safrokolimba*, Sierra Leone) supreme being.

Kurumasaba (*Temne*, Sierra Leone) supreme being.

Kush page 137 and **129.**

Kwoth (*Nuer*, Sudan) supreme being.

Kyala (*Ngonde*, borders of Malawi, Zambia and Tanzania) supreme being.

Lamurudu (*Yoruba*, Nigeria) legend says he was king of Mecca and his son Oduduwa, (q.v.) the ancestor of the *Yoruba*, while his other sons became kings of the neighbouring *Gogobiri* and *Kukawa* peoples.

Lebé Sérou 22, 27–29.

Legba 88.

Leve see Ngewo.

Leza (*Baila, Tonga* and other peoples in Zambia, Tanzania and Zaïre) the supreme being. His name may be derived from a word meaning 'to cherish'. To the *Tonga* he is the fount of all things. The *Baila* see him as the moulder of the universe and founder of their tribal customs. He is all pervasive, the essence of all natural phenomena. Thunder is caused by him beating his rugs. He is an old man now and more remote from man than once he was. Just as old people's eyes water, so do Leza's and this is what causes rain.

Libanza (*Upoto*, Congo) supreme being.

Lisa (*Fon*, Dahomey) according to some myths, the male primaeval twin born to Nana Buluku (q.v.). He married his sister Mawu (q.v.). Other stories say he was Mawu's son and sent to earth to clear the forests with his metal sword and teach men how to make tools. Realising that man could not survive on

earth without metal, of which there then was none, he recreated the order of things to include metals. On his return to heaven Mawu gave him the sun to reign over.

Lizard 41, 70–71.

Loba (*Duala*, Cameroon) supreme being.

Loma (*Bongo*, Sudan) supreme being.

Long Juju the name European slave-traders gave to a feared oracle at Aro in eastern Nigeria. A priest of the cult stood in a cave above the river, supplicants in the water below. Any declared guilty of a crime had to go into the cave, to be 'eaten' by the oracle. They were then sold into slavery.

Longar (*Dinka*, Sudan) according to some myths the name of a hero, the first ancestor of the people and eldest son of God. He was the first person to emerge from the river in which till then all people had lived. A version of Aiwel, see **108–114.**

Lova (*Kpe*, Cameroon) supreme being. Also called Lové.

Lyambilo see Ngeketo.

Macardit (*Dinka*, Sudan) divinity of suffering and bad luck.

Mahrem (*Axum*, Ethiopia) ancient god of war, referred to in a fourth-century inscription of King Ezana.

Makishi (*Mbundu*, Angola) man-eating monsters. See Sudika-Mbambi.

Maklandjalu Al Mas'udi, a tenth-century traveller from Baghdad, wrote in his *Murj al Dhabab wa Ma'adin al-Jawhar* that the people of Zanj (the coastal areas between the Cape and Mozambique) called the ruler of heaven and earth Maklandjalu, meaning 'supreme ruler'.

Malandela (*Zulu*, S. Africa) legendary hero, father of Ntombela, who was the founder of the *Zulus*. It is said Malandela led his people south in a great march. His strength failing, the old man made his wives and children enter a great round basket and with a mighty last effort he pushed them on their way; then fell back dead. The basket rolled on and finally came to rest in the Umhaltuze valley.

Malava (*Vugusu*, Kenya) one of the tribe's first ancestors, the other being Umngoma.

Maluth (*Nuer*, Ethiopia) spirit.

Mandakha 127.

mangabanga bana (*Barongo*, Congo) one-legged flying spirits.

Mapico (*Maconde*, Mozambique) a mask symbolic of highly-feared evil spirits. These are driven out of villages by dancers.

Mariam (*Kafa* and other peoples, Ethiopia) Mary the mother of Jesus. Although many of the *Kafa* have been nominally Christian since the sixteenth century Mariam is also treated as a fertility goddess. It is said she created man while God gave him life. At the annual Atero festival in her honour senior women of the clan pour libations of beer into special jars and an animal is sacrificed, its blood being smeared on a kind of altar. The rites are intended to preserve the continuity of life. Similar ones are performed by the *Janjero* people.

Masai (*Masai*, Kenya) son of Murungu, the supreme being, and founder of the *Masai* people. See also **83.**

Masilo (*Basuto*, Lesotho) legendary fratricide. He killed his brother Masilonyane for the sake of his cattle. The murder was revealed by a small speckled bird, which Masilo also tried, unavailingly, to kill. In another version of the tale the murder was revealed by Masilonyane's dog.

Massim Biambe (*Mundang*, Congo) supreme being and creator of the male and female Phebele and Mebeli (qq.v.).

Matu (*Efé* pygmies, Zaïre) mother of the hero Efé (q.v.).

Mawu, (*Fon*, Dahomey and Togo) supreme being. Usually male or sexless, but some stories say Mawu was the female moon-goddess and one of the primaeval twins born to Nana Buluku (q.v.). In these stories Mawu and her twin Lisa (q.v.) the sun, at first were childless but an eclipse brought them together and subsequently they made love whenever there was an eclipse. They bore seven pairs of twins, the first men. See also **31–33, 86–88.**

Mbale (*Baganda*, Uganda) a fertility divinity and together with Nkulu gave men children.

Mbasi see Ngeketo.

Mbega (*Shambala*, Kenya and Tanzania borders) a legendary hero. His father was a Moslem from an offshore island who married the daughter of a *Shambala* chief. His parents died young and Mbega, rejected by his swindling kinsmen became a great hunter and medicine-man. He was invited to become chief of the *Bumburi* and *Vuga* tribes. His son Buge succeeded him.

Mbori (*Agande*, Zaïre) supreme being.

Mbumba Luangu 51.

Mebeli (*Mundang*, Congo) primaeval mother. Wife of Phebele (q.v.).

Meder (*Axum*, Ethiopia) ancient divinity of the earth, referred to in fourth-century inscription of King Ezana.

Membe (*Lugbara*, Zaïre, Angola and Uganda) one of the tribe's first ancestors. The other was Gborogboro.

Meroë page 137 and **129**.

Mikael see Gabriel.

Minepa (*Macouas* and *Banyis* peoples, Zambia) evil divinity in opposition to Muluku, the supreme being.

Mirimu (*Baganda*, Uganda) son of Mukasa (**89–90**), brother of Nende and Kirabira (qq.v.). His chief function is to help men capture their enemies' weapons during a battle.

Miseke (*Banyarwanda*, Rwanda) a girl who married the Thunder. Her pregnant mother had promised her to the god in return for his kindness in coming down and kindling a fire which prevented the woman from dying of cold while her husband was away at war.

Moelo (*Bushongo*, Zaïre) twin brother of Woto (q.v.).

Molimo (*Basuto*, Lesotho) supreme being. His name also connotes light and can mean 'paternal guardian'. The variant Morimo is found in Botswana.

Mombasa 128.

Moombi 104–107.

Mother Earth see Earth.

Muhongo 74, 76–77, 79.

Mujaji (*Lovedu*, Transvaal) hereditary queen and rain queen of the tribe, the inspiration of Rider Haggard's novel She. The queen must always have enjoyed perfect health and have perfect physique. Her first illness is her last for she then commits ritual suicide.

Mukasa (i) (*Banyarwanda*, Rwanda) son-in-law of Ryang'ombe (q.v.). According to some stories he killed his wife by maltreating her, but other tales give him a gentle and benevolent character and the first may reflect intertribal disputes.

(ii) **89–90**.

Muluku variant of Mulungu and Murungu (q.v.).

Mulungu see Murungu.

Mumbi (i) see Moombi.

(ii) (*Akamba*, Kenya) name of supreme being in his role as creator.

Mupe (*Bambuti*, Zaïre) one of the tribe's two first ancestors. His wife was Uti.

Murile (*Chagga*, Tanzania) following the murder of a baby he had charmed from a tuber, the boy Murile raised himself up to the sky by a stool on a rope pulley. In the country of the moon he won great honour and wealth by teaching the people how to make fire by friction. Returning home to visit his parents he was given a ride by a bull and promised in return never to eat of

it, but a foolish trick of his mother led him unwittingly to break his vow. Reproved by a voice from his dish, he slowly disappeared into the ground.

Murungu this name and its variants Mulungu and Muluku is given to the supreme being by some 25 East African tribes. See also **104–105**.

Musikavanhu (*Budju*, Tanzania) supreme being. See also Mwari.

Musisi see Wanema.

Musoke (*Baganda*, Uganda) one of the two great gods of the elements, the other was Gulu (q.v.). See also **50**.

Mutangakugara see Mawri.

Mwambu (*Luyia*, Kenya) the first man, created by God so that the sun should have something to shine for. God made Mwambu a wife, Sela for his companion and forbade the couple to eat any crawling thing or carrion bird. He presented them with a pair of young buffalo, which they pastured on an anthill. Fearing monsters, the couple lived in a house on stilts but their more confident children built houses on the ground.

Mwari (*Shona*, Tanzania) (i) the supreme being. He is also known as Nyadenga— the great one of the sky—Mutanga-kugara—the one who existed in the beginning—Musikavanhu—the creator of mankind;

(ii) oracle divinity of a small cult, served by hereditary priestly caste in Matopo hills.

Mwatuangi (*Akamba*, Kenya) a name of the supreme being. It means 'the carver'. See also Mumbi (ii).

Mwenembago (*Wazaramo*, Tanzania) lord of the forest, once a man.

Nabende (some *Gisu* peoples, Uganda) supreme being.

Nagadya (*Baganda*, Uganda) goddess mother of Kibuku (q.v.). During droughts, people went to Entebbe to pray to her to intercede with the other gods and send them rain.

Nagawonyi (*Baganda*, Uganda) goddess of hunger. In times of drought she was also asked to intercede with Musoke and Gulu (qq.v.) the great gods of the elements.

Naijok (*Lotuko*, Sudan) supreme being.

Nakwube (*Toposa*, Kenya) supreme being.

Nambi 118–126.

Nana Buluku (*Fon*, Dahomey and Togo) the primordial mother. She created two children, a daughter, Mawu, the moon, and a son, Lisa, the sun. Mawu lived in the west and controlled night, Lisa in the east and ruled day. All other

gods descend from them. See also Lisa, Mawu.

Nap of Napata 130–131, 135.

Nasilele 58–59.

Ndorombwike (*Ngonde*, Malawi, Zambia and Tanzania borders) name of the supreme being to some groups of these people.

Ndriananahary 60–62.

Ndwanga 89.

Nenaunir (*Masai*, Kenya and Tanzania) an evil spirit and storm demon.

Nende, (*Baganda*, Uganda) war-god, son of Mukasa (**89–90**), brother of Kirabira (qq.v.).

'Ngai (*Masai*, Kenya and Tanzania) supreme being who gives everyone a guardian spirit to protect him in this world and, at death, guide him to the next.

Ngeketo (*Ngonde*, Malawi, Zambia and Tanzania borders) once, it is said, Ngeketo was a god of the *Ngonde* but his two older brothers, Lyambilo and Mbasi grew jealous of him because he introduced maize to the people. They conspired with tribal elders to kill him. Three days later Ngeketo re-appeared as a snake. This they decimated, but its parts rejoined. Killed a third time, again he revived. Some people saw him it is said, but he went away to the coast and became the god of the white people there. Possibly the story recalls a deified hero who introduced maize sometime after or during the sixteenth century, when the Portuguese brought it to Africa from S. America.

Ngewo (*Mende*, Sierra Leone) supreme being. He is omnipotent but not immanent. He created all things and fills the universe with a power which is manifest in such phenomena as lightning and, occasionally, in specially gifted men.

Ngi see Zamba.

Nguleso (*Kakwa*, Sudan-Zaïre border) supreme being.

Ngun-lo-ki (*Bari* and *Fajulu* peoples, Sudan) supreme being. The name means 'God in the sky above'.

Ngunza Kilundu (*Mbundu*, Angola) a hero who, after the death of his brother Maka caught Kalungangombe (**76**), king of the underworld, in a mantrap. Kalungangombe showed him that the dead always ascribed their ends to human agents, not to him, and were happy in their new lives. He gave Ngunza Kilundu the seeds of all the useful plants cultivated in Angola and promised to visit him. Apparently the hero failed to keep some promise he had made the king, for when Kalungangombe came he hurled a hatchet at Ngunza Kilundu and turned him into a water spirit.

Ngworekara (*Panhouin*, Gabon) ruler of the dead. He is very ugly and evil and can condemn a spirit to the terrible punishment of a second, final death. His subjects have long, sparse hair, asymmetrical eyes, long noses, mouths like elephants' trunks and dirty ears. They feed on noxious-smelling ants and can be frightened away by dancing.

Nhialic (*Dinka*, Sudan) supreme being.

Nimba (*Baga*, Guinea) the earth mother; cf. Nyame.

Njinya (*Bamun*, Nigeria) supreme being. Also called Nrui (Nruwi).

N'kokn, see Zamba.

Nruwi (*Bamun*, Cameroon) supreme being. See also Njinyi.

Ntangaire (*Baziba*, Tanzania) a giant whom the hero Ryang'ombe attacked and swallowed, but the giant cut his way free, killing Ryang'ombe. (q.v.).

Ntubugez (*Baziba*, Tanzania) man-eating giant defeated by Ryang'ombe (q.v.).

Nummo 11, 14–16, 18–19, 21–26.

Nyadenga (*Shona*, Rhodesia, and *Budja*, Tanzania) supreme being. His name means 'great one of the sky'. See also Mwari.

Nyambe a name for the supreme being. It is found among many peoples from Cameroon to Bechuanaland. See also **53, 58–59.**

Nyame (*Ashanti*, Ghana and Ivory Coast) is held to have created three realms of the universe. He rules the sky as Nyankopon, symbolised by the sun, by a cross indicating four points of the compass and by scarabs, golden discs and birds. In another aspect Nyame the great mother, rules the earth. Her symbol is the moon. The third aspect of Nyame, Old Mother Earth, rules the underworld as monarch of the dead, who lie buried in her womb or pocket. Other forms of the name, Nyam, Nyonomo, Nyama are widespread. They probably have a different philological root from Nambe, Nyambe (qq.v.), says Parrinder. See also **82.**

Nyamia (*Agni*, Guinea) supreme being.

Nyankopon see Nyame.

Nyasi (*Luo*, Kenya) supreme being.

Nyengebule (*Xhosa*, S. Africa) a legendary figure who battered his wife to death in a fit of temper. A bunch of feathers she had been wearing in her hair turned into a bird and revealed the murder to her relatives, who killed the husband.

Nyikang (*Shilluk*, Sudan) legendary first king and ancestor of the *Shilluk*, now an intermediary between them and

Dance mask of the *Baga* people of Guinea, used in rituals of the Simo society. It represents the goddess Nimba. Musée de l'Homme, Paris. (*Photo: Giraudon.*)

God, in whose nature he participates. He is said to have been descended from a man who either came down from heaven or was specially created by God in the form of a cow. Nyikang married a crocodile woman. She represents all river creatures and offerings are still made to her. Any water creature behaving in an unusual way is said to be her temporary incarnation. She is the patronness of birth and protectress of babies.

Nyiragongo see Ryang'ombe (i).

Nyonmo (*Ga*, Ghana) the supreme being. His name may be translated 'Providence'. He is expressed particularly in rain.

Nzame variant of Nyame, found among the *Fang* peoples (Gabon).

Nzua Dia Kimanaweze (*Mbundu*, Angola) mythical hero who married the daughter of the sun and moon and became the father of the twins Sudika-Mbambe and Kabundungulu (qq.v.).

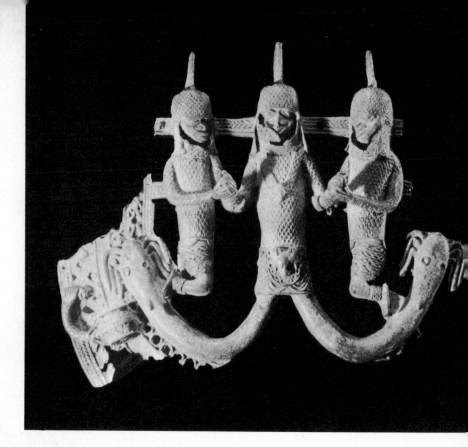

Seventeenth-century bronze
from Benin city of Oba Ohe and
attendants. The Museum of
Mankind, the British Museum.
(*Photo: Werner Forman Archive.*)

Bronze armlets with representations of Olokun, used in Ogboni society rituals. Museum of Mankind, British
Museum. (*Photo: British Museum.*)

184

Oba Ohe (*Yoruba*, Nigeria) a legendary king of the mid to late fourteenth century. He became paralysed in his legs and was said to have become possessed by Olokun whose worship he particularly encouraged.

Obang (*Banen*, Cameroon) supreme being.

Obtatala (*Yoruba*, Nigeria) synonym of Orishanla (q.v.).

Oduduwa (*Yoruba*, Nigeria) According to some stories Oduduwa is female, but more usually he is spoken of as male. Some myths make him the creator of the earth. God had sent Orishanla (5–10) to do the job and when he did not return Oduduwa came to look for him, discovered him in a drunken stupor under a palm tree and so took the tools and did the work for him. According to some legends Oduduwa is the founder of the *Yoruba* people and the name seems to have been given to the leader of those immigrants who came to Nigeria from the east, intermarrying with the indigenous *Nok* people.

Ogboni (*Yoruba*, Nigeria) secret society dedicated to the bull-god Oro.

Ogun (*Yoruba*, Nigeria) god of war and hunting. When the gods first came to earth they were led by Orishanla (5–10) but his bronze axe proved useless against the thick forests so the other gods asked Ogun to clear a path for them with his iron matchet. Later when they had built the city of Ilé Ifé (q.v.) they rewarded him by making him its king but he preferred hunting and fighting and spent most of his time alone on the mountainside, where he could spy out his prey. When at length he returned to the other gods they shunned him in his blood-stained clothes, so he made himself fresh garments from palm-tree bark and went away alone.

Ohe (*Egede*, Nigeria) supreme being and sky-god.

Olodumare (*Yoruba*, Nigeria) supreme being also known as Olorun (5–10, 85) and Olofin. See also **4**.

Olokun (*Edo* and *Yoruba* peoples, Nigeria) sea divinity. Among *Edo* he is spoken of as male, among *Yoruba* usually as female. See also **2–3**.

Olorun see Olodumare and see also **5–10, 85**.

Omumborombonga (*Herero*, Namibia) the primordial tree from which men and cattle emerged. In 1933 it was still believed to exist in the veldt to the north of the River Ugab. The *Herero* said that the *Bushmen* and sheep and goats did not emanate from the tree but came out of holes in the ground. See

Terracotta head from Ifé, excavated next to the altar of Olokun Walode, goddess of wealth. Property of Sir Adesoja Aderemi, the Oni of Ifé. (*Photo: Herbert List.*)

also **37**.

Onyame (*Akan*, Ghana) supreme being.

Oranyan (*Yoruba*, Nigeria) legendary second king of the people who stuck his staff into the ground and it changed into the twenty-foot pillar which can still be seen in Ilé Ifé (q.v.).

Oreluere (*Yoruba*, Nigeria) leader of the first men to come to earth. His authority was later challenged by Oduduwa (q.v.).

Orisha (*Yoruba*, Nigeria) pantheon of divinities. According to some traditions they number 1700, according to others 201, 401, 600. See also **4, 6**.

Orishanla (*Yoruba*, Nigeria) chief of the lesser gods and God's earthly deputy. See **5–10**.

Oroko 85.

Orunmila (*Yoruba*, Nigeria) oracle divinity whose messages are revealed through the Ifa divination (**85**). A great doctor and linguist, he can understand every language of mankind. According to some traditions he, not Orishanla (5–10), created the earth. See also **4**.

Osai Tutu (*Ashanti*, Ghana and Ivory Coast) legendary fourth king of the Ashanti, during the eighteenth century. First owner of the Golden Stool (see Anotchi).

185

Osanobwe 2–3.
Oshowo see Ebutokpabi.
Otkut see Zamba.
Owo (*Idoma*, Nigeria) supreme being. The word also connotes rain.
Oya (*Yoruba*, Nigeria) fierce bearded goddess, consort of Shango (q.v.).

Pemba 128.
Phebele (*Mundang*, Congo) male god created by Massim Biambe (q.v.). His wife Mebeli bore man, to whom Massim Biambe gave a soul, breath and life. Every time a man or creature dies its soul enters a deep hole and then goes into the body of a female and forms a new being. Human souls can only create human beings, animal souls animals.
Poro 100.

Rainbow 50–53.
Rainbow Snake 30–35, 51.
red anthill 14.
Rock Sene (*Serer*, Gambia) these people's only god. His anger is revealed in the thunderstorm, his kindness in rain and good harvests.
Rubanga (*Alur*, Sudan) supreme being.
Ruwa (*Chagga*, Tanzania) the supreme being. His name also connotes the sun.
Ryang'ombe (i) (*Banyarwanda*, Rwanda) a deified hero of this and neighbouring tribes. He became king of the *imandwa* (q.v.) and met his death by being gored by a witch who had transformed herself into a buffalo. He has since lived mainly in the volcano Muhavura, sometimes in Karisimba. Eruptions were caused by his attacks on the neighbouring volcano Mirkeno, home of Nyiragongo. Ryang'ombe cleft this mountain with a burning sword and Nyiragongo fled to the nearby volcano. Ryang'ombe sliced off its summit, threw Nyiragongo into the crater and piled rocks upon him.
Ryang'ombe (ii) (*Baziba*, Tanzania) a hero who spoke even before his birth, and ate an ox immediately after it. He frightened the man-eating giant Ntubugezi into giving him eleven cattle, which Ryang'ombe ate at once. He met his death when he attacked and ate the ogre Ntangaire. The latter cut his way out of the hero, thus killing him.

Sakarabru (*Agni*, Guinea) a greatly feared god of darkness. He is blood-thirsty, but just and a great healer.
Sali-fu-Hamr 131–133.

Sande (*Mende*, Sierra Leone) a secret society concerned with female initiation rites. A parallel with the Poro (**100**).
Sechobochobo (*Ila*, Zambia) monstrous half-man with one eye and arm. He lives in forests and according to some accounts brings good luck to those who meet him and shows them medicinal trees. Other stories say it is fatal to glimpse him. cf. Chiruwi, Kollo, Sikulokobuzuka.
Sela (*Luyi*, Kenya) wife of Mwambu (q.v.).
Shamba Bolongongo (*Bushongo*, Zaïre) Shamba of the Bonnet, a legendary king said to be descended from Woto, ninety-third king of the *Bushongo*. He lived in *c.* 1600 and is renowned for his skill and wisdom.
Shango (*Yoruba*, Nigeria) storm-god. His symbol, the double-bladed axe, connotes the thunderbolt. The ram is sacred to him. According to some stories he was the fourth king of Oyo but so fierce that he had to exile himself into the forest. Some accounts say he there hanged himself, others that he went up to heaven and now rules from there. He has gradually taken over many of the attributes of the older divinity Jakuta (q.v.).
Shaugu 127.
Shehrzad 129.
Sheshu (*Gbari, Edgar, Sheko* and *Esse* peoples, Nigeria) supreme being.
Shiraz 128.
Shopona (*Yoruba*, Nigeria) terrible god of smallpox.
Si (*Bambileke*, Cameroon) supreme being.
Sikulokobuzuka (*Subiya*, Zambia) legendary monster half made of wax. His other leg is an animal's. He feeds on wild honey and is said to live in a hut with an elephant's-tusk frame and python-skin covering. He roams the forest carrying wax weapons and an axe. Some stories say he has a wife and children like himself. His other name is Chilube. Cf. Kollo, Sechobochobo, Chiruwi.
Simo (*Konde*, Guinea) secret society.
skyey heaven home of the supreme being. Once so close to earth that men might touch it. Later it moved away. See **80–84**.
Snake 28, 30–36, 51.
Soko (*Nupe*, Nigeria) supreme being.
Sokogba (*Nupe*, Nigeria) god of wrath. His name means 'God's axe'.
Spear Masters 108, 114.
Sudika-Mbambi (*Mbundu*, Angola) hero, whose name means 'thunder-stone'. The son of Nzuadia Kimanaweze (q.v.). Before his birth his parents' village had been ravaged by Makishi monsters. Sudika-Mbambi, a wondrous child who

spoke before his birth was born with a knife, a gun and a *kilembe* (tree of life) in his hand. Leaving his twin brother at home to guard the *kilembe* Sudika-Mbambi pursued the Makishi, accompanied by four boastful assistants, the Kipalende. He foiled and killed a witch, married her daughter, descended to the underworld and there killed the five-headed snake Kinyoka but was swallowed by the fish Kimiji. However his brother Kabundungulu rescued and revived him and Sudika-Mbambi then married the daughter of the king of the underworld as his second wife. This occasioned the jealousy of his brother, who was unmarried, and after an inconclusive battle the twins separated, one going east, the other west. Some stories say Sudika-Mbambi is now the thunder in the eastern sky, Kabundungulu the echo which replies from the west.
Swahili 127.

Tamukujen (*Didinga*, Sudan) supreme being. His name is closely associated with the word for rain, 'tamu'.
Tano (various peoples in Togo and Ghana) a river-god. The creator of men and son of the supreme being. Like Jacob he disguised himself and tricked his father into giving him his elder brother's patrimony. See Bia.
Tembo (*Baganda*, Uganda) legendary early king. He killed his grandfather Kimera, for contriving his father's death, and ruled in his stead.
Tilo (*Baronga*, S. Africa) supreme being. He sends rain, lightning, locusts and twins to earth. See also Balungwana.
Tore (i) (*Bambuti*, Zaïre) god of death.
　　(ii) (*Logo*, Zaïre-Sudan border) supreme being.
Tororut (*Suk*, Kenya-Uganda border) supreme being. See also Ilat.
Trowo (*Ewe*, Dahomey) divine pantheon.
Tsetse' Bumba 48.
Tsoedi (*Nupe*, Nigeria) legendary first king of the people, now semi-divine.
Tsui-goab (*Hottentot*, S. Africa) rain-god and hero. He fought chief Gaunab, sometimes identified with death, and finally killed him but in his death throe Gaunab slashed the hero's knee, hence his name, which means 'wounded knee'. It was once thought that Tsui'goab was the supreme being of the *Hottentots*, but recent scholars have rejected this interpretation of the evidence.
Turtle 72.
Twins 14, 18–19, 94–95. See also Sudika and Mbambi.

186

King Shamba Bolongongo,
ninety-third king of the
Bushongo, Zaïre. Museum of
Mankind, the British
Museum. (*Photo: British
Museum.*)

Simo society mask of the *Banda* people, Guinea. Rietbergmuseum, Zurich. (*Photo: Rietbergmuseum, Zurich.*)

which are almost as important as their inherited names.

Wo see Zamba.

Word, the first, **16–17.**

Woto (*Bushongo,* Zaïre) oldest son of Bombasi (q.v.) and twin brother of Moelo. A great medicine-man he released the pygmies from the trees with his magically sweet music and eventually became father of all the Bushongo people.

Yamba (various Nigerian peoples) name for the supreme being.

Yanbu 127.

Yaruba (*Tangale,* Nigeria) supreme being.

Yero (*Kafa,* Ethiopia) formerly the sky-god, now the name given to the Christian God.

Zamba (*Yuande,* Cameroon) supreme being. After creating the earth he descended to it from the sky and fathered four sons: N'kokn the learned, Otkut the idiot, Ngi the gorilla and Wo the chimpanzee. He taught the *Yuande* how to look after themselves and allotted special duties to each man.

Zambi (various Angolan peoples) supreme being and judge of the dead.

Zar (*Agau,* Ethiopia) ancient sky-god. Following the *Agau's* adoption of Christianity in the fourteenth century he became demoted to the rôle of a common spirit.

zin (*Songhay,* upper Niger area) water-spirit. The word is possibly derived from 'jinn', 'genie'.

Zin-Kibaru 91–92.

Zwisi (*Shona,* Tanzania) holy days sacred to Mwari (q.v.).

PART 4

Bibliography

BURNE, C. S. *The Handbook of Folklore.* New ed. rev. and enlarged. Sidgwick & Jackson for the Folk-Lore Society. 1914.

*CALAME-GRIAULE, GENEVIÈVE *Ethnologie et langage, La parole chez les Dogon.* Paris: Éditions Gallimard. 1965.

CAMPBELL, J. *The Masks of God. Vol. 1 Primitive Mythology.* London edition: Souvenir Press. 1973.

*DAVIDSON, BASIL *The Africans: An Entry to Cultural History.* Penguin Books. 1973.

——*The African Past, Chronicles from Antiquity to Modern Times.* Longmans. 1964.

EVANS-PRITCHARD, E. E. *The Nuer: A description of the modes of livelihood and political institutions of a Nilotic people.* Oxford: The Clarendon Press. 1940, reprint of 1968.

FAUCONNET, MAX 'Mythology of Black Africa' in *New Larousse Encyclopaedia of Mythology.* New ed. Paul Hamlyn. 1968.

*FORDE, DARYLL (ed.) *Ethnographic Survey of Africa* (work in progress) 60 vols. International African Institute. 1950–73. A pamphlet is available from the Institute at 210 High Holborn, London WC1V 7BW.

GAISSEAU, PIERRE-DOMINIQUE *The Sacred Forest. The Fetishist and Magic Rites of the Toma.* Trans. Alan Ross. Weidenfeld and Nicolson. 1954.

HALLET, JEAN-PIERRE and PELLE, ALEX *Pigmy of Kitabu.* New York: Random House. 1973.

HALLPIKE, C. R. *The Konso of Ethiopia, A Study of the Values of a Cushite People.* Oxford: The Clarendon Press. 1972.

IDOWU, E. BOLAJI *African Traditional Religion, A Definition.* S.C.M. Press. 1973.

Olódúmarè, God in Yoruba Belief. Longmans. 1962.

JONES, A. M. *Africa and Indonesia: The Evidence of the Xylophone and Other Musical and Cultural Factors.* Leiden: E. J. Brill. 1964.

KENYATTA, JOMO *Facing Mount Kenya: the Tribal Life of the Gikuyu.* Secker & Warburg. 1938.

KRIGE, E. JENSEN, and KRIGE, J. D. *The Realm of a Rain Queen: A study of the Pattern of Lovedu Society.* Oxford University Press. 1943.

MacDERMOT, B. H. *The Cult of the Sacred Spear.* [Nuer of Ethiopia]. Robert Hale. 1972.

*MBITI, JOHN S. *African religions and philosophy.* Heinemann Educational. 1969.

MURPHREE, MARSHALL W. *Christianity and the Shona.* Athlone Press. 1969.

MUTWA, VUSAMAZULU CREDO *Indaba My Children.* Stanmore Press. 1966.

——*My People.* Anthony Blond. 1969.

ORENT, AMMON *Lineage and the Supernatural: the Kafa of Southwest Ethiopia.* Ann Arbor: University Microfilms Inc. 1970.

PANKHURST, RICHARD K. P. (edit.) *The Ethiopian Royal Chronicles.* Addis Ababa: Oxford University Press. 1967.

PARRINDER, GEOFFREY *African Mythology.* Paul Hamlyn. 1967.

*——*African Traditional Religion.* 3rd ed. Sheldon Press. 1974.

*WAUTHIER, CLAUDE *The Literature & Thought of Modern Africa: A Survey.* Pall Mall Press. 1966.

*WERNER, ALICE *Myths and Legends of the Bantu.* Frank Cass. 1933. New imp. 1968.

*These books include detailed bibliographies.

The International African Institute's *List of publications* offers an up-to-the-minute guide to further reading. It is obtainable from the Institute at 210 High Holborn, London, WC1V 7BW.